D0938733

Politics and Punishment

Politics and Punishment

THE HISTORY OF THE
LOUISIANA STATE PENAL SYSTEM

Mark T. Carleton

LOUISIANA STATE UNIVERSITY PRESS
BATON ROUGE
1971

ISBN 0-8071-0940-1
Library of Congress Catalog Card Number 78–165067
Copyright © 1971 by Louisiana State University Press
Manufactured in the United States of America
Printed by Franklin Press, Inc., Baton Rouge, Louisiana
Designed by J. Barney McKee

Dedicated to the Memory of
David M. Potter
1910-1971

Contents

Illustrations

Preface

L OUISIANA'S penal system, established during the 1830s, has been largely neglected by historians. The aggregate of secondary literature on the subject consists of a brief historical sketch, written in 1930 by a student of social welfare, and several master's theses, all but one of which were written by sociologists. In terms of historical content and value, all of these previous writings are incomplete and superficial. This volume, therefore, is the first extensive history of Louisiana's penal system from any scholarly point of view.

Because the Louisiana penal system has always been enmeshed in politics, the study has been focused upon the origin and evolution of the state's penal policy as established and modified by public officials from 1835 to 1968. Publications of the state of Louisiana have been examined thoroughly, as have been major Louisiana newspapers. Several excellent monographs dealing with Louisiana's political history have afforded valuable perspective. Scattered works in comparative penal history—a field which remains generally unexplored—have been of limited value.

This study was researched and written in Louisiana where I have been a member of the history faculty at Louisiana State University in Baton Rouge since 1965. For cheerful and unfailing assistance in providing official source material, a special debt of gratitude is due Miss Evangeline M. Lynch and her staff in the Louisiana Room of the Louisiana State University Library. Useful criticism and encouragement were offered from time to time by Professor Charles B. Dew and Professor Jo Ann Carrigan, now of the University of Missouri and the University of Nebraska, respectively. Professor Carl N. Degler of Stanford University read the manuscript in its original form as a doctoral dissertation. The numerous helpful comments and suggestions he offered are sincerely appreciated.

My father Roderick Lewis Carleton, a memorable scholar of Louisiana government, died when I was two years old. The difficult task of raising me was performed splendidly and alone by my mother Helen Parker Carleton, who has stood by me in every way for the past thirty-four years, and without whose help and encouragement this work would never have been initiated.

Since this project was undertaken, my one-year-old son has reached school age, while two more little boys have joined the "seminar." These fine fellows have endured through five years of what, to them, has meant little more than too many daddy-less bedtimes and weekends. My wife Maureen O. Carleton would have been similarly victimized had she not contributed enthusiastically to the project from start to finish. In many ways she is as much the author as I am. What is now due these four wonderful people simply cannot be verbalized.

Nor can I adequately express my debt to Professor David M. Potter, whose death occurred shortly after the manuscript was accepted for publication. For the last thirty years of his life Professor Potter was a truly distinguished member of the history faculties at Yale and (from 1961) Stanford universities. As an undergraduate at Yale and as a graduate student at Stanford, I was a most privileged beneficiary of David Potter's readily shared wisdom and of his sympathetic and yet thoroughly professional guidance. Whatever merit this work possesses is due in ample measure to his having been the best of advisors and a most loyal and patient friend.

Finally, I must thank Mrs. Ruth B. Hubert of the Louisiana State University Press for making this work clearer and more readable, and Mrs. Nan E. Nakos for typing revisions of the original manuscript.

Politics and Punishment

CHAPTER I

Punishment for Profit
1835-1880

S HORTLY AFTER Louisiana entered the Union in 1812, Edward Livingston, an adopted son and eminent jurist, was commissioned by the General Assembly to codify the state's jurisprudence. A bewildering hodgepodge, indeed, was Louisiana law, "inherited with little legal logic from the Corpus Juris Civilis, the Pandects, the Code of Justinian, various laws and codes of France and Spain, criminal and commercial laws and the law of evidence from England, the Code Napoleon, and various Federal and state laws of the United States."[1] Clearly, the entire body of Louisiana law had to be untangled, simplified, and brought up to date. Livingston addressed himself conscientiously to this task. By 1824 he had completed a Civil Code, a Code of Procedure, a Commercial Code, and his widely acclaimed *System of Penal Law*. The last was a project over which Livingston had labored most enthusiastically. He sought not only to clarify Louisiana's criminal jurisprudence but also "to ameliorate punishment and not to avenge society; to reform the criminal and to prevent crime."[2]

These progressive and humane views were most extensively

[1] Edwin A. Davis, *Louisiana: A Narrative History* (Baton Rouge, 1965), 197.

[2] William B. Hatcher, *Edward Livingston: Jeffersonian Republican and Jacksonian Democrat* (Baton Rouge, 1940), 263.

embodied in the Code of Reform and Prison Discipline, one of four codes within Livingston's *System of Penal Law.* Convinced that capital punishment had failed everywhere as an effective deterrent to further criminal behavior, Livingston urged its abolition in favor of life imprisonment.[3] Theft, in one form or another, has always been the most frequently committed criminal act, and Livingston was equally convinced that ignorance and poverty (rather than inherent criminal tendencies) were what induced persons to steal. He suggested that imprisoned felons be taught useful trades, reading and writing, and be rewarded for good behavior. He also recommended separation of first offenders from hardened criminals and believed that prisoners under the age of eighteen should be detained in special institutions.[4] The influence of philosophes and other reformers, such as Beccaria, Diderot, Montesquieu, Voltaire, and Bentham, is apparent in Livingston's *System of Penal Law.* "He was desirous," according to his biographer, "that Louisiana should lead the age in humanitarian legislation."[5]

But Louisiana was not inclined to accept such leadership, either in Livingston's own time or subsequently. The General Assembly adopted only his Civil Code and Code of Procedure.[6] It failed even to take action on the *System of Penal Law.* Louisiana, as a colony of absolutist France and Bourbon Spain, "had not participated in the progressive events of the eighteenth century and was hostile to them. The social basis was not liberal. . . . The truth is [in the judgment of a legal scholar,] that Louisiana was only interested in Edward Livingston to the extent that [Livingston] satisfied the needs of the existing system of production through slave labor. That, possibly, is why the criminal codes, with their advanced characteristics, never were adopted."[7] Livingston himself pronounced a caustic appraisal of Louisiana when he observed that the

---

[3] *Ibid.,* 269–70.   [4] *Ibid.,* 279–80.   [5] *Ibid.,* 267.
[6] Mitchell Franklin, "Concerning the Historic Importance of Edward Livingston," *Tulane Law Review,* XI (1937), 210.
[7] *Ibid.,* 210–11.

concerns to which the state gave priority were "security to property, stability to personal rights, certainty to commercial contracts, a decrease in the number of litigated questions [and] dispatch in their decision when they arise."[8] A more recent observer views the disinclination of antebellum Louisiana to endorse penal reform as part of a regional pattern, concluding that "acceptance of slavery necessarily destroyed the philosophical basis for a prison reform movement." In the North, abolition of slavery and penal reform "were both part of the greater humanitarian movement," a fact which probably "caused the Southern people to look askance at both."[9] If, therefore, penal reform outside the South was vigorously implemented during the 1830s, the rise of abolitionism to the forefront of the general reform movement did much to retard other efforts in the direction of betterment, including prison reform, within Louisiana and throughout the South during the same period.

Perhaps, then, active promotion of humanitarian legislation was too much to expect of socially conservative, property-minded, slave-owning Louisiana. Negro slavery, however, has long since vanished from the American scene. Several generations of reformers, moreover, have sent their various spokesmen to Washington (and to Baton Rouge) since the late nineteenth century. And the fields of criminology and penology have risen to become respected professions as well as recognized areas of academic investigation. Have these and related developments furthered the cause of penal reform in Louisiana? Or, on the other hand, has Louisiana remained immune to them? The historical record indicates that the first question should receive a qualified yes, the second an equally qualified no.

Penal reform in Louisiana has rarely inspired sustained

[8] Quoted in *ibid.*, 211.

[9] Hilda Jane Zimmerman, "Penal Systems and Penal Reforms in the South since the Civil War" (Ph.D. dissertation, University of North Carolina, 1947), 48–49. A comprehensive discussion of southern prisons and southern prison reform (or rather the lack of it) during the antebellum period may be found on pp. 14–49.

popular support, probably because "law-abiding" Louisianians, like such people anywhere, fear criminals, make little or
no effort to understand causes of criminal behavior, and certainly find it difficult to identify openly or to sympathize with
criminals. Hampered by these negative and persistent attitudes, friends of penal reform in Louisiana have often been
frustrated by the forces of habit, hostility, fiscal conservatism,
and official inertia. The overall result since 1835 has been a
collection of bits and pieces snatched up here and there along
a road more conspicuously marked by rhetoric than by substantial achievements.

Among the other codes contained in Livingston's *System of
Penal Law* were those of Criminal Procedure and Crimes and
Punishments. Louisiana did not enact a Code of Criminal
Procedure until 1928; the criminal law itself remained in
disorder, tangled, contradictory, and uncodified, until 1942.
Although the state has not put anyone to death since 1961,
capital punishment remains on the statute books, and subsequent executions are therefore not altogether unlikely.
"Convicts" as young as seven years of age remained in the
penitentiary until 1910. Louisiana's manner of dealing with
juvenile offenders has improved substantially since that time,
although shortages of qualified personnel, buildings, and other
necessities must still be overcome. The state's parole system
evolved from the commutation law of 1886 and the first parole
law of 1914. Rarely, however, have parole boards been free
of political or professional criticism. Parole officers have always, in addition, been too few in number to be able to
supervise their numerous cases satisfactorily.

It is the penitentiary itself, however, which remains the
largest and most venerable complex of nineteenth century
ideas and practices still at work in the twentieth century. In
that institution, located on a remote plantation adjacent to
the Mississippi River, many of the prisoners spend their time
cultivating sugar cane and engaging in other agricultural pursuits, activities in which convicts have been continuously
engaged (in one part of Louisiana or another) for more than

a century. Plantation work was adopted after the Civil War at a time when the vast majority of convicts were Negroes. There was much cotton picking and cane cutting to be done in the 1870s, and because most of the inmates (as slaves) had become experts in this line of work, sending many of them back to the fields seemed the natural (and most profitable) policy to pursue. Also, the survival of agricultural operations within the penal system into the 1960s suggests that the terms "convict," "slave," "Negro," and "farm work" have remained unconsciously interchangeable in the mind of institutional Louisiana.

From 1844 until 1901, almost without interruption, Louisiana leased her convicts to a number of private operators, if possible for profit; but if profit was not possible, leasing was at least a means of avoiding the expense of maintaining the prisoners. Genuine programs of reform or rehabilitation are difficult to implement when making or saving money become the most important objectives of a penitentiary. During the lessee era, needless to say, there was no commitment to reform or rehabilitation. This long and dismal experience gave rise, nonetheless, to the still-fashionable notion that the penal system should be made to "pay for its own keep." Lessees made considerable profits by working the convicts on farms and plantations—so considerable that the state, on resuming control of the penitentiary in 1901, put prisoners to work on its own plantations, where they have been engaged in similar tasks (but at not quite the same rate of profit) ever since. Finally, it may not be irrelevant to question the rehabilitative value of agricultural work (if any such value is claimed for it), when it is realized that the farm dwellers of Louisiana in 1960 comprised only 7.2 percent of the state's total population.[10]

Since the Louisiana penal system was established, penal reform in the state has had to combat an apathetic, vengeful, and sometimes hostile public, a thoroughly politicized

[10] James R. Bobo and Sandra A. Etheridge, *Statistical Abstract of Louisiana,* (3d. ed.; New Orleans, 1969), 15.

penal system, and a ubiquitous profit motive. Reforms have been achieved, but certainly not as readily nor in as substantial a form as Edward Livingston visualized them a hundred and fifty years ago.

Construction of Louisiana's first "official" state penitentiary was completed at Baton Rouge in 1835. Up to that time convicted state prisoners had been lodged in an old, vermin-infested New Orleans jail, condemned by no less an authority than Alexis de Tocqueville. In 1831 the French observer commented: "We saw there men thrown in pell-mell with swine, in the midst of excrement and filth. In locking up criminals, no thought is given to making them better but simply to taming their wickedness; they are chained like wild beasts; they are not refined but brutalized."[11] Transfer of all prisoners to the new facility was soon effected, and it was assumed that management of the "model" penitentiary would result in marked improvements over the shortcomings of its predecessor. No longer permitted to languish idly in their cells, the inmates were put to work manufacturing various cotton, leather, and woolen products. Engaged in this potentially rehabilitative activity (perhaps inspired by the ideas of Edward Livingston) were "three-hundred convicts, of whom two-thirds were white and only one-third foreign-born. Murder was the crime for which a third . . . had been convicted; larceny and burglary were charged to the rest. Their sentences . . . ran from one to five years for larceny, twenty years for manslaughter, and life for murder."[12]

All that was wrong with this smoothly functioning and humanely motivated penal factory was that it cost the state

[11] Quoted in George Wilson Pierson, *Tocqueville and Beaumont in America* (New York, 1938), 622. See also Elizabeth Wisner, *Public Welfare Administration in Louisiana* (Chicago, 1930), 141–43; and Leon Stout, "Origins and Early History of the Louisiana Penitentiary" (M.A. thesis, Louisiana State University, 1934).

[12] Roger W. Shugg, *Origins of Class Struggle in Louisiana: A Social History of White Farmers and Laborers During Slavery and After* (Baton Rouge, 1939), 60–61.

too much to operate. In 1844, after only nine years of state control, the legislature "abandoned the idea of reformation" altogether and—imitating the example set by Kentucky twenty years earlier—leased the penitentiary for five years to a private firm, McHatton, Pratt and Company.[13] Except for two instances—an interval between subsequent leases during the 1850s and the disruptive interlude of the Civil War—Louisiana's convicts would remain under private control and management until 1901.

Between 1830 and 1844 construction and maintenance of the penitentiary consumed $450,000 of the state's funds. (It should be remembered that during the latter years of this period the nation, and Louisiana, were afflicted by a major economic depression.) As the number of prisoners increased, the physical plant had to be expanded and extra personnel hired.[14] These improvements required additional money which penitentiary earnings were unable to provide. State control of the institution was proving to be "an expensive luxury," as recalled in later years by the official state journal.[15]

Compared to post-Civil War contracts, which required lessees to pay annual rentals as high as $50,000, the McHatton, Pratt lease was modest indeed. The lessees were required to pay nothing for the privilege of working the state's convicts, but were only to relieve Louisiana of the "expensive luxury" which state support of the penitentiary had become. In 1844,

[13] Wisner, *Public Welfare Administration*, 147; State of Louisiana, *Acts Passed at the Second Session of the Sixteenth Legislature* (New Orleans, 1844), 41–44. Published legislative actions are hereinafter cited as *Acts of Louisiana*, with appropriate year indicated. The lease measure was entitled "An act to provide for the better administration of the Louisiana Penitentiary."

[14] Wisner, *Public Welfare Administration*, 147. See also Zimmerman, "Penal Systems and Penal Reforms in the South since the Civil War," 22–25. Of all southern penal systems, Louisiana's was the most sketchily researched in this otherwise commendable pioneer study.

[15] Baton Rouge *Daily Advocate*, January 13, 1901; Clement Eaton, *The Growth of Southern Civilization, 1790–1860* (New York, 1963), 281–82.

therefore, economy replaced rehabilitation as Louisiana's principal objective in penal policy.[16]

Although the state sought to reduce her expense, she was
still concerned with rehabilitation and sought no profit. In
fact, she advanced large sums to the lessees. But the lessees
were not at all committed to rehabilitation. Profit was their
sole objective. And if the lessees were to prosper, little time
could be devoted to reforming or rehabilitating the convicts,
for such distractions would cut deeply into working hours
and thus decrease profits. Nor could large numbers of doctors,
nurses, clergymen, or other professional people be employed
to attend the prisoners; large payrolls also gnawed into profits and were to be avoided. Finally, the convicts themselves
would have to be dealt with in a more businesslike manner:
leisure time must be minimized, food and clothing cut down
to a subsistence level, and discipline administered more thoroughly in order to maintain a profitable level of operation.
Not long after the lessees took over, the legislature was informed that the convicts were being treated "like slave[s]."[17]

It had previously come to the legislature's attention that
the lessees were making a great deal of money. Accordingly,
in 1850, a new five-year lease was negotiated with the rear-
ranged firm of McHatton, Ward and Company. The lessees
would thereafter be obliged to pay the state an annual rental
of one-quarter of the profits.[18] Although the lease was signed

[16] Wisner, *Public Welfare Administration*, 148–51. The legislature
in 1844 had agreed to lend the lessees $15,000 to set up additional manu-
facturing machinery. By 1849, however, $57,000 had been advanced.
Economy soon proved to be an elusive objective insofar as leasing the
penitentiary was concerned. See *Acts of Louisiana* (1844), 44; and State
of Louisiana, *Legislature, Journal of the Senate* (Baton Rouge, 1852),
123–24. Published proceedings of the senate are hereinafter cited as
Senate Journal, with appropriate year indicated.

[17] *Senate Journal* (1852), 123. Before the Civil War most of Louisiana's convicts were Caucasian, a fact which may have fired the indignation of the senator presenting the report.

[18] *Senate Journal* (1850), 10. The lessees had to guarantee that annual
profits would be no less than $4,000, which would guarantee the state,
in turn, a minimum annual revenue of $1,000 from the penitentiary
lease.

in 1850, formal ratification by the legislature would be required in order for the contract to be operative legally. Once again Louisiana had embarked upon a new course of penal policy. For the next half-century the objective of the state would be identical with the motive of the lessees themselves—to make money.

But why not *all* of the money? The same legislator who complained that convicts were being treated like slaves suggested in 1852 that the lease be terminated and the state resume control of the penitentiary. "If this profit [estimated in 1852 at $15,000 annually] can be made by [the lessees]," he asked, "why should so considerable a sum be withdrawn . . . from the public treasury, which needs it so much?"[19] This conscientious public servant, Senator G. W. Watterston of Baton Rouge, apparently failed to realize that the lessees' methods, to which he was so strongly opposed, were in fact what made profits possible. Moreover, if the state was unwilling to adopt the lessees' methods, it should not expect to make the lessees' profits.

There is no evidence to suggest that other legislators were so solicitous of convict welfare as their colleague from Baton Rouge. Most probably agreed with Senator J. W. Butler of Natchitoches who said that "without some means to make the prisoners stand in fear, it would be utterly impossible to maintain any discipline or subordination, and we know of no mode of punishment less cruel, and more effective, than a proper amount of flogging."[20] There is evidence to suggest, on the other hand, that Watterston's concern for the "public treasury" was shared by the legislature—on a no-risk basis, at any rate—for the lease to McHatton, Ward and Company was duly ratified. Five years later, in 1857, still another lease, even more attractive from the state's point of view, was made with J. M. Hart and W. S. Pike. This arrangement provided that annual profits were to be divided evenly between the

[19] *Ibid.* (1852), 125.   [20] *Ibid.*, 128.

state and the lessees.[21] The Civil War ended this lease. Following a period of federal supervision, Louisiana's convicts were returned to the custody of the state, which in 1868 promptly leased them all off her hands again.

There was much controversy before 1861—more than has been discussed here—concerning the lease system and related problems. How badly were the convicts being treated by lessees? To what uses beneficial to the convicts might lessee rentals be put? How might the state retain some control over convict rehabilitation and convict welfare?[22] The same questions were asked during the course of post-Civil War contracts and were no more satisfactorily resolved in the later years than before. For so long as lessees remained in control of the Louisiana penal system, humane treatment and rehabilitation of convicts took a distant back seat to profit making. Rentals paid by lessees were seldom if ever reinvested in the penal system. State officials comprising a Board of Control, appointed to safeguard "convict welfare," discovered that "convict welfare" was nothing but a euphemism within a penitentiary run for profit by private individuals whose quasi-official authority could be neither disputed nor overridden.

A prison under relatively humane state management, with reform and rehabilitation of convicts its ostensible objectives, had failed to support itself, much less yield any profits, between 1835 and 1844. The state of Louisiana viewed this situation as unacceptable and sought to correct it by leasing the penitentiary to private contractors, first with the objective of saving money, and later with the objective of making money. For eighteen years, up to 1862, the penitentiary remained in private hands. During this time the state actually made little money, but was spared the burden of expenditures to have been expected from continued state management. To this extent, the prewar leases fulfilled the state's purposes. At the same time, there continued to be criticism of lessee treatment of convicts and concern expressed that

[21] Wisner, *Public Welfare Administration*, 148–51.
[22] For a more detailed summary of this controversy, see *ibid.*, 151–60.

rehabilitation was being ignored. Concerned Louisianians were discovering that both aims could not go hand in hand: lessees could not be expected to make money (both for themselves and for the state) and also carry out programs of reform and rehabilitation, responsibilities which the state itself had cast away in favor of the profit motive.

The most decisive event in the history of southern penology was the Civil War. The conflict itself, of course, had no direct bearing upon penal law or practices, but the war changed the status of half of the population—the slaves—who were most liable to penal action, and it thus created a wholly new situation for the penal system to deal with. Negro slaves became free Negroes and, subsequently, citizens. From this sizable component in the population came a correspondingly large group of Negro criminals. Insofar as such persons had previously committed offenses defined as crimes, they had, as slaves, been punished largely on the plantations; but after 1865 they were jammed into overcrowded and dilapidated penal facilities constructed in antebellum days primarily "for whites only." Even if nothing was done to alleviate these conditions—and nothing was—the added expense of feeding, clothing, and guarding so many more prisoners, white as well as colored, was an undertaking that southern state and county governments viewed with concern. Faced with these real and immediate problems at a time when their economies were prostrate, southern legislatures considered the lease system an attractive proposition, particularly when it seemed possible to avoid the financial embarrassment of supporting convicts and, in addition, to derive a revenue from the transaction as well.

Southern penal systems were affected on two levels, therefore, by the sudden influx of Negroes into the prison population after 1865. The sheer numbers of convicts to be maintained within inadequate facilities and on meager budgets strongly recommended the lease system as both an economical and potentially profitable alternative to state maintenance and responsibility. And as Negroes were experienced agri-

cultural workers, most of them were eventually employed by
the lessees as cotton and fruit pickers, sugar cane cutters, and
vegetable gardeners. From these circumstances arose the
penal farm, an institution uniquely southern, which in
Louisiana still serves as the sacrosanct nucleus of penal
operations.

While prison reform made headway elswhere in the nation during the latter nineteenth century, in the South no
comparable progress would be evident for decades to come.
Private contractors, eager to obtain cheap labor for a variety
of projects ranging from levee and railroad construction to
plantation work, found southern legislatures equally eager
to accommodate them. By 1870 most arrangements had been
made.[23] For more than a generation in some states the convict lease system would remain the dominant feature of southern penology.

Louisiana was briefly in charge of her penitentiary during
the period immediately following the Civil War. In January,
1868, penitentiary officials submitted a detailed report on
conditions within the institution, the last such detailed report, in fact, for almost thirty years.

There had been 228 convicts within the pentitentiary on
January 1, 1867. Admitted during the ensuing year were
229 more. Within this same year 167 convicts were released,
11 were pardoned, 41 escaped, and 16 died. Half of the
deaths resulted from scurvy, which authorities ascribed to lack
of fruit in the prison diet.[24] No data were provided on the
number of white and black prisoners, but a subsequent report,

[23] Fletcher Melvin Green, "Some Aspects of the Convict Lease System
in the Southern States," in Fletcher Melvin Green, ed., *Essays in Southern
History presented to J. G. deRoulhac Hamilton by his Former Students*
(Chapel Hill, 1949) , 115–19; Blake McKelvey, "Penal Slavery and Southern
Reconstruction," *Journal of Negro History,* XX (1935) , 153–55; Dan T.
Carter, "Prisons, Politics and Business: The Convict Lease System in the
Post-Civil War South" (M.A. thesis, University of Wisconsin, 1964) , 40.

[24] State of Louisiana, *Annual Report of the Board of Control of the
Louisiana State Penitentiary: January 1, 1868* (New Orleans, 1868) , 3, 32.
Published annual reports of the board are hereinafter cited as *Report,
Board of Control,* with appropriate date indicated.

issued several months later, listed 85 white males, 203 black males, 9 black females (but no white females) in the penitentiary as of June 14, 1868.[25]

Crimes for which 229 prisoners admitted during 1867 had been convicted included: 198 against property (of which larceny alone counted for 131); and 31 against the person, of which three were for murder, three for rape, five for manslaughter, and the rest for various forms and degrees of assault.[26] By occupation, most of those admitted, 191, were "laborers."[27]

While no correlation was given of race-to-crime-to-occupation, it can be seen that a majority were laborers, a majority were Negroes, and a majority had commited no crime more serious than larceny, for which the average sentence was four months to one year. Prison officials asked, indeed, if the legislature would not "inquire into the reason why so many are sent to this institution for the term of three, four, and six months, upon the most trivial charges? Does there not lurk beneath, the low, mean motive of depriving them of the right[s] of citizenship?"[28]

Of the 222 convicts in the penitentiary on January 1, 1868, 116 were under the age of twenty-five, 73 having been in the twenty-to-twenty-five year age group, 40 between the ages of fifteen and twenty, and 3 between ten and fifteen years of age.[29] The penitentiary had cost the state of Louisiana $61,838.88 to operate during 1867. An appropriation of $210,000 was requested for the following year.[30] On March

[25] Ibid. (November 17, 1868), 111.
[26] Ibid. (January 1, 1868), 63–71.   [27] Ibid., 93.
[28] Ibid. (November 17, 1868), 52. Charges of political racism against judges and juries do not seem to have been investigated, even though Radical Reconstruction had been established in Louisiana, and many legislators by 1868 were Negroes. For an interesting commentary upon the behavior of juries in Louisiana during early Reconstruction, see Ella Lonn, Reconstruction in Louisiana after 1868 (New York, 1918), 354–55.
[29] Report, Board of Control (January 1, 1868), 96. On September 26, 1870, Samuel Wilson of Bienville Parish was admitted into the penitentiary to serve a life sentence for murder. He was nine years old at the time. Wilson's race was not specified. See Senate Journal (1873), 147.
[30] Report, Board of Control (January 1, 1868), 6.

18, 1868, Governor Joshua Baker signed a contract leasing the penitentiary to John M. Huger and Colonel Charles Jones. The contract would, however, have to be ratified by the legislature.

In the meantime, Louisiana had been placed under military supervision, as provided for by the Reconstruction Acts of 1867. A new state constitution had been written, adult male suffrage established, and elections set for state executive offices and seats in the legislature, henceforth (until 1921) to be called the General Assembly. The elections were held in 1868, and when the lease came up for ratification the following year it faced an assembly in which there was a majority of white and Negro Republicans. Louisiana's new chief executive was a handsome, twenty-six-year-old "carpetbagger," Henry Clay Warmoth, who had been inaugurated on July 13, 1868.

The lease of the penitentiary to Huger and Jones was ratified by the assembly in January, 1869, but was vetoed by Governor Warmoth, who issued this morally outraged message: "There is too much power given to the lessees over the institution, and the Board of Control is ignored. The health, comfort, food, religious training and discipline of the prisoners should be under the charge of disinterested officers of the Government. . . . Where the lessees have absolute power over the prisoners the tendency is to work them too much and feed them too little and give no attention to their comforts and instruction."[31]

The Board of Control, a legacy from antebellum days, consisted of five gubernatorial appointees who were supposed to ensure that humane standards of convict welfare were maintained by the lessees. Before the war the board had not been too successful: "humane standards" conflicted with the objective of the lessees, which was to make money. The lessees, moreover, rather than the board, possessed the authority to manage the penitentiary. Between 1865 and 1868 the state Board of Control had actually managed the penitentiary; but

[31] *Senate Journal* (1869), 6.

now, in 1869, Huger and Jones appeared determined to relegate this agency to limbo in order that the convicts might be worked at the lessees' pleasure. The governor found this attempt distressing. Later in the session, however, a modified bill, which became Act 55 of 1869, legalized the arrangements made previously between Baker and the new lessees. The Board of Control was given the "direction and control of the health and religious regulations of the convicts," although final authority remained with the lessees.[32] Warmoth signed the bill granting a lease to Huger and Jones for five years (from 1868). Annual net profits would be divided evenly between the state and the lessees. Finally, in order to get the penitentiary into operating condition again following wartime damage, $500,000 worth of state bonds were authorized for the purpose of buying new manufacturing machinery.

Act 55 was signed by Governor Warmoth on March 5, 1869. Hardly before the ink had dried, Huger and Jones were packing their bags. Were they disappointed? Were they not making money? They had just made a great deal of money—probably in excess of $100,000—by having sold out to a firm calling itself James, Buckner and Company. For the next eleven months James, Buckner and Company managed the penitentiary and worked the convicts without legal authorization, either from Warmoth or the General Assembly. When the assembly convened in January, 1870, James and his associates were in New Orleans to do business.

House member O. H. Brewster of Ouachita Parish sponsored a bill proposing that "Samuel L. James, C. B. Buckner and T. Bynum, having purchased from Messrs. Huger and Jones, the lease [of the penitentiary] . . . be and the same are

[32] *Acts of Louisiana* (1869), 57. The full measure of the board's impotence was revealed in a subsquent clause: "Provided, that nothing in this act shall be construed into a right to impair the efficiency in the labor, or to interfere with the employment of the convicts in accordance with the terms of the lease." By 1894 salaries of the board members were being paid by lessees. See *Senate Journal* (1894), 14. It is more than likely that Huger and Jones "employed" the Board of Control at this earlier date as well.

hereby substituted and placed instead of [Huger and Jones] as lessees of the Louisiana State Penitentiary.[33] The measure further proposed to award a twenty-one-year lease to S. L. James and Company. On January 28 the bill was reported favorably (6–1) by the House Penitentiary Committee. The dissenting member, however, expressed dissatisfaction with the length of the contract, believing that it should be reduced to ten or even five years and "be given to the highest responsible bidder."[34] The vote on final passage three days later revealed a crossing of party lines as some Democrats and some Republicans supported, while others opposed, the bill. Of the twenty-five Negroes who were present and voting, however, all but one were in favor. Forty-seven white members supported the bill, while thirteen opposed it.[35] In the upper house, Senator John Lynch sought first to amend the bill by providing for an annual rental of $35,000. When this was voted down, he suggested $20,000. This, too, failed. The bill as passed on February 24 retained the twenty-one-year contract and provided for a graduated scale of annual rentals, $5,000 being due the first year, $6,000 the second, and so on, until by 1891 the lessees would have paid the state $25,000 for the final year of their lease. All four Negro senators favored the bill, which became Act 56 of 1870 when signed by Governor Warmoth a week later.[36] One motive behind passage of this measure was to obtain a revenue for the state from the labor of her convicts. But other "inducements" seem to have been applied as well.

[33] *Acts of Louisiana* (1870), 85.

[34] State of Louisiana. *Journal of the Proceedings of the House of Representatives of the General Assembly, Regular Session* (New Orleans, 1870), 118. Published proceedings of the house are hereinafter cited as *House Journal*, with appropriate year indicated.

[35] *Ibid.*, 135–36. The bill passed by a vote of 71–14. The authority on Negro membership in the Louisiana General Assembly during the latter nineteenth century is A. E. Perkins, "Some Negro Officers and Legislators in Louisiana," *Journal of Negro History*, XIV (1929), 523–28.

[36] The senate approved the bill 20–7, with five Democrats and fifteen Republicans voting in favor and six Democrats and one Republican opposed. *Senate Journal* (Regular Session, 1870), 212. The James bill contained no reference to the Board of Control, an agency which, by 1870, was totally without influence.

A financial victim of the clandestine "switch" from one set of lessees to the other charged that, while the James bill was being debated, the bonds issued a year earlier had in fact been obtained and used by James as a colossal bribe: $100,000 worth had gone to Huger and Jones to sell their equity in the lease, and part of the remainder to members of the General Assembly, with the understanding that all necessary transactions and endorsements should be legalized.[37] The documented performance of latter-nineteenth century Louisiana politicians, during and after Reconstruction, lends substantial credibility to these charges.[38] Insofar as Louisiana was concerned, the leasing of convicts originated in antebellum days and was readopted following the Civil War. Reconstructionists, therefore, were not to blame for instituting the system in Louisiana, as was the case elsewhere in the South. But within the assembly of 1870, white Democrats had joined white and black Republicans in adding the nasty odor of corruption to the traditional motives of fiscal conservatism and indifference to humanitarian considerations.

Samuel Lawrence James, who by 1870 had become Louisiana's dominant postbellum lessee, was born in Clarksville, Tennessee, in 1834. A competent civil engineer at twenty, James, in 1854, moved to New Orleans where he became associated with P. G. T. Beauregard and helped construct the United States Custom House, a hospital, and the city's first streetcar lines.[39] When the Civil War broke out, James assisted in raising an Irish brigade from New Orleans and was commissioned a captain in the Sixth Louisiana Infantry Regiment, with which he fought at First Manassas. Promoted soon thereafter to major, James was believed in later years to have served "valiantly" throughout the remainder of the conflict in the Trans-Mississippi Department. (The official rec-

[37] See P. Winfre, "The Penitentiary Bill," New Orleans *Times*, January 19, 1870.

[38] Shugg, *Origins of Class Struggle*, 225–26. See also William Ivy Hair, *Bourbonism and Agrarian Protest: Louisiana Politics, 1877–1900* (Baton Rouge, 1969), 7–9, 132–33.

[39] New Orleans *Daily Picayune*, July 28, 1894.

ords disclose, however, that James resigned from the Confederate army in December, 1861.)[40]

The major's activities for the next few years are vaguely documented. He traveled abroad after the war and managed somehow during the late sixties to accumulate a considerable amount of money, which he used in part to purchase Angola, an extensive cotton plantation in West Feliciana Parish, and to purchase the convict lease in 1869 from Huger and Jones. That he may also have "purchased" members of the General Assembly the following year was not acknowledged.[41]

Physically, the major was an impressive specimen of the Gilded Age: with the features and sideburns of a beefy Chester A. Arthur, from the neck down James could double equally well for Grover Cleveland. But the major's affinities with the time were not merely symbolic. A man of property and influence in 1870, James continued to demonstrate that he possessed the means to secure for himself an abundance of good things in this life. When he died in 1894 newspaper obituaries described James as having been a "singularly sagacious man of business," "gifted with indomitable will," "eminently successful in all that he undertook," and "endowed with a nature that knew no defeat."[42] Rendered by friend and enemy alike, these post-mortem tributes to Samuel L. James rather fairly portray the man who initiated and personally maintained for twenty-five years the most cynical, profit-oriented, and brutal prison regime in Louisiana history.

With the penitentiary comfortably out of its hands, and with twenty-one years of revenue anticipated, the Louisiana General Assembly returned to the "normal" business of Reconstruction politics in the early 1870s. Amidst party and factional squabbling, few persons bothered to keep an eye on the lessees or concern themselves with the matter of convict

40 *Ibid.*; New Orleans *Times-Democrat*, July 28, 1894; Andrew B. Booth (comp.) , *Records of Louisiana Confederate Soldiers and Louisiana Confederate Commands* (New Orleans, 1920) , III, Book 1, p. 427.

41 New Orleans, *Daily Picayune,* New Orleans *Times-Democrat,* July 28, 1894.

42 *Ibid.*

welfare. In 1873, however, a joint committee of senators and representatives inspected the penitentiary in Baton Rouge and submitted the following report: "Bucking, gagging, and [the] shower-bath had been abandoned . . . Whipping was still used, also the dark cell . . . in extreme cases . . . . The guards generally were competent men, and not malicious or cruel . . . . White as well as colored convicts were whipped; they made no discriminations as to race in the punishments inflicted."[43] None of the lessees was at the penitentiary; the clerk of the institution, one Matta, "did not know who the owners of the lease now were, except Major Samuel James." The warden was not on hand either, but his deputy, Captain F. Guidry, informed the committee that "the warden . . . had authority to punish convicts for misconduct without special directions from the board." Guidry further "suppose[d] that the board of control knows the character of punishments used by the warden and his deputies; they ought to know if they did not."[44] Action taken on this report by the assembly consisted of having it printed in the journal. Perhaps Major James still had a number of legislators in his pocket.

Where was Major James? Where was the warden? Where, for that matter, were most of the convicts? The committee had found the penitentiary nearly deserted. A year later, in 1874, Senator Thomas Cage, a Negro from Terrebonne Parish and chairman of the senate Committee on Parks and Public Buildings, submitted his report on the status of the penitentiary:

The penitentiary building was found in much better repair [than was supposed]. It is true the building is going to wreck [sic] in many particulars, and looks much forsaken

[43] *House Journal* (1873) 121–23. To "buck" someone was to tie his wrists together, next placing the arms over the bent knees. A stick was then placed over the arms and through the angle made by the knees. One was "gagged" by being made to wear an iron frame over the head with a metal bit, or "gag," in the mouth. The "shower bath" was a version of the ancient "water torture," in which water was poured over a person for an extended time. The "dark cell" was a form of solitary confinement.

[44] Quoted in *ibid.*

and weather-beaten, mouldy and dilapidated, but still it is more than amply sufficient for all that is going on within its walls or inclosures [sic]. Almost all the convicts arc now constantly farmed out—sent promiscuously, it seems, to different portions of the State to work in competition with free labor—so that there would seem scarcely any use any more for any Penitentiary building at all, and if matters go on for a few more years as they have been going on . . . we shall have none, except as a den or hiding place for owls, bats, and reptiles.[45]

In 1875 the president of the Board of Control disclosed that "the walls and buildings . . . have been but very little used since the last report [of the Board, submitted in 1872], most of the prisoners being outside the walls working on the levees, railroads, plantations, etc."[46]

Convict leasing in the nineteenth century conformed to one or the other of two basically different patterns. The contract system, strictly applied, left state officials directly responsible for feeding, clothing, and guarding the convicts, who remained (and were worked by the lessees) within the prison structure. Under this type of arrangement, lessees hired only convict labor, and not the convicts themselves. South Carolina, Texas, and Virginia had adopted this system by the 1880s.[47] The lease system required that lessees maintain the convicts but empowered them to work convicts outside the prison structure. All other southern states, plus Nebraska and the New Mexico Territory, were using the lease system by the 1880s. Louisiana's antebellum arrangements had combined features of both systems, for while the lessees had been responsible for convict maintenance, they had also worked the prisoners "within the walls" at Baton Rouge. And in the early 1870s state authorities had assumed, or had pretended to assume, that James also would work the convicts within the penitentiary in the customary manner as

[45] Senate Journal (1874), 213.
[46] Report, Board of Control (1875), 3.
[47] Report of the United States Commissioner of Labor, House Executive Documents, 49th Cong., 2nd sess., No. 1, Part 5, pp. 269–74.

"manufacturers," utilizing the machinery therein. Although some of this machinery was antiquated, all of it was not. According to the president of the board, $300,000 worth of new textile machinery was available and in excellent condition. But aside from a few elderly convicts who were assigned the job of oiling and polishing, no one came near this equipment.[48]

James had been working the prisoners at more lucrative employment from the very beginning. Between March and November, 1869—even before his lease had been legally ratified—James had made almost $100,000 from working his convicts on the state's Mississippi River levees.[49] "Experienced" Negro convicts could be worked almost as profitably on farms or plantations, while any able-bodied convict could be subcontracted for railroad construction. James and his associates worked the prisoners under their control on all three of these projects from the moment prisoners were "bought" from Huger and Jones until they were returned to the state in 1901. The system that prevailed in Louisiana from 1869 to 1901 was, therefore, the pure lease system, and not the hybrid system of prewar years. And anyone wishing to locate the major, by the way, might have inquired either at Angola or at Lagona plantations, the latter a sugar estate in St. Mary Parish also owned by the enterprising lessee and worked, not surprisingly, by convicts.[50]

In general, it made no difference to white legislators how James worked the convicts or where, so long as the penitentiary was not the state's responsibility. But to many of the Negro senators and representatives, this matter was of genuine concern, for low-priced convict labor at work throughout the state frequently deprived their constituents of jobs. It was one thing to establish a convict lease by which the state might avoid expense or even derive revenue, but it was highly undesirable to see convicts at work "in competition with free

[48] *Report, Board of Control* (1875), 4–5.
[49] *Ibid.* (1870), 9–19.
[50] William Ivy Hair, "The Agrarian Protest in Louisiana: 1877–1900" (Ph.D. dissertation, Louisiana State University, 1962), 192.

labor," as Senator Cage had expressed it in 1874. The apparent logic of this argument convinced enough legislators, white as well as Negro, to result in the passage of Act 22 of 1875 which prohibited the lessees from employing or permitting employment of the convicts outside the penitentiary itself. Penalties for violation could include a $5,000 fine and abrogation of the lease.[51]

Major James found himself harassed from two directions during the spring of 1875. Act 22, which could be invoked to put him out of business, was actually the less formidable of the two obstacles placed in his path. On March 20 the district attorney for East Baton Rouge Parish filed a lawsuit against James demanding that he pay immediately two years' delinquent rentals for his use of the convicts and that he forfeit the lease.[52] Thus, James could lose the convicts if he continued to work them profitably outside the penitentiary. At the same time, he stood to lose them anyway.

On January 3, 1876, Governor William Pitt Kellogg submitted his annual message to the General Assembly. Part of his address was devoted to Act 22 and its effect on the status of the penitentiary. After recommending that the convicts be authorized to work on the levees, as if they had not already been engaged in this work for several years, Kellogg got down to the dilemmas occasioned by the passage of Act 22:

> An attempt to enforce the law developed the fact that there was no appropriation for the support of the convicts within the walls of the penitentiary, and that the machinery and other appliances for manufacturers previously provided . . . could not be made available in their existing condition without a large outlay of money for which there was no

[51] *Acts of Louisiana* (1875), 54.

[52] State of Louisiana, *Report of the Senate Committee on Penitentiary to the Senate, Session of 1878* (New Orleans, 1878), 9. See also "Statement of the Auditor of Public Accounts," in State of Louisiana, *Journal of the Proceedings of the Constitutional Convention of 1879* (New Orleans, 1879), 180–81. One can only speculate concerning James's delinquency. The number of contracts may have fallen off, or he may have been convinced that he really need not pay his rentals (so long as he maintained the penitentiary) or there may have been any number of other reasons.

authority of law, and even with such an outlay, would in all probability fail to render the institution self-sustaining for some years to come. . . . The convicts are now nearly all working on the line of the New Orleans Pacific railroad [*sic*], a work of great importance to the State. I believe that they are as well provided for and as humanely treated as is practicable under the circumstances. Unless the State should make some arrangements otherwise to utilize their labor and ma[k]e it self-sustaining, I am convinced . . . that it is better to permit the present lessees to continue working the convicts under their existing lease.[53]

Thinking perhaps of the lawsuit pending against James, Kellogg concluded his discussion by suggesting that "some provision should be made . . . to meet an exigency that might be presented in the future by reason of the convicts being thrown upon the State."[54] Whatever virtues the governor's analysis may have possessed, certainly frankness and honesty were not among them. Kellogg failed to explain why he himself had signed Act 22 one year earlier. Surely, if he had read the bill, he would have noticed that it contained no appropriation. As for the condition of machinery in the penitentiary, Kellogg had either been misinformed or was telling a lie. Unless James had deliberately sabotaged the machinery (a distinct possibility under the circumstances), it is most unlikely that $300,000 worth of new equipment would have deteriorated to uselessness within one year. How could Kellogg possibly know, moreover, that James would *not* prosper by working the convicts within the walls? Finally, to whose advantage would violation of Act 22 really accrue—to the state's, to the railroad's, or to Major James's?

The house of representatives, in which there were a number of Negro members, briefly defied the governor. On February 7, William Murrell, a Negro representative from Madison Parish, proposed a resolution which ordered the penitentiary committee to investigate the matter and to determine if legal

[53] *Senate Journal* (January, 1876) , 12–13.   [54] *Ibid.*

grounds existed for canceling the lease.[55] The resolution passed but no further action on it was reported. Nor was there any attempt made in either chamber to provide for the "exigency," alluded to by Governor Kellogg, of the convicts "being thrown upon the State."

The "Home Rule" administration of Governor Francis T. Nicholls had no more intention of interfering with the lessee than its predecessor. Nicholls spoke frankly and to the point in his message of 1878: "As matters now stand [that is, with the lease still in financial arrears and most of the prisoners still working on the New Orleans Pacific Railroad] though the State gains nothing in money from her convicts she is at no expense for their support, and . . . I think that the present arrangement should continue." In case there might be legislators so unrealistic as to desire an abrogation of the lease, Nicholls concluded with a remark calculated to render the situation crystal clear: "I am not aware of a desire on the part of any one to lease the Penitentiary should the present lease be set aside."[56]

During an extra session, convened two months later, a bill to resolve the dilemma was rushed through the senate and arrived in the house on March 15. It provided that the amount due the state from S. L. James and Company be set by arbitration and, in addition, that the convicts continue to work on the New Orleans and Pacific Railroad.[57] Once again, as in the Kellogg episode, the house—in which there were more Negroes than in the senate—rebelled. Immediately following introduction, the bill was tabled by a vote of 49–24, without being read.[58] For one reason or another, the members were in a more receptive mood three days later. To quote the *House Journal*'s description of what took place, the bill "was taken up on its first reading, passed to a second reading, and under a suspension of the rules the bill was read a third time

[55] *House Journal* (January, 1876), 144.
[56] *Senate Journal* (Regular Session, 1878), 11.
[57] *House Journal* (Extraordinary Session, 1878), 64.
[58] *Ibid.*, 47–48.

and passed."[59] No votes are given for any of these august deliberations. The following year Governor Nicholls reported that an arbitration committee had fixed the sum owed by the lessees at $44,833, and that S. L. James and Company had begun to settle acounts.[60] Not until 1881, however, did the major actually make a payment.[61]

What of the legal proceedings filed against James in 1875? During the assembly session of 1878 a senate committee disclosed that Governor Kellogg, followed by Governor Nicholls, had urged officials in Baton Rouge "not to press the suit."[62] Two administrations, one Radical Republican, the other Home Rule Democrat, had considered it less prudent to evict the lessee than to settle with him out of court. Between 1873 and 1878 Major James violated one law six times and another at least once. (He failed to pay his rent for six consecutive years and continued to employ convicts outside the penitentiary between the passage of Act 22 and its repeal three years later.) The state of Louisiana, therefore, possessed legal grounds on at least seven counts for cancelling the James contract. State officials, however, whether Republican or Democratic, found it as easy to abandon their sworn obligation to enforce the law as they had earlier abandoned their official responsibility to support the penitentiary. Both the institution and its inmates remained securely in the contrtol of Major James during the transition from one state regime to another, so anxious were both to avoid that dreaded "exigency" of having the convicts "thrown upon them."

There is the additional possibility that James, in order to ensure absolutely his continued tenure in Baton Rouge, might have seen that various sums of money reached appropriate individuals at critical times. It is always difficult to prove

[59] *Ibid.*, 64.   [60] *Ibid.* (1879), 16.

[61] State of Louisiana, *Biennial Report of the State Treasurer to the Governor of the State of Louisiana: 1880–81* (Baton Rouge, 1882), 103–104. Published biennial reports of the treasurer are hereinafter cited as *Biennial Report, State Treasurer*, with appropriate years indicated.

[62] State of Louisiana, *Report of the Senate Committee on Penitentiary, 1878*, pp. 9–13.

that public officials have been bribed. Neither the source nor the recipient of such a transaction is likely to disclose his guilt or to leave written evidence thereof lying about. There is considerable evidence, however, to substantiate the general charge that bribery in late nineteenth century Louisiana was as popular a sport as football has become in the twentieth, with almost as many participants.[63] Traditionally, the most corrupt, and corrupting, agency in the state at that time was the notorious Louisiana State Lottery Company, an organization which "with its gigantic 'slush' fund . . . debauched legislators, muzzled the press, [and] made and unmade public officials."[64]

The lease, like the lottery, was a vested interest, and relations between the heads of these unsavory organizations remained as close after 1877 as beforehand. Charles T. Howard and John A. Morris, chiefs of the lottery, were both personal friends of Major James. All three of these gentlemen, moreover, were boon companions of Edward A. Burke, the state treasurer from 1878 to 1887. Burke, who also carried the title of "Major," had played an important role in the negotiations which sent Rutherford B. Hayes to the White House. In Louisiana, where he soon had "his fingers in scores of pies," Burke acquired the New Orleans *Times-Democrat*, which he converted into a stanch pro-lottery organ.[65] With the possible exceptions of the New Orleans *Daily States* and the Shreveport *Weekly Caucasian*, Burke's newspaper was the

[63] C. Vann Woodward, *Origins of the New South, 1877–1913* (Baton Rouge, 1951), 11–14.

[64] Henry E. Chambers, *A History of Louisiana* (3 vols.; Chicago, 1925), I, 707. Chartered in 1868 during the administration of "carpetbagger" Henry Clay Warmoth, the lottery was able to write itself into the Democratic Constituion of 1879, and to secure from the General Assembly of 1890 a joint resolution renewing its original charter. But the proposal was rejected by the electorate in 1892 and after a number of other troubles beset it, the lottery company moved to Honduras in 1894.

[65] C. Vann Woodward, *Reunion and Reaction: The Compromise of 1877 and the End of Reconstruction* (rev. ed.; Garden City, 1956), 208. In 1874 Burke and Governor Kellogg exchanged gunfire on a New Orleans street corner after Kellogg had made "an insulting gesture at Burke 'with his finger.'" Hair, *Bourbonism and Agrarian Protest*, 28.

most reactionary sheet in postbellum Louisiana. Rounding out this coterie were two other men, Louis A. Wiltz, governor of Louisiana from 1880 to 1881, and his successor, upon his death, Samuel Douglas McEnery, the state's chief executive between 1881 and 1888.

The lessee had, indeed, made friends in high places. But they were not his only supporters. Within the General Assembly those members who voted for the lottery also stood by Major James, with very few exceptions, when both enterprises were renewed in 1890.[66]

It has been shown that James also might well have "debauched legislators" in the process of ratifying his lease in 1870. His ability to continue the practice would depend, in large measure, upon his being able to afford it. An examination of the major's financial condition—to the extent that he let it be known—sheds considerable light on this question.

The annual report of the Board of Control for 1870 contains a long and lavish "General Balance Sheet of the Books of the Louisiana Penitentiary, under the Lease of James, Buckner and Co., on the first day of November, 1869" (three months before the major's lease was officially confirmed). Within eight months James and his associates had worked up a debit-credit balance of $478,456.75. Among the more revealing individual entries are the following:

	Debit	Credit
Company account	$90,141.99	$133,311.50
S. L. James	10,931.67	7,463.80
Lessees' cash acount	36,931.59	36,762.46
Levee account	50,900.01	147,449.30
Expense account	57,806.05	4,298.15
Provision account	21,481.33	7,894.71[67]

James had received almost $150,000 for working convicts

66 Renewal of the lottery and the James lease are discussed in chapter three below.

67 Report, Board of Control (1870), 9–19.

on levees; their labor had cost him a third of that amount, leaving a net profit for levee work alone of a tenth of a million dollars. Personally, the major himself had already drawn more than $10,000 from his new enterprise, while both the "Expense account" and the "Lessees' cash account" seem to have been actively employed, although for what purposes was not indicated.

It was officially known, therefore, by members of the General Assembly of 1870 that Major James had already done a half million dollars worth of business in less than a year. No wonder it was suggested in the house that the lease be cut to five years and sold to the highest bidder. No wonder Senator John Lynch recommended, for openers, that James be charged an annual rental of $35,000. But, as it developed, James emerged with a twenty-one-year contract, obliging him to pay, as his initial rental, a sum equal to approximately one-one-hundredth of the magnitude of business he was known to have carried on. How the major had been able to secure official endorsement of a contract so advantageous to himself can be easily imagined.

Once established in the penitentiary, James closed his books to both public and official scrutiny. No other report of the Board of Control during the subsequent thirty-one years of the major's regime contains any financial information relative to the lessees whatsoever. No reports of any sort, in fact, emerged from the penitentiary in 1873, 1874, 1876, 1877, or during the inclusive period from 1879 to 1889.

However, some idea of what was going on, financially and otherwise, within the major's domain may be gained from scattered available figures taken from official sources:

Year	Number of Convict Deaths Reported	Rental Paid the State	Debit-Credit Balance
1870	19	$ 5,000.00	$478,456.75
1871	21	6,000.00	Unknown
1872	9	7,000.00	Unknown
1875	53	None	Unknown

1878	31	None	Unknown
1888	99	5.00	Unknown
1889	68	17,181.49	Unknown
1896	216	48,553.70	Unknown[68]

As we have seen, before the Civil War, leasing of convicts in Louisiana was undertaken for reasons of economy. If the state could acquire a share of lessee profits, this, too, was desirable but not really necessary, because the principal objective in contracting with lessees was to spare the taxpayers the "expensive luxury" of maintaining the penitentiary.

However, by 1870, fiscal conservatism had begun to serve as a mask for official avarice and personal greed, both of which sought through convict labor a most reprehensible form of monetary enrichment. In such an atmosphere, rehabilitation of convicts became an utterly dead letter—as dead in fact, as an increasing number of convicts themselves.

Samuel Lawrence James acquired control of the penitentiary from a state administration dominated by Radical Republicans of both races. But white Democrats had also supported the major at the outset. They continued to do so, in greater numbers and with sustained effect, following their self-proclaimed redemption of Louisiana in 1877 from the other "evils" of Reconstruction. The Louisiana State Penitentiary was not redeemed until 1901, and even then only partially. In the meantime, and with James still in command, punishment for profit continued to be Louisiana's objective in penal policy.

[68] *Ibid.* (1871), 34; (1872), 8–34; (1875), 15; (1878), 47; (1890), 85–87; (1896–97), 160; *Biennial Report, State Treasurer* (1888–89), Statements "B" and "G"; (1896–97), 12; *Journal of the Proceedings of the Constitutional Convention of 1879*, pp. 180–81.

CHAPTER II

"This Species of Slave Labor"
1880-1890

THOSE WHO HAD "redeemed" Louisiana in 1877 from the "excesses" of Radical Reconstruction were soon to demonstrate their own inadequacies and limitations as administrators and public servants. "Bourbon misrule," as one recent study has disclosed, "followed . . . Radical misrule."[1] An oligarchy of businessmen, lawyers, and planters "remarkably powerful, backward, and corrupt,"[2] the Louisiana Bourbon Democrats were perhaps the epitome of the southern conservative type that returned to power throughout the region during the 1870s. Bourbon Democratic administrations in every southern state generally pursued the same objectives—to attract foreign and Yankee capital, to minimize taxation, to restrain the political influence of the Negro (and, when neces-

---

[1] William Ivy Hair, *Bourbonism and Agrarian Protest: Louisiana Politics, 1877–1900* (Baton Rouge, 1969), 107. This is the first study of late nineteenth century Louisiana derived from comprehensive and critical examination of the sources. Abundantly documented and persuasively constructed, Hair's revisionist interpretation has been long overdue. For a thoroughly researched, yet somewhat superficial analysis of Populism and Bourbon reaction in Louisiana, see Henry C. Dethloff, "Populism and Reform in Louisiana" (Ph.D. dissertation, University of Missouri, 1964).

[2] Hair, *Bourbonism and Agrarian Protest*, 107.

sary, of lesser whites), and to maintain themselves in office.[3] In Louisiana, however, certain aspects of this policy were advanced with singular zeal and resulted in some uniquely disastrous consequences.

Between 1878 and 1896 the Democratic Party in Louisiana debased the democratic process itself by stealing every closely contested state election and several congressional elections.[4] Most parish election officials and registrars of voters were creatures of the Bourbon Democratic governors, in whose interests widespread stuffing of ballot boxes, bribery and intimidation of voters, and frequent violence at the polls were carried on. All of this was justified by the dogma that Louisiana should remain under "white" (that is, Bourbon Democratic) control. In reality, what the Bourbon Democrats wished to preserve was the supremacy of *some* whites— themselves—over less affluent whites and all blacks. Finally, in 1898 the Louisiana Bourbon Democrats sought to deal once and for all with the problem of dissent by eliminating from the voting rolls as many potential dissenters as possible. The new state constitution of that year, by means of literacy and property qualifications, either discouraged or directly prevented the subsequent registration of nearly all Negro voters and a significant number of white electors as well.[5]

Disfranchisement of many white and most black voters reached a climax in Louisiana during the Populist decade of the 1890s. In other southern states, notably North Carolina, white and Negro Populists were able to score impressive, if temporary, victories over the Bourbon Democratic machines. But Populism gained no victories in Louisiana. A careful scholar has concluded that in fact "nowhere else in the South did Populism encounter so many obstacles or as much bru-

[3] C. Vann Woodward, *Origins of the New South: 1877–1913* (Baton Rouge, 1951), 51–52, 56–66, 292, 304, 308, 328, 331–33.

[4] Hair, *Bourbonism and Agrarian Protest*, 113–114, 234, 237, 241, 242–43, 247, 262–65.

[5] Black voter registration in Louisiana declined from 130,344 in 1897 to 5,320 in 1900; white registration from 164,088 to 125,437. By 1904, after the addition of a poll tax, Negro registration stood at 1,342, white registration at 91,716. Woodward, *Origins of the New South*, 342–43.

tality" as in Louisiana.[6] For almost a generation following
the end of Reconstruction, therefore, Louisiana experienced
the absolute and uninterrupted rule of a small group of fiscal
archconservatives who utilized race, electoral fraud, physical
violence, and, eventually, disfranchisement to sustain themselves in office.

One of the few positive results of Bourbon Democracy in
Louisiana was the reduction, if not the elimination, of pro-
fligate spending, which had so discredited Radical Reconstruction. But, in overreacting, the Bourbons curtailed legitimate, as well as illegitimate, state expenditures. In so doing
they became immovable cornerstones of the status quo, insen-
sitive to the needs of those below them and thus responsible
for the untoward delay of a host of necessary social reforms.
Louisiana, it was officially claimed, was impoverished and
needed time to recover from the ravages of the Civil War and
the plundering of Reconstructionists. The state could not
afford "to take chances with liberal ideas or liberal legislation."[7]

The federal census of 1880—which ranked Louisiana thirty-
seventh in per-capita wealth among states and territories of
the nation—revealed that most Louisianians, black and white
alike, were poor. On the other hand, "immensely wealthy
persons" lived throughout the state; by 1892 thirty-five mil-
lionaires resided in New Orleans alone. A number of affluent
corporations were also domiciled in Louisiana.[8] The Bour-

[6] Hair, *Bourbonism and Agrarian Protest*, 234. For a convincing account of how Democratic Governor Murphy J. Foster defrauded his Populist-Republican opponent in the election of 1896, see pages 259–65. Hair's
version should be contrasted with the assessment of Foster's biographer,
Sidney J. Romero, Jr., "The Political Career of Murphy J. Foster," *Louisiana Historical Quarterly*, XXVIII (1945), 1180–83.

[7] Edwin A. Davis, *Louisiana: A Narrative History* (Baton Rouge,
1965), 283. A widely used textbook in Louisiana history courses, this
work generally praises the Bourbons.

[8] *Tenth Census, 1880*, VII, *Valuation, Taxation and Public Indebted-
ness*, 5, 12, quoted in Hair, *Bourbonism and Agrarian Protest*, 34; New
Orleans *Times-Democrat*, May 11, 1892, quoted in Hair, *Bourbonism and
Agrarian Protest*, 120.

bons' "plea of poverty," consequently, "was purposely exaggerated" so that the "privileged few" could "use the poverty of the majority as the specious excuse for avoiding taxation upon themselves."[9] Professing sympathy with taxpayers, the Louisiana Bourbon Democrats actually desired "a government of should-be taxpayers who paid little or nothing."[10]

Among the worst of Bourbon Democratic crimes against the public interest in Louisiana was the willful neglect of state-supported institutions, all of which were allowed to languish because of insufficient appropriations for their support. Schools, asylums, and hospitals fell victim to Bourbon Democratic social indifference. The largest group of martyrs to fiscal conservatism in Louisiana were the state's young people, both white and Negro. In 1880 Louisiana was the fifth most illiterate state in the nation. By 1890 she had "climbed" to the unenviable status of first, with 20.33 percent of her white and 72.14 percent of her black citizens unable to read or write.[11]

The school children of Louisiana were not the only ones for whom life had been better during Reconstruction than it would be under Bourbon Democracy. Major James continued to operate the penitentiary, and convicts under his supervision were subjected after 1880 to an increasingly brutal confinement.

While the 1870s had been a trying decade for James, he had managed to retain his lease and to keep out of the spotlight because the turmoil of Reconstruction monopolized the attention of both press and public until 1877. Only within the General Assembly itself had pointed criticism of the lessee arisen. But the critics (in this instance, black legislators) did not object to the major's system of convict management. The employment of prisoners "in competition with free labor" was the source of distress, as noted above. James paid the state no rentals for eight years, and for three years ignored a law

[9] Hair, *Bourbonism and Agrarian Protest*, 119–20.
[10] *Ibid.*, 119.   [11] *Ibid.*, 122–23.

which obliged him to work the convicts within the penitentiary. None of these infractions caused the major to be driven from the penal system. Official Louisiana, seemingly terrified at the prospect of having the convicts "thrown upon" them, went to excessive lengths to maintain the lessee in business: the restrictive statute, Act 22 of 1875, was repealed in 1878, and James was given until 1881 to pay a sum of $66,010.34, which was about 72 percent of what he legally owed by then in delinquent rentals.[12]

With his accounts in order, with his good friend[13] Samuel McEnery in the executive mansion, and with no restrictions placed upon his employment of prisoners, Major James must have felt comfortably secure by 1881. More work camps were established, frequently near towns, railroad lines, or plantations. Convicts, driven at their tasks in broad daylight, were increasingly viewed by women, children, and travelers. The lease began to receive public criticism, which grew louder as the major and his subcontractors continued to work, mutilate, and kill prisoners throughout Louisiana. In 1886 a newspaper in Clinton "described what was (by then) common knowledge" when it stated that the

> men on the [James] works are brutally treated and everybody knows it. They are worked, mostly in the swamps and plantations, from daylight to dark. Corporeal [sic] punishment is inflicted on the slightest provocation. . . . Anyone who has travelled along the lines of railroads that run through Louisiana's swamps . . . in which the levees are built, has seen these poor devils almost to their waists, delving in the black and noxious mud. . . . Theirs is a grievous

---

[12] Had the major's delinquent rentals not been previously reduced by arbitration, he would have owed $92,000 by 1881, State of Louisiana, *Biennial Report of the State Treasurer to the Governor of the State of Louisiana: 1880–81* (Baton Rouge, 1882), 103–104. Published biennial reports of the treasurer are hereinafter cited as *Biennial Report, State Treasurer*, with appropriate years indicated.

[13] James was known to have been one of several prominent Louisiana businessmen who were able to manipulate McEnery. Hair, *Bourbonism and Agrarian Protest*, 109.

lot a thousand times more grievous than the law ever contemplated they should endure in expiation of their sins.[14]

In the same year a committee of the General Assembly visited some of the major's work camps in order to see for themselves how the convicts were treated. The legislators' attention focused upon Theophile Chevalier, a black convict who was observed to have no feet. Chevalier had been forced to work outdoors, without shoes, during the winter of 1884–85. Afflicted with frostbite, which soon led to gangrene, Chevalier next endured the amputation of one of his feet by means of a penknife. (The other foot had meanwhile rotted off.) The committee was told that Chevalier was serving a five-year sentence for the theft of five dollars.[15]

A leading critic of the Louisiana convict lease was the *Daily Picayune* of New Orleans. During the 1880s this paper commented frequently on the horrors Major James inflicted upon his charges. It was the editor's belief that a more humane course would be to impose the death sentence immediately upon anyone sentenced to a term with the lessee in excess of six years, because the average convict lived no longer than that anyway.[16]

Joseph E. Ransdell was a young North Louisiana attorney in 1898. Engaged as defense counsel in a murder trial, the future United States senator assured the jury of the inevitability of his client's early demise if sentenced to the penitentiary. Ransdell stated that "a gentleman told me that in 1885

[14] Clinton (La.) *East Feliciana Patriot-Democrat*, n.d., quoted in New Orleans *Daily Picayune*, March 22, 1886. See also Hair, *Bourbonism and Agrarian Protest*, 129–33.

[15] New York *Times*, May 22, 1886, quoted in William Ivy Hair, "The Agrarian Protest in Louisiana, 1877–1900" (Ph.D. dissertation, Louisiana State University, 1962), 191.

[16] New Orleans *Daily Picayune*, June 30, 1884. The editor of the *Daily Picayune* during the 1880s, C. Harrison Parker, later managed the successful campaigns of Democratic governors Nicholls, Foster, and Hall. A man who "rendered incalculable services to his party," Parker in 1901 became president of the state Board of Control which took over the penal system upon expiration of the last James lease. See Alcée Fortier, *Louisiana: Comprising Sketches of Parishes, Towns, Events, Institutions, and Persons, arranged in Cyclopedic Form* (n.p., Century Historical Association, 1914), 785.

or 1886, he saw 42 convicts buried at one camp . . . and the
death[s] were nearly all caused by overwork, exposure and
brutality."[17] No official reports were made public by the
Board of Control during 1885 or 1886, but their report for
1896, as noted above, (two years before Ransdell addressed
the jury) admitted 216 convict deaths for that year alone, the
highest toll officially on record during the James lease.[18]

Critics of the lease attacked it from two directions. Negro
workers remained hostile because cheap convict labor continued to rob them of employment on farms and plantations.
Irish laborers, too, became anti-lease because convicts took
away their jobs on railroad construction projects. Such traditional opposition became more genteel (and formidable) when
merged with the indignation of many Louisianians who were
genuinely revolted by the major's treatment of convicts. It
was not long before this coalition of displaced laborers and
the morally outraged became a public threat to the lessee's
interest.[19] The organization to which these anti-lease elements
took their case was nothing less than the state Democratic
Party.

At the party convention in Baton Rouge during December
of 1883, a floor fight occurred when the majority of the platform committee read its report, for there was nothing said
therein concerning the lease. The minority objected and
moved that the following be inserted:

> . . . That the employment of convicts outside the walls
> of the Penitentiary is detrimental to the interests of the

[17] Joseph E. Ransdell Papers (Department of Archives and Manuscripts, Louisiana State University), p. 23.

[18] State of Louisiana, *Biennial Report of the Board of Control of the
Louisiana State Penitentiary to His Excellency Murphy J. Foster, Governor of Louisiana* (Baton Rouge, 1898) , 160. Published biennial reports of
the board are hereinafter cited as *Biennial Report, Board of Control*,
with appropriate year indicated.

[19] Laborers in Baton Rouge before the Civil War had complained
briefly, and unsuccessfully, of competition with leased convict labor. See
Roger W. Shugg, *Origins of Class Struggle in Louisiana: A Social History
of White Farmers and Laborers During Slavery and After* (Baton Rouge,
1939) , 115–16.

honest labor portion of the . . . State, and to the proper care and custody of the convicts themselves, subjecting them to hard and cruel treatment and enhancing their opportunities of escape; that it brings this species of slave labor in competition with honest industry to the great pecuniary profit of the penitentiary lessee, but with disastrous results as far as the honest free labor of our State is concerned.[20]

A substitute for both reports was proposed, and adopted by a vote of 228–139. It condemned both the Louisiana State Lottery Company and the convict lease system, the latter in even more sweeping terms than those employed by the minority report. It was now the official position of the Democratic Party of Louisiana, "that the convict labor of the State should be appropriated and assigned to labor on the public levees, under the direction and control of the State authorities, by such legislation as may be necessary."[21]

On the face of it, it appeared that a reorientation of Louisiana's penal policy was imminent, for the majority political organization of the state had formally committed itself to ending the lease. Another promising result of this party convention was a tacit but enduring alliance between those who opposed the lease and the enemies of the Louisiana State Lottery Company. Indeed, Louisiana seemed on the verge of cleaning house.

But Louisiana's convict "slaves" were not soon emancipated from the custody of Major James. Eighteen years of the most tortuous and cynical political maneuvering in the state's history would precede the eviction of the James Company from the penal system. While this story will be analyzed in detail, a preview of the events will serve to illustrate their interrelated complexity: bills to abolish the James lease were sponsored by four different legislators in every biennial session of the General Assembly between 1884 and 1890. All of the measures were defeated. Both the lease and the lottery were actually renewed in 1890, the latter by constitutional

---

[20] Quoted in New Orleans *Daily Picayune*, December 21, 1883.
[21] *Ibid.*

amendment. The lottery amendment, however, was defeated in the election of 1892. Not until 1894 did the assembly vote to abolish the lease, by means of another constitutional amendment. This amendment was in turn rejected by the voters in the election of 1896. Leasing of convicts to private firms or individuals was finally prohibited by the Constitution of 1898—to take effect only after the existing ten-year lease had run its course in 1901. Meanwhile, the lessees paid their rentals, the state avoided expense and continued to make money, and perhaps as many as two thousand convicts perished.[22] Even in the face of mounting and determined opposition, Major James could clearly depend upon powerful allies.

In addition to having been anti-lease and anti-lottery, the Louisiana Democrats who carried the convention of 1883 against the aforementioned institutions were "anti-Governor McEnery" also. The governor himself was a notorious supporter of the lottery[23] and smiled favorably upon the lease as well. His close association with these enterprises, through friendship with the men who headed them, burdened McEnery with an unsavory image. Enemies within his own party sneeringly referred to the governor as "McLottery." (Perhaps "McLeasery" would have been a more inclusive and precise label.) At any rate, while able to attack his friends in the convention, the anti-McEneryites were unable to derail the governor's own nomination. In 1884 he was easily elected to a four-year term in his own right. (It will be remembered that McEnery, as lieutenant governor, had succeeded upon the death of Louis A. Wiltz in 1881.) Until 1888, when he was at last denied renomination by a disgusted and apprehensive party leadership, McEnery could be relied upon to defend the lease with rhetoric when it came under public

[22] Available reports of the Board of Control indicate that an average of about a hundred convicts died annually between 1883 and 1901.

[23] In 1890, as a justice of the Louisiana Supreme Court, McEnery supported the lottery in a crucial case. See Berthold C. Alwes, "The History of the Louisiana State Lottery Company," *Louisiana Historical Quarterly*, XXVII (1944), 1052. As the acknowledged pro-lottery Democratic gubernatorial candidate in 1892, McEnery was defeated by the anti-lotteryite, Murphy J. Foster, also a Democrat.

attack and to protect it behind the scenes with his gubernatorial power and influence.[24]

McEnery was elevated to the Louisiana Supreme Court in 1888.[25] His successor in the executive mansion was Francis T. Nicholls, the "maimed brigadier," who had been called from retirement to restore a façade of honor and respectability to party leadership. In office for the second time, Nicholls would prove to be implacably against the lottery and ill-disposed toward the lease. The major's pipeline to the governor's office had been choked off, and it is more than likely that he turned for assistance to his other good friend, John A. Morris, chief of the Louisiana State Lottery Company. Morris' resources were immense. While neither he nor Major James publicly discussed their financial affairs, it is reasonably estimated that the lottery's annual profits averaged about twelve million dollars by 1890.[26] Both the James lease, due to expire in 1891, and the lottery were renewed during the assembly session of 1890. Democrats who supported one, generally favored the other. White and black Republicans, who during Reconstruction had voted in large numbers for the creation of both, again supported the lease and the lottery in 1890. As a result of sudden and serious misfortunes, however, the lottery ceased doing business in Louisiana in 1894. That same year the General Assembly, dominated by anti-lotteryites, voted

[24] No reports were released by the Board of Control during McEnery's administration. In 1888 McEnery virtually eulogized the lessee in his message to the General Assembly and also threatened implicitly to veto anti-lease legislation. See State of Louisiana, *Official Journal of the Proceedings of the Senate of the General Assembly, 1888* (Baton Rouge, 1888), 23. Published proceedings of the senate are hereinafter cited as *Senate Journal*, with appropriate year indicated.

[25] For an amusing contemporary account of the shenanigans behind this appointment, see Henry Clay Warmoth, *War, Politics, and Reconstruction: Stormy Days in Louisiana* (New York, 1930), 251–53. Warmoth, the Republican nominee for governor in 1888, charged that the irate McEnery was offered a seat on the court *before* the election if the governor "in turn promised to see to it that every ballot box should be stuffed to the limit in favor of General Nicholls and his ticket." For evidence substantiating Warmoth's accusation, see Hair, *Bourbonism and Agrarian Protest*, 140.

[26] Hair, *Bourbonism and Agrarian Protest*, 201–202.

to abolish the lease, but not until 1901, at the termination of
the existing ten-year contract. This concession to the lessee,
it was explained, would "keep the faith of the State intact."[27]
It would also keep intact $350,000 of anticipated revenue
from the major, although this point was not brought out.[28]

Money was also, therefore, a most consistent and reliable
factor between 1883 and 1901 in keeping at bay the hounds
of dissolution and criticism. To be sure, a personal friend in
the executive mansion was of demonstrated value during part
of this period, while a possible alliance with the lottery in
1890 could have helped James secure a new lease. But it was
through his rentals which, though frequently short, were paid
much more regularly than during the 1870s, that the lessee
most endeared himself to the Bourbon Democratic oligarchy
in Louisiana. Even when enemies within the party came to
power, the lessees were given generous official notice of seven
years in 1894 and three years in 1898 that their days at the
penitentiary were numbered.

Prior to 1881 both economy and profit had been the state's
apparent motives for leasing its convicts. Official Louisiana
had soon admitted, however, that economy alone would suffice. Whether or not James paid his rentals (and he did not
for eight consecutive years) was secondary to the burden of
expense which his continued operation of the penitentiary
spared the state. The Bourbon Democrats apparently demanded that James adhere to the original terms of his lease.
However viciously exacted from convicts, the revenues furnished by Mayor James were absolutely painless to taxpayers.

The desire to make money from convict labor was in fact
so compelling and popular throughout Louisiana that the
advocates of reform themselves were infected by it. In 1884
the New Orleans *Daily Picayune* attacked the manner in

---

27 State of Louisiana, *Report of the Special Committee on Amendments to the Constitution Authorized by the General Assembly of 1892
with the Accompanying Amendments* (Baton Rouge, 1894), 28.

28 The second James lease, a ten-year contract extending from 1891
to 1901, obliged the major to pay an annual rental of $50,000, due
every January 1.

which Major James was victimizing the "taxpayer": "If Messrs. James & Co. can hire [convicts] to the State [for levee work] and get rich out of their wages, why cannot the State work them to advantage and save the bonus that has to be paid to these lessees? It is an outrage upon the taxpayer to levy a contribution upon him to pay James . . . for the use of these convicts, when their labor belongs to the State."[29] The paper went on, of course, to condemn the known forms of mistreatment inflicted by the lessee upon prisoners. But then so had Senator Watterston some thirty years earlier. Like that well-meaning but shortsighted legislator, other Louisianians persisted in believing that the state could reap lessee profits without depending upon lessee methods. This point of view tended to strengthen the major's position rather than weaken it. His spokesmen could persuasively argue, and did, that in view of the fact the state was already deriving a regular revenue from the lessee (at no expense), the costly experimentation of state control had best be avoided. One other significant point favored the lessee's case during the latter nineteenth century. "Profits" derived from the convict lease were usually allocated to some objective other than the penal system, the maintenance of which, after all, was the lessee's responsibility. If the state were to resume this responsibility, most of the "profits," even under efficient management, would necessarily have to be reinvested in the system and would thus cease to be profits at all.

In any event, neither the penitentiary nor convict welfare were matters of immediate concern to most Louisianians. Here and there, agricultural workers or construction laborers might, as previously noted, denounce the lessee for reasons of self-interest, but rarely was sympathy for the convict himself a prime source of complaint. And while indignant humanitarians might frequently express themselves in print, they seemed not to have spoken for the majority of their fellow citizens, who (according to George Washington Cable) remained convinced "that to punish crime, no matter how is to

[29] New Orleans *Daily Picayune,* June 30, 1884.

deter crime; that when broken laws are *avenged* that is the end; that it is enough to have the culprit in limbo, if only he is made to suffer and not to cost."[30]

It should also be emphasized that after the Civil War the "crime problem" had become in all southern states confused with the "Negro problem," insofar as black convicts began greatly to outnumber white convicts in all penitentiaries. This fact could be gleefully cited by racists as proof of the Negro's inherent criminal nature, of his innate inferiority to, and need to be closely supervised by, his white superiors. A more realistic view might have pointed out that Negroes still constituted a majority of the population in Louisiana, Mississippi, and South Carolina, and that they remained an ignorant and largely poverty-stricken majority at that. Hardships endured by blacks on account of enforced ignorance and economic peonage were seldom discussed openly in public, much less acknowledged by Bourbon Democratic politicians. One notable exception to this rule in Louisiana was a speech delivered by Aurel Arnaud, member of the General Assembly in 1886. A poor man himself, of Acadian lineage, Arnaud rose to condemn a law requiring all adult males in every parish to work on the roads for twelve days annually or contribute, in lieu thereof, a specified sum of money. Negroes, he said, were especially hurt by this statute as the amount of cash earned by a black tenant or laborer for an entire year rarely exceeded forty dollars. Then, no doubt to the amazement of his colleagues, Arnaud offered a surprisingly candid analysis of the criminal motives of black Louisianians: "Can you not see that this amount is not sufficient to support the laborer? And every day you divest him from a chance of earning something is a robbery of his daily bread? Should any one . . . be surprised to hear that negroes steal? I am only surprised that they do not steal more."[31]

[30] George Washington Cable, *The Silent South: Together with the Freedman's Case in Equity and the Convict Lease System* (New York, 1885) , 125.

[31] Arnaud completed his speech by observing that "there is an immense difference between the two [races], but this difference exists

Negroes did steal. Frequently they committed crimes of violence as well. And in steadily increasing numbers they were sent to the penitentiary, where they worked—and died—for the lessee.[32] But few Louisianians perceived the causes of black criminal behavior as objectively as Aurel Arnaud. Most preferred to account for Negro crime on the basis of racial assumptions alone. Like other Southerners living in an age of mounting tension between whites and blacks, Louisianians demanded more rather than less proscription of the Negro, and they were either unwilling or unable to comprehend that the further subordination and restriction of opportunity they desired to impose upon him were, in the end, what induced many Negroes to become criminals.

Treatment of black convicts by southern lessees was frankly described by a "southern man" in 1883. "Before the war we owned the negroes. If a man had a good negro, he could afford to take care of him: if he was sick, get a doctor. He might even get gold plugs in his teeth. But these convicts: we don't own 'em. One dies, get another."[33] Convicts were indeed a "species of slave labor" in postwar southern prisons under lessee control. In a sense, therefore, Major James was "the largest slaveholder in post-bellum Louisiana."[34] But convicts, unlike antebellum chattels, cost lessees nothing. They

only in the fancy of unscrupulous and rascally politicians: in every respect the white laborer stands exactly on the same footing as the negro." Baton Rouge *Weekly Truth*, May 28, 1886, quoted in Hair, *Bourbonism and Agrarian Protest*, 192–93.

[32] By 1900, the last full year of the James lease, there were 840 black convicts but only 149 whites within the Louisiana penal system. See *Senate Journal* 1900, 6. In 1868 there were 212 black prisoners to 85 whites. It is impossible to determine precisely how many convicts had been "framed" as a result of false arrest, hostile judges or juries, indifferent defense, and the like.

[33] The statement was made in 1883 at the National Conference of Charities in Louisville, Kentucky. Quoted in Hilda Jane Zimmerman, "Penal Systems and Penal Reforms in the South since the Civil War" (Ph.D. dissertation, University of North Carolina, 1947), 93. See also Dan T. Carter, "Prisons, Politics and Business: The Convict Lease System in the Post-Civil War South" (M.A. thesis, University of Wisconsin, 1964), 54–55, 63.

[34] Hair, *Bourbonism and Agrarian Protest*, 109.

were furnished free with regularity by southern courts and magistrates. In Louisiana, Negro convicts were furnished in large numbers, and the major's system of "slave" management was unencumbered by considerations of cost and maintenance. Between 1870 and 1901, three thousand Louisiana convicts, most of them blacks, may well have died under the lessee's regime. Barely a handful of planters ever owned as many as a thousand slaves before the war, and there is no record of any antebellum slaveowner allowing three thousand valuable chattels to perish. But if Negroes were regarded as unworthy of humane treatment, they were also equated with convicts, and the latter, whether white or black, became generally regarded as unworthy of humane treatment, too. This identity between blacks and criminals in the minds of many Louisianians not only helped to perpetuate the lease system but survived long afterward as an impediment to penal reform.

Despite the fact that a number of citizens in the 1880s had begun to condemn the lease for various reasons, it should be remembered that seventeen years elapsed between the introduction of the first anti-lease bill in the General Assembly and the lessees' departure from Baton Rouge. This prolonged and unseemly delay resulted in the main from a combination of the durable factors noted above, all of which favored the status quo: the major's personal connection with the mighty (both in and possibly out of government), the traditional and universally respected profit motive, and a vengeful and racist-minded public opinion. In a subtle but real sense, however, among the chief architects of indecision and procrastination, to say nothing of the mounting annual death toll from lessee brutality, were the reformers themselves. However strongly they may have felt in private about the need to make reform and rehabilitation of convicts the objectives of Louisiana's penal system, those who opposed the lease failed until 1900 to stress any practicable aspect of this philosophy in their public statements, whether in the press or in the General Assembly. All that the "reformers" advocated was termination of the lease and restoration of state control. This financially vulnerable objective played directly into the major's hands, and his spokesmen were able to resist it effectively for years.

Guided and inspired by the state Democratic platform of 1883, several legislators joined forces in the General Assembly the following year in an attempt to put James out of business. A bill providing for immediate abolition of the lease was sponsored by Senator Charles Parlange of Pointe Coupee Parish. The measure further provided for working the convicts, under state control and supervision, on the levees and on railroad construction projects. Financial support would come from the state levee fund and from whatever fees could be earned by the state-supervised employment of convicts on railroad work.

This bill was not a thoroughgoing reform measure, an unhappy circumstance which critics readily perceived and criticized. "The Parlange Bill," complained Senator George Kelly of upland Winn Parish, "simply makes the State . . . a contractor of convict labor, and all the sentimental issues and ideas upon this question of ameliorating the condition of the convict [fall] to the ground."[35] The same kind of work, the same harsh treatment of prisoners would continue, agreed Negro Republican Simon Toby of New Orleans; only the taskmasters would change.[36] "If the State wants to improve the condition of convicts," Senator Kelly resumed: "[she should not] place them upon railroads and levees under political taskmasters, but put them within the walls of the penitentiary; make an appropriation of $150,000 annually . . . to support them; and, thereby, place herself in the position of a humanitarian and reformer."[37] The state had no intention of embarking upon this expensive course in penal policy. Senator Kelly, convinced that she should not, fired the ultimate weapon of Bourbon Democratic Louisiana when he said: "The people who now propose all this fine sentiment no doubt

[35] *Senate Journal* (1884), 270.
[36] *Ibid.*, 270–71.   [37] *Ibid.*

will not object to extra taxation for this purpose."[38] Senator G. H. Braugh of New Orleans warned that "the State [was] not in a condition to make costly experiments, prompted solely by sentimental motives which under [the Parlange bill] can have no practical realization."[39]

What the reformers had proposed was not "fine sentiment" at all, but basically a continuation of the lease system minus the lessee. Even this aspect of Parlange's proposal evoked grave misgivings from Senator C. C. Cordill of Tensas Parish. A one-time Scalawag, Cordill had become by 1884 the stanchest of Bourbon Democrats. For him economy was the primary consideration, and

> on the question of economy, the State now draws a revenue from the lease. . . . I am sure that the present bill proposes to submit the State to a grave loss; a loss which in the present state of our finances we cannot stand. After all, the question of economy would present no urgency to my mind, if the funds were in the Treasury to maintain the convicts. . . . [But in] the present state of our finances we have not the resources, [and] every dollar going to the convicts would be a dollar taken from the blind, the insane, the sick.[40]

Cordill's gloomy description of Louisiana's financial condition was exaggerated. At no time during the Bourbon period did the state's annual expenditures exceed her revenues, a condition that would have prevailed even if no income whatever accrued from a penitentiary lease.[41] State control and management of the penal system would certainly have required expenditure of additional public funds. But whether such expenditures would have necessarily bankrupted Louisiana, or

[38] *Ibid.* The Baton Rouge *Daily Advocate*, Louisiana's official journal, printed Kelly's comments in full, observing that "we consider them so weighty that in view of the grave importance of the measure we have thought proper to reproduce them for the information of our readers." No remarks of other legislators, pro or con, were quoted. Baton Rouge *Daily Advocate*, July 2, 1884.

[39] *Senate Journal* (1884), 271.   [40] *Ibid.*, 267–68.

[41] See State of Louisiana, *Biennial Reports, State Treasurer*, 1880–1900, inclusive.

would have automatically stricken the blind, the insane, and the sick, as Cordill stated, remain questions impossible to resolve.

One enemy of the Parlange bill, Senator S. S. Carlisle of New Orleans, expressed his conservatism with an eloquence that might have unnerved Edmund Burke. Carlisle became highly indignant as Senator Murphy J. Foster of St. Mary Parish made frequent reference, in defense of the Parlange bill, to the anti-lease writings of George Washington Cable, at that time Louisiana's foremost author—and critic. Cable, said Carlisle, was a "Quixotic moral reformer, who, mounted upon the ass of public credulity, [rides] against the immovable windmills of fixed institutions. . . . The lease is a legally vested interest."[42] Negro Republican Jordan Stewart of Terrebonne Parish echoed this opinion, if not the exact wording, when he cautioned that "the lease of the penitentiary [was] a contract binding upon the State."[43]

By the time Parlange's bill came up for final action, few senators would speak in its defense. One who did was Edgar Sutherlin of DeSoto Parish, who, as a loyal Democrat, felt himself committed to the bill by the 1883 party platform.[44] Nineteen votes in the affirmative were required to pass the measure. It received eighteen, with sixteen senators opposed and two absent (one of whom was the bill's sponsor, Parlange). Senator Foster changed his vote to no in order that he might move for reconsideration the next day.[45] With Parlange again among the absentees, Foster's motion to reconsider was tabled

---

[42] Quoted in New Orleans *Times-Democrat*, June 27, 1884. See also Arlin Turner, *George W. Cable: A Biography* (Durham, 1956), 144. Cable was a vocal and persistent critic of the lease system during the 1880s. But the extent of his influence remains questionable, because the Louisiana lease seems to have been finally terminated for political rather than humanitarian reasons, while elsewhere in the South most convict leases were abolished during the twentieth century, long after Cable had retired from active social criticism.

[43] *Senate Journal* (1884), 268.   [44] *Ibid.*

[45] New Orleans *Times-Democrat*, July 2, 1884. The secretary of the senate apparently failed to note Foster's change of vote, as he recorded the final tally as 17–17–2. *Senate Journal* (1884), 267.

by a vote of 16–15–5.[46] All five Negro senators opposed the bill; Stewart and Toby for reasons cited above, Henry Demas, R. F. Guichard, and Richard Simms for reasons known only to themselves, as these legislators chose not to explain their votes. The crucial absences of Parlange himself remain unexplained and mysterious to this day. Possibly as he became aware of the hostility toward his proposal, Parlange became personally disillusioned and left the field. Or perhaps he felt some obligation to refrain from supporting his own bill. At any rate, while he was later a member of the Anti-Lottery League, he played no leading role in further opposition to the James lease. On July 2, 1884, the same day that the senate tabled reconsideration of the Parlange bill, the house indefinitely postponed a measure to prohibit employment of convicts outside the penitentiary.[47] Efforts to end or even to restrict the lease in 1884 had met with complete failure, and not for the last time, by any means.

In 1886 the Prison Reform Association of Louisiana was organized in New Orleans, where it soon established itself as the spokesman and coordinator of statewide reform sentiment aimed toward abolition of the lease. Composed of a "few earnest men, resident chiefly in the alluvial district," the association, according to one of its members in later years, "demonstrated to successive State administrations and legislatures that under the proper [state] management the convicts could be employed on public works, such as levee and road building and cultivation of State farms, to far greater advantage to the State and to the physical and moral benefit of the prisoners."[48] "Demonstrated" was a misleading choice of terms. "Attempted to convince" would have been more accur-

46 *Ibid.*, 286.
47 State of Louisiana, *Official Journal of the Proceedings of the House of Representatives of the General Assembly, 1884* (Baton Rouge, 1884), 444. Published proceedings of the house are hereinafter cited as *House Journal*, with appropriate year indicated. No vote is recorded on this action. The bill was sponsored by Benjamin Ewell, a black Republican from Assumption Parish.
48 F. S. Shields, *Prison Reform: Its Principles and Purposes—What It has Accomplished—Work Yet to be Done* (New Orleans, 1906), 17.

ate, because the association could only assume that state control of the penal system would be as financially rewarding to Louisiana as lessee control.

These "few earnest men" could, and did, accomplish little more than to focus attention on the major's brutal methods of handling prisoners and to suggest that possibly the state could engage them in the same work, treat them more kindly, and still make money. Because the major had the convicts all the while and was, in fact, submitting a revenue to the state, the Prison Reform Association found itself in the dilemma of past critics of the lease system, such as Watterston and Parlange, whose promises of more humane (and yet equally profitable) convict management suggested costly experimentation to more practical minds. If the Prison Reform Association had more boldly attacked the whole system and had called for a sweeping reevaluation of penal policy, perhaps results would have come more quickly and substantially. On the other hand, it is equally possible (and indeed more likely) that such an advanced policy would have made members of the association appear even more ridiculous in the eyes of their Bourbon Democratic contemporaries. The lease, after all, was the present enemy. Further reform could be urged after the lease had been disposed of. This was the eventual policy pursued by the association, which continued to advocate abolition of the lease and claimed the credit for its demise (which the group did not really deserve). After restoration of state control in 1901, the association, for a brief period, was moderately influential. In the meantime, according to the same source quoted above, "despite persistent agitation and the enlistment of some of the State press, little was accomplished even in the mitigation of the evil practices of the [lease] system" (for a long time).[49]

The assembly session of 1886 witnessed another attempt to dislodge the major from his enterprise. This effort originated in the house, before which Representative R. M. Downing of New Orleans placed a measure identical to the Parlange bill

[49] *Ibid.*

of 1884. Frightened by the near success of abrogation two years before, friends of the lease scurried about to make the necessary arrangements for battle. Their conduct must have been both obvious and offensive to other members of the assembly, for soon complaints were heard concerning a "penitentiary ring" whose efforts in behalf of Major James had proved discreditable to a number of personal reputations.

Did such a ring exist? "No." said Representative G. W. Munday of East Feliciana Parish, who, as chairman of the House Penitentiary Committee, spoke from a somewhat vulnerable position. At once the Baton Rouge *Daily Advocate* came to "the General's" assistance. In a supremely condescending editorial, the state journal reduced a matter of legitimate inquiry to an unwarranted and scurrilous attack upon a southern gentleman: "The character of General Munday for rectitude and honorability is so generally established throughout the State, that his remarks need only to be read by the people to dissipate the many evil reports that are persistently circulated, to the great injury of the good name of the State and its government."[50]

On June 18, the Downing bill was indefinitely postponed by a house vote of 49–38–10.[51] The New Orleans delegation was almost solidly behind the measure, blacks and white Republicans opposed, while reaction from other members was mixed. Many of the same reasons for voting one way or another were given as had been expressed on the Parlange bill: members supported the Downing proposal out of loyalty to the 1883 party platform or because they genuinely wished to end the lease; others opposed it because they felt the state could not afford to maintain the convicts or because they considered the lease a contract which the assembly had not the authority to abridge.

Negro Republican Thomas Cage of Terrebonne Parish opposed the bill because he feared that convicts would derive no benefit from it. Like several senators in the Parlange episode,

---

50 Baton Rouge *Daily Advocate*, June 20, 1886.
51 *House Journal* (1886), 399–400.

Cage saw in this identical piece of proposed legislation merely an extension of the lease system without the lessee. On the other hand, had the Downing bill agreed to confine the prisoners "within the walls," Cage would have supported it.[52] So, presumably, would Benjamin Ewell, a black Republican from Assumption Parish. As a senator in 1874, Cage had been the first to raise the issue of convict labor in competition with free labor. Ewell, ten years later, had attempted to revive the principle of the unsuccessful Act 22 of 1875, which had prohibited the major from employing convicts outside the penitentiary. Both of these men and other black legislators continued to be disturbed by the practice of farming out convicts, which forced their constituents into the ranks of the unemployed. But until and unless reform legislation proposed to correct the situation (which it consistently failed to do), there seemed to be nothing left for the Negroes but to let "the contract stand as fixed by law," as Ewell expressed it during the Downing debates.[53] However grudgingly rendered, support of Major James by black legislators left him free to abuse and kill more black convicts, a prerogative that could not have been further enhanced even if Negroes had supported the lessee enthusiastically.

But the assembly session of 1886 was by no means a total disaster for the cause of penal reform in Louisiana. For the first time in her history the state was given a basic, though reasonably flexible, commutation-of-sentence law, sponsored and endorsed by two usually indifferent supporters of convict welfare—Senator C. C. Cordill and Governor Samuel Douglas McEnery.

Article 66 of the Constitution of 1879 had created a state pardon board, composed of the lieutenant governor, the attorney general, and the presiding judge at the trial of the convict whose case might come up for review. The governor could neither pardon nor commute sentence independently of this unwieldy board; in fact, he had to concur in the board's recommendation whether he desired to or not. Governor Mc

[52] *Ibid.*, 400.   [53] *Ibid.*

Enery did "not approve of the system," believing that "the entire responsiblity for pardoning should rest upon the Executive."[54] Professing further to believe that "the punishment of criminals should be accompanied by inducements for reformation," McEnery urged the assembly to enact legislation which would create more adequate machinery for the commutation of sentences.

Sponsored by Cordill, Senate Bill 99 passed both houses over nominal opposition to become Act 72 of 1886.[55] A new system was created, applying both to penitentiary convicts and to felons confined in parish jails. Liberal commutation of sentence was granted to first offenders—second and subsequent offenders were excluded, as were escapees. First offenders who were sentenced to life imprisonment, however, had to serve fifteen years before becoming eligible, and no more than 20 percent of the convicts under life sentences could receive commutation in one year. A three-man board composed of the governor, lieutenant governor, and attorney general would supervise commutation of penitentiary sentences, while lesser boards composed of sheriffs, district attorneys, and clerks of criminal courts dispensed commutations on the parish level. Combined with Act 112 of 1890, also sponsored by Cordill, this legislation enabled a number of otherwise doomed persons legally to escape from the clutches of Major James.[56] By 1896, for example, the worst year of the James lease in terms of convict deaths—216—144 convicts were "released for good behavior."[57]

---

[54] *Senate Journal* (1886), 21.

[55] The senate vote was 31 for, none against, and five absent; the house vote 71–8–18. Of the eight opponents in the house, six were white Democrats, one a black Democrat, and one a black Republican. *Senate Journal* (1886), 235; *House Journal* (1886), 647.

[56] State of Louisiana, *Acts of the General Assembly of 1886* (Baton Rouge, 1886), 109–10. Published legislative actions are hereinafter cited as *Acts of Louisiana*, with appropriate year indicated. *Acts of Louisiana* (1890), 153–54. James himself was credited in 1894 with having originally sponsored these commutation laws. Whether he did or not remains an open question. See New Orleans *Daily Picayune* and *Times-Democrat*, July 28, 1894.

[57] *Biennial Report, Board of Control* (1898), 160. There is no way of ascertaining how many were returned as subsequent offenders because

Three additional items of forward-looking legislation were proposed in 1886. The senate briefly considered, but then rejected, bills to establish a code of criminal procedure, a code of criminal evidence, and a penal code for Louisiana.[58] All things considered, however, and despite the major's victory over the Downing bill, 1886 had come off as a potential turning point in criminal and penal policy in Louisiana. Some persons in the state, other than convicts themselves, had actually demonstrated interest in convict problems and rehabilitation. Others, if perhaps only for reasons of procedural efficiency, were disposed to modernize Louisiana's criminal and penal laws.

By 1888, conditions had returned to "normal." Both Cordill and McEnery were back in the major's corner as two further attempts to end the lease were made within the General Assembly. Senator O. O. Provosty, Parlange's colleague from the alluvial parish of Pointe Coupee, took up the banner of reform from his frustrated predecessors and sponsored an abolition bill identical to the proposals which had been voted down in 1884 and 1886. In the house, Representative J. W. Bossier of St. Tammany Parish put forth a companion measure. Under attack this time on two fronts, Major James received the unequivocal public support of Governor McEnery, whose message to the assembly included a section devoted to the lease, which he suggested should be retained. (One might well ask why, particularly from the financial point of view, for in that year, the major made a rental payment to the state of $5, which sum was precisely $21,995 short of what he owed.[59])

"You are familiar," McEnery said, "with the history of this institution. The convicts . . . are well taken care of, humanely treated, well fed and clothed and not overtasked in their

---

official records were made public irregularly and kept erratically by the Bourbons.

[58] Senate Journal (1886), 194. After several subsequent efforts also failed, Louisiana finally adopted a code of criminal procedure in 1928 and a code of criminal law in 1942. Penal laws were codified, to a degree, in the Revised Statutes of 1950.

[59] Biennial Report, State Treasurer (1890), Statement "B," 14. Why the major's 1888 rental was not paid in full when due is not known.

labor." Having uttered this official lie, the governor got down
to the real essence of the matter: "The question what to do
with the convicts is an embarrassing one," he continued, elabo-
rating upon the necessity for a "vast outlay of money" if the
convicts were to be maintained in the penitentiary; how their
work therein would involve them in competition with "honest
and skilled labor"; and how, if they were worked instead upon
the levees, the state could not provide enough labor to keep
them busy the year round. "It would be embarrassing to any
State administration," he concluded, "to have the convicts now
thrust upon it for care, support and employment. I think the
best solution . . . under present circumstances would be to let
the convict labor system remain as now fixed by law."[60]

McEnery had apparently concluded that the best offense
should consist of a sound and traditional defense and, therefore, he reverted to the logic of the 1870s. Borrowing a page
each from Kellogg and Nicholls, the governor stressed economy rather than revenue as the reason why Major James should
be left unmolested. It might also have been embarrassing for
the governor to defend as a source of revenue an institution
which had lately paid into the treasury the contemptible sum
of five dollars. Another supporter of the lease, Senator Charles
T. Soniat of New Orleans, was not as circumspect. Soniat,
though opposed on "general principles" to the practice of
leasing convicts, was even more opposed to ending the lease
"as a matter of expediency." He thought it unwise to repudi-
ate the contract made with James and, as a further "expedi-
ent" argument, Soniat believed that Louisiana should not
abandon the "revenue" provided by the lessee.[61]

Threatened implicitly with a gubernatorial veto, supporters
of the Provosty bill nonetheless went ahead with what the
Daily Advocate had come to describe as "the customary on-
slaught upon the penitentiary lease."[62] On June 26 they again

---

Five dollars, however, is better than nothing, which is what the state had
received from James between 1873 and 1881.

[60] *Senate Journal* (1888), 23.
[61] Baton Rouge *Daily Advocate*, June 22, 1888.
[62] *Ibid.*, June 23, 1888.

went down in defeat. Despite a final concession to James, in the form of an amendment postponing abolition until his contract expired in 1891, friends of the lessee were successful in defeating Provosty's measure by a vote of 21–13–2.[63] On July 6 Bossier's bill met the same fate in the house.[64] The usual coalition of hard-core Bourbon Democrats plus white and black Republicans had sustained the major for the third time in four years. Not to be minimized is the performance of Governor McEnery who, though a lame duck, still possessed the power to render the major a final, and necessarily overt, act of service.

A footnote to the principal events of 1888 reveals much about the insensitivity of Louisiana Bourbon Democrats to the plight of unfortunates. Once again, Senator C. C. Cordill had voiced his opposition to ending the lease, no doubt as proof of his continued solicitude for "the blind, the insane, [and] the sick," from whom state control of the penitentiary would unavoidably take many dollars, as the senator had himself warned four years earlier. Having upheld the cause of these helpless people by acquiescing in the further exploitation of other helpless people, Cordill proceeded in 1888 to demonstrate more precisely the genuineness of his concern for the "blind" and some of the "sick." He voted for Senate Bill 107, which, like many items of legislation, carried an innocuous title: "An act to unite the institutes for the deaf and dumb and the institute for the blind under one general superintendent, to be known as the Institute for the Deaf, Dumb and Blind."[65] The bill became law, which made Cordill a party to crowding these variously afflicted persons "all under one roof. Instead of two dilapidated buildings as previously, the deaf, dumb, and blind, after 1888, occupied one dilapidated building."[66] How Cordill may have eased the torments of the insane has yet to be revealed.[67]

[63] *Senate Journal* (1888), 256. The bill was indefinitely postponed.
[64] *House Journal* (1888), 234.
[65] *Senate Journal* (1888), 234.
[66] Hair, *Bourbonism and Agrarian Protest*, 129; *State Journal* (1888), 178–80.
[67] An item of Bourbon propaganda published in 1898 described Cordill

Samuel Lawrence James emerged as unscathed from his second decade in command of Louisiana's penal system as he had from his first. Barbarous treatment of convicts had jeopardized his secure position no more than had flagrant violations of law during the 1870s. After 1890, however, the major's fortunes quickly deteriorated, despite his having secured in that year a ten-year renewal of his lease. By 1901 the practice of leasing convicts had been terminated in Louisiana—not primarily for humanitarian reasons nor because penal reformers had suddenly acquired genuine influence, but rather because the lessee (together with the lottery, black voters, and Populism) had become politically intolerable to the new ruling faction of the state Democratic Party. And in 1894, the same year during which an anti-lease proposal was at last endorsed by the General Assembly, James himself died, leaving successors who were unwilling or unable to stem the tide of adverse circumstances.

---

as "an active worker, quick at reaching decisions, [who] knows exactly what to do, and the best, shortest and simplest way of doing it." *The Convention of '98: A complete Work on the Greatest Political Event in Louisiana's History, and a Sketch of The Men Who Composed It* (New Orleans, 1898), 49.

CHAPTER III

Profits and Politics
1890-1901

C ONTRACTED IN 1870 during Radical Reconstruction, the lease of Louisiana's penal system to S. L. James and Company was due to expire in 1891. Thus the assembly session of 1890 afforded the state's Bourbon Democrats a timely opportunity to redeem themselves from their unbecoming association with the major's disgraceful regime, which had survived the era of its inception by serving the interests of Bourbon fiscal conservatism. The assembly could refrain from granting James another contract, let his existing one run out, and provide for resumption of state control the following year. On the other hand, legislators could continue leasing the state's convicts, either to James or to anyone else who might offer a more attractive proposition. All of these possible courses of action were duly sponsored in 1890 and James, although hard pressed by anti-lease elements and a competitor, managed to vanquish each threat in turn. But the major's triumph soon proved to be a pyrrhic victory—in 1892 his enemies came to power and began at once to move against him.

Among those already disenchanted with James by 1890 was Governor Francis T. Nicholls, whose message to the General Assembly demonstrated that his regard for the lease had cooled since 1878: "The present system is open to very serious and great objections, but I see no way of dealing with this matter other than by either continuing it for a time, making the new lease as short as possible, or by placing the convict force upon the levees and making the levee and drainage fund effect a double purpose."[1] While the balance of his remarks indicated that Nicholls preferred the latter alternative—resumption of state control in the manner previously suggested by Parlange, Downing, and Provosty—the governor's willingness to sign a compromise measure was made abundantly clear. Neither James nor his critics was likely to be entirely satisfied with a short-term lease, the former because he was accustomed to a contract of twenty-one years' duration and the latter because they were opposed to any further contracts. But each, presumably, could learn to live with such a settlement, James remaining in business for a time and his opponents taking solace from the limited duration of his tenure. The state, meanwhile, would continue to make money and Nicholls himself could avoid the responsibility for terminating an easy source of revenue without having to appear as another McEnery. The governor's proposal contained something for everyone.

James apparently understood and accepted the rules of the game as laid down by Nicholls. On May 21, 1890, a bill proposing a renewal of the major's lease for ten years at $25,000 annually was introduced by Senator William Robson, "an extensive levee contractor and builder" from Caddo Parish, who may well have been one of the lessee's subcontractors.[2] A second lease bill was sponsored by Republican Senator K. A. Cross of East Baton Rouge Parish; this measure proposed to award the concession to one C. G. Ellis, a former associate of the Texas lessee. And once again Senator O. O. Provosty of Pointe Coupee Parish proposed that the state resume con-

[1] State of Louisiana, *Official Journal of the Proceeding of the Senate of the General Assembly, 1890* (Baton Rouge, 1890), 5–6. Published proceedings of the senate are hereinafter cited as *Senate Journal*, with appropriate year indicated.

[2] *Biographical and Historical Memoirs of Louisiana* (Chicago, 1892), II, 498; New Orleans *Times-Democrat*, July 2, 1890; *Senate Journal* (1890), 293.

trol of the penal system. All bills originated in the senate, which for more than a month conducted itself on the level of what two members described as an "auction mart."[3] The house behaved similarly when the status of the penal system came before its members for deliberation.

Provosty's bill resembled previous anti-lease measures in two respects: (1) it provided for employment of the convicts on levees under state control and supervision; and (2), because the bill called for no basic changes in convict management or penal policy, it was not committed, in any forthright sense, to reform or rehabilitation. Unlike its predecessors, however, the Provosty measure of 1890 sought to appropriate $50,000 as the initial balance in a penitentiary fund. The last annual rental due from James under the old lease, $25,000, would also be credited to the fund upon receipt. These proposals, if enacted, would not only deprive Louisiana's taxpayers of $50,000 at the outset, but would commandeer, for convict maintenance, $25,000 of anticipated revenue which could doubtless be applied to more popular objectives. The James proposal, by contrast, was infinitely more sensible from a financial point of view. When it was revealed that Ellis intended to match the major's proffered rental of $25,000 per year, James raised his bid to $35,000, provoking Ellis in turn to make a formal offer of $45,000 annually. By this time Provosty's cause was under great pressure. On June 28 his bill was defeated by a vote of 11–12–13, with Provosty himself one of the many unexplained absentees, any two of whom, had they been present and voting in favor, could have saved the measure.[4]

Now the bidding began in earnest. By July 2, when the James bill came up for final passage, Senator Robson announced that the current lessee had agreed to match the annual rental offered by Ellis. This information prompted Senator Lloyd Posey of New Orleans to observe that the pur-

[3] The two represented adjoining parishes in South Louisiana, John M. Avery of Iberia and Murphy J. Foster of St. Mary. See *Senate Journal* (1890), 357, and New Orleans *Times-Democrat*, July 3, 1890.

[4] *Senate Journal* (1890), 293.

pose of the lease was not to make money but merely to insure that the penal system remained self-supporting. In order to pay $45,000, he continued, the lessee would have to work the convicts harder and abuse them more. "The lash," he advised his colleagues, "would have to be applied all the more vigorously."[5] The James bill passed the senate by a vote of 21–12–3, with the amount to be paid remaining at $35,000 per year.[6] Among the yeas were the four Negro senators, although it should be stated that two, Senator Thomas Cage and Senator Richard Simms, had voted earlier for the Provosty bill while the other two, R. F. Guichard and Henry Demas, had been away from the chamber with eleven other members while Provosty's measure went down in defeat.

In the house, a majority of the penitentiary committee reported the bill favorably, with a proviso that James be required to pay $45,000 per year. Ellis at this point countered with an offer of $50,000. Five days later, on July 8, a floor amendment raising the major's annual fee to $50,000 was proposed and adopted. C. G. Ellis was now in a desperate situation. Action on his own bill had been stalled in the senate; on this same day it was "ordered to lie over, subject to call," which meant that it was being killed. Somehow, Ellis had to work himself into the James bill, now before the house, or accept defeat. His spokesman, Representative C. W. Seals of Claiborne Parish, offered a last-ditch amendment to the James proposal which would, in effect, transform it into an Ellis proposal: the name "C. G. Ellis" would be substituted for "S. L. James," while "$50,000.00," would be replaced, as a final inducement, by "$55,000.00." The amendment was rejected.[7] James, more than likely, had seen to it from the

[5] New Orleans *Times-Democrat*, July 3, 1890.

[6] *Senate Journal* (1890), 357. But Senator Posey, along with fellow New Orleanian Charles T. Soniat, supported the bill only with the understanding that a house amendment would raise the James fee to $45,000 a year.

[7] State of Louisiana, *Official Journal of the Proceedings of the House of Representatives of the General Assembly, 1890* (Baton Rouge, 1890), 594. Published proceedings of the house are hereinafter cited as *House Journal*, with appropriate year indicated.

beginning that his bill should prevail, no matter how much Ellis might offer to pay the state in either chamber.

The James proposal was now the sole survivor of the three penitentiary bills. One last matter had to be settled before the house was polled. Negro Republican T. T. Allain of Iberville Parish rose to ask the James manager "if there was anything in [the] bill which allowed convicts to work on cotton or sugar plantations." (A clause within the bill specifically forbade the lessee to engage convicts in farm or plantation work—as bait for black support.) In reply to Allain's question, Anthony Wayne Faulkner of Caldwell Parish said, simply, "No, sir."[8] With that the James bill passed by a vote of 74–19–4, nine out of ten Negro members voting in favor.[9] James, of course, had no intention of terminating lucrative contracts for cotton picking and cane cutting. He continued to accept them and just before his death in 1894 prevailed upon the General Assembly to repeal the inconvenient portion of his lease which prohibited him from doing so. By that time there were no more black senators and only three blacks in the house, all of whom voted silently and hopelessly against repeal.

The effectiveness with which James's interests had been handled throughout the session of 1890 received ample credit in the comments of house members. Representative S. O. Shattuck of Calcasieu Parish found himself compelled to support renewal of the major's contract because it was "the only [bill] before the Legislature; the present lease is about to expire and something must be done with the convicts. I strongly favored the Provosty bill, *and regret that he allowed*

[8] New Orleans *Times-Democrat*, July 9, 1890. Democrat Faulkner had voted for the first James lease in 1870. He had also "owned and worked many Negroes, having 101 at the beginning of the Civil War." *The Convention of '98: A Complete Work on the Greatest Political Event in Louisiana's History, and a Sketch of The Men Who Composed It* (New Orleans, 1898), 28.

[9] *House Journal* (1890), 604. Republican Victor Rochon of St. Martin Parish was the only black member of the General Assembly in 1890 to oppose the James bill. For additional evidence of the character and outspokenness of Rochon during this session, see *ibid.*, 201–204.

it to be killed in the Senate."[10] Representative G. W. Bolton of Rapides Parish also felt obliged to vote for James, "for in the event no lease is passed now, the convicts would be thrown upon the Governor, with no means provided for their support."[11] Representative A. A. Batchelor, from the traditionally anti-lease parish of Pointe Coupee, offered a comprehensive summary of the dilemma created by events of the session:

> I am opposed to the lease system, but the exigencies of the situation require that some disposition shall be made of the State convicts in order that the Governor may not be placed in an embarrassing situation. And as the friends of this [James] bill have defeated that bill [by Provosty] placing them under the control of the State . . . and have also refused to consider an offer of C. G. Ellis for $50,000 more than is obtained in this bill, I see no other practical solution of the question; and no other alternative than voting for this bill.[12]

To no one's surprise, Representative Seals of Claiborne Parish opposed the James proposal. The defeated Ellis manager condemned the brutality of the current lessee, charging that "the death rate [in the Louisiana penal system] is about four times as great in proportion to the number of convicts as the death rate in any other penitentiary in the United States."[13] Seals also opposed the bill because the "lease under the James regime is fast becoming a political combine dangerous to the welfare of Louisiana."[14] While hardly a disinterested commentator, Seals was essentially correct on both counts.

Typical of the perennial ambivalence of "reformers" was the observation of Representative Placide P. Sigur of St. Mary Parish, who, though he wished to end the harsh conditions

---

[10] *Ibid.*, 605. Shattuck in 1890 sponsored the lottery amendment. Italics added.   [11] *Ibid.*, 606.

[12] *Ibid.*, 607. Shortly afterward, Batchelor noted "Gov. Nicholls says he think[s] I voted right." Albert A. Batchelor Papers (Department of Archives and Manuscripts, Louisiana State University).

[13] *House Journal* (1890), 605–606.   [14] *Ibid.*

prevailing under the lease, also desired that Louisiana should receive all the money from the labor of its convicts: "I vote no upon this measure, because I think the system of hiring out the convicts . . . is wrong and inhuman, and for the reason that the State is fully competent to control and retain supervision over its own wards. The State being sadly in need of revenue, it should receive itself any benefit or profit that can or may be derived from convict labor."[15] For its part, the upper chamber concurred in the house version with indecent haste, voting on the same day to award Major James a ten-year contract obliging him to pay the state $50,000 a year. Among those in favor was Senator Posey, who only a week before had been so concerned about having to apply the lash.

During the session of 1890 both chambers also approved a re-charter of the Louisiana State Lottery Company. Just as the institution had been written into the Louisiana Constitution of 1879, "where it would be beyond the reach of fickle legislatures and ungrateful governors,"[16] so again the re-charter bill was passed as a proposed constitutional amendment subject to popular ratification at the next (1892) state election. In the house, of the seventy-four members who voted to renew the major's lease, sixty also supported the lottery. Of the nineteen who opposed the lease, thirteen also opposed the lottery. Twenty of the twenty-one senators who favored the lease voted for the lottery, and ten of the twelve senators who opposed the lease also opposed the lottery.[17] Republicans, especially black Republicans, were nearly unanimous in their support of each institution. All four Negro senators voted for both, while in the house the entire black delegation supported the lottery and all but one voted for the lease.

The relationship between Negroes and the convict lease system in post-Civil War Louisiana was compounded equally of cynicism and tragedy. All four Negro senators and twenty-four of twenty-five Negro representatives helped award the major his first contract during the assembly session of 1870. Many undoubtedly had been bribed. Between that time and 1890 both the number and proportion of black convicts, together with the number and proportion of convict deaths, steadily increased. By 1890 the lurid details of the lessee's operation were well known, as was the race of a majority of his victims. Nonetheless, all four Negro senators in 1890 and nine of ten Negro representatives acquiesced in the extension of the lease.

James could have secured his first contract, and probably his second lease as well, without Negro support in the General Assembly. White Republicans and Democrats voted in sufficient numbers on each occasion to comprise majorities in his favor. (Although without black votes in 1890, the majority in the senate favoring the lease would not have been an absolute one. In addition had Senator Demas and Senator Guichard supported the Provosty bill, it would have passed the upper house. James surely would not have liked that.) But without Negro support against the Parlange and Downing bills, in 1884 and 1886 respectively, Major James might have been evicted from the penitentiary. In each case the vote was close, and in each case black legislators held the balance of power and provided the lessee with his margin of victory.[18] State control of the penitentiary, if restored at any time between 1884 and 1890, might not have been less harsh or brutal than lessee control. Surely it could have been no worse. But no one will ever know, because black votes in the

18 The vote in 1884 on Parlange's bill was 18 for, 16 against (including the five Negro senators), and 2 absent (including Parlange himself). Had any one of the Negroes voted in the affirmative, the bill would have passed the senate and might have become law. The vote in 1886 to postpone Downing's bill was 49 for (including 11 Negro representatives), 38 against (including one Negro), and 10 absent (including one Negro). Had 11 Negroes voted not to postpone, the bill might have passed the house later in the session and might have become law. Only in 1888 was there likelihood of a gubernatorial veto of an abolition bill. Even then, and more possibly in 1884 or 1886, McEnery might have signed a compromise measure endorsed by both houses.

General Assembly were decisive in enabling the James enterprise to remain in business until 1901.

While consistently opposed to the lessee's practice of employing convicts in competition with free labor, Negro legislators in each chamber nonetheless stood by the major in all
of his darker hours between 1884 and 1894. Some were probably insincere when they spoke out against the lessee (and
would sell their votes when the major was in need of them),
while others found themselves, despite their personal detesta-
tion of the system, torn between concern for Negro convicts
at the mercy of James and Negro constituents at the mercy
of prison labor competition. Some, no doubt, fell into each
category. In either event, their votes could be controlled.

Act 22 of 1875, which prohibited employment of convicts
outside the penitentiary, had caused the major great incon-
venience. The bill had been sponsored, handled, and passed
largely by black members of the General Assembly. James
ignored it until he could secure its repeal three years later.
The experience, however, furnished him a potentially valuable lesson in the art of managing conscientious black legislators. There was always the other kind who, with their white
counterparts, could be purchased. Money had been liberally
used to "buy" the first James lease in 1870. It was, no doubt,
again distributed as required to kill abolition bills in 1884,
1886, 1888, and perhaps in 1890, also.

In 1890, faced simultaneously with another anti-lease bill,
a competitor, and the task of renewing his own contract,
James needed to gather up every available endorsement.
But not all legislators, whether white or black, would accept
cash. Another level of inducement, from past experience,
seems to have come to mind. By playing upon the genuine
fears of responsible Negroes for the jobs of their constituents, the major might bring these legislators into his camp.

Written into the James bill was a clause stipulating that
"under no circumstances shall [convicts] be hired, sub-let,
or rented out, or be used by the lessee himself in the cultiva-

68 POLITICS AND PUNISHMENT

tion, planting, or gathering of any agricultural crop."[19] This ruse, as has been demonstrated, accomplished its objective. Given confidence by the "legal" assurance that convicts would no longer displace their constituents from agricultural work, black legislators who were honestly concerned about this matter serenely proceeded to underwrite ten more years of horror in the major's work camps. What was nothing more than a tongue-in-cheek facsimile of Act 22 had been disinterred and cynically twisted to serve the purpose of the man against whom it had originally been applied.[20] By 1894, as noted previously, this temporarily self-imposed nuisance was off the books.

In the end, therefore, whenever he needed them (or thought he did), James was able to rake in almost all Negro legislators, by one means or another, for as long as they continued to sit in the General Assembly. Many of these same blacks also supported the lottery, as did many more whites. But the lease and the lottery, though both were corrupt (and corrupting) institutions, were not really engaged in the same line of business. And from this difference the tragedy emerges. For all the years that the lessee was supported by some blacks, who in turn were either "supported" or manipulated by him, thousands of other blacks (and many whites) were being whipped, maimed, and killed. But perhaps too much has been expected of Negro legislators—in Louisiana—during the troubled decades of the late nineteenth century.[21] James cer-

[19] State of Louisiana, *Acts of the General Assembly of 1890* (Baton Rouge, 1890), 157. Published legislative actions of the General Assembly are hereinafter cited as *Acts of Louisiana*, with appropriate year indicated.

[20] A recent and otherwise valuable sociological study of Louisiana's penal system interprets Act 114 of 1890—the James lease renewal—as a legislative reform and credits its passage to effective lobbying by the Prison Reform Association of Louisiana! Joseph Clarence Mouledous, "Sociological Perspectives on a Prison Social System" (M. A. thesis, Louisiana State University, 1962), 66–67.

[21] In Georgia and South Carolina, by contrast, blacks in and out of politics vigorously and consistently opposed the practice of leasing convicts. See Clarence Bacote, "Negro Proscriptions, Protests, and Proposed Solutions in Georgia, 1880–1908" in Charles E. Wynes (ed.) *The Negro in the South Since 1865: Selected Essays in American Negro History*

tainly bribed and hoodwinked a number of white legislators, too, as did the Louisiana State Lottery Company.

In 1875 a weary and disillusioned Henry Clay Warmoth had commented upon conditions then prevailing in Louisiana under the even more excessive regime of his widely despised successor, and personal enemy, Governor William Pitt Kellogg. "Why, damn it," Warmoth exclaimed, "everybody is demoralizing down here. Corruption is the fashion."[22] The kind of corruption Warmoth described remained fashionable in Louisiana long after he, Kellogg, and Reconstruction passed from the political scene.

Governor Nicholls signed the second James lease without any enthusiasm whatever. A message to the senate, rebuking the entire General Assembly, expressed the Governor's indignation:

. . . . I attach my signature to this bill solely for the reason that the subject matter of the disposition of the convicts was acted upon so late that I am either forced to approve this bill or find myself at the close of the present lease of the Penitentiary [in 1891] between two sessions of the Legislature without directions or instructions as to how to deal with the convicts, and without means at my command to provide for them in the interim.

I am strongly opposed to the granting by legislative act a contract to a particular individual, and I disapprove of the manner [in which] the lease contained in this act has been thus adopted.[23]

On this note of gubernatorial vexation commenced the

(Tuscaloosa, 1965), 162–66; and George B. Tindall, *South Carolina Negroes, 1877–1900* (Columbia, S. C., 1952), 267–73.

[22] Quoted in Roger W. Shugg, *Origins of Class Struggle in Louisiana: A Social History of White Farmers and Laborers During Slavery and After, 1840–1875* (Baton Rouge, 1939), 227.

[23] *Senate Journal* (1890), 446. Compared with his earlier statements to the Assembly and considering the comment of Representative Batchelor (note 12 above), Nicholls' final commentary leaves one in doubt concerning the governor's consistency on the lease question. Or perhaps Nicholls, jealous of his reputation for integrity, was simply attempting to disassociate himself from the sordid proceedings behind passage of the James bill.

third decade of the major's control of Louisiana's penal system. From the convict's point of view it would be the worst decade. In terms of revenue furnished the state, it would be the best decade, and, as a result of political developments over which the James company exercised no influence, it would be the last decade.

Only two years elapsed between the major's impressive victory in 1890 and the initiation of an ultimately successful campaign to end the convict lease system in Louisiana. The architect and director of this undertaking was State Senator Murphy J. Foster of St. Mary Parish, who was elected to the governorship in 1892 and served until 1900. Although Foster's youth had excused him from service in the Confederate Army—he was only twelve when the Civil War began—few veterans by 1877 could have surpassed him in his passionate dedication to "white supremacy." And for Foster, who had grown to maturity during Reconstruction, the indispensable fortress of stability and security for his class (Foster was a wealthy planter) was the Democratic Party.

Elected to the state senate in 1879 at thirty, Foster embarked upon his long political career only two years after Democratic "home rule" had replaced Radical Reconstruction in Louisiana. With Republicanism on the defensive in the state, and with Republicans, both in and out of office, too few to pose an immediate threat, it seemed in 1879 that the numerically superior and wealthier Democrats could anticipate many serene years in power.

Five years later, however, there appeared an unhealthy symptom of division within the party as white Democrats in the senate split almost evenly over the Parlange anti-lease bill. The five Negro Republicans thus became the decisive factor, and when all of them sided with the opposition, the bill fell short of passage by only one vote. Always an anti-lease Democrat, Foster had enlisted in the cause initially as a humanitarian disciple of George Washington Cable, whose criticism of the convict lease system had been cited by the young senator in support of the Parlange bill. But as Negro

Republicans continued to provide the lessee with his margin of victory over three subsequent anti-lease measures, Foster's aversion to Major James took on an extra dimension: not only was the lessee conducting a brutal and repulsive enterprise, he was also objectionable as a source of division and potential weakness within the Democratic Party.

Foster's apprehensions must have been severely aggravated by the events of 1890. Pro-lease Democrats in alliance with some Negro Republicans had defeated the Provosty bill and given James another contract. Pro-lottery Democrats in alliance with all Negro Republicans had produced the two-thirds vote required in each house for passage of the odious lottery amendment. Viewed from the perspective of Foster and other Bourbon purists, the James lease was indeed a "political combine dangerous to the welfare of Louisiana," as Representative Seals had described it, for with Democrats badly divided over the James lease and lottery measures, a handful of Negro Republicans acquired the balance of power in Louisiana's General Assembly—thirteen years after "white supremacy" had supposedly been established.

Meanwhile, agrarian discontent was becoming worrisome to Bourbon Democracy in Louisiana. Initially, as members of the Farmers' Alliance and later as Populists, many ordinary Louisianians of both races voiced increasing opposition to the unsympathetic policies of their wealthy and reactionary Bourbon leaders. The old slogans of "white supremacy," so useful in the past as rallying cries against Radical Reconstructionists, had begun to lose much of their potency in keeping poorer whites and Negroes politically apart.[24] Faced with an emerging and disaffected "biracial Proletariat," Louisiana's Bourbon Democrats could no longer afford to tolerate the divisions within their ranks caused by the lottery and the James lease. Nor could the beneficiary of Democratic discord, Negro Republicanism, be permitted

[24] For a scholarly analysis of the origins, composition, grievances, and difficulties of Louisiana Populism, see William Ivy Hair, *Bourbonism and Agrarian Protest: Louisiana Politics 1877–1900* (Baton Rouge, 1969), chapters 7 and 9.

any longer to capitalize on the weaknesses of the majority party. Thus, by 1892 Murphy J. Foster was the gubernatorial candidate of those Democrats who grasped these political realities most clearly. The ultimate objectives of the Foster Democrats, as demonstrated by their 1892 campaign and by their subsequent performance in office, were to destroy the lottery, terminate the James lease, and remove the Negro from Louisiana politics. Not until 1901 were all of these objectives finally achieved. The groundwork in all cases, however, was completed by 1892, the year in which Foster— enemy of the lottery, the lease, and black voters—was elected governor of Louisiana.

First to be assaulted was the lottery, which became the principal issue in the 1892 gubernatorial campaign. While the Negro vote, and subsequently the biracial Populist vote, remained the most dangerous of the three nemeses of Bourbon Democracy, the lottery in 1892 was the most vulnerable, and therefore the most useful for Foster's immediate purposes, which were to win the governorship for himself and to gain a majority in the General Assembly for the foes of the lottery, the Foster Democrats.

In order for the company to survive, the lottery amendment would have to be approved by the people, and the people could be bombarded with the truth about the lottery— how it corrupted public officials, extorted hard-earned money from innocent citizens (white and black), and was therefore a disgrace to the good name of Louisiana. The lease, on the other hand, had been legally extended for ten years by Governor Nicholls (however reluctantly) and the General Assembly (however shamefully). Rentals due the state under this new agreement, moreover, would subsequently amount to a half million dollars. And finally, at a time when thousands of poorer voters of both races were suspicious enough of Foster's sincerity and devotion to their interests, there was no political capital to be gained (commensurate with the risks involved) from posing as the advocate and protector of convicted felons. It was the lottery, therefore, and not the

lease nor even the Negro vote, which was condemned and
disparaged by the Fosterites in 1892. Once in power, however, Foster and his associates could proceed against the lessee
and black voters in turn.

Early in 1892 the federal government prohibited the lottery
from using the mails. This was a mortal blow because there
was no other practical way for the company to distribute its
tickets or advertisements. This disaster from without was
compounded by a disaster at home. To oppose Foster for
the Democratic gubernatorial nomination, the lottery had
prevailed upon its old friend, Samuel D. McEnery, to descend
from the bench of the Louisiana Supreme Court and reenter
the lists once again, this time as an avowed pro-lottery candidate. It was soon demonstrated, however, that McEnery
suffered from an "obvious lack of popularity." Lottery officials, "convinced . . . that their cause within the state was
also hopeless," left the field. Their request for re-charter
was withdrawn.[25] Foster went on to defeat McEnery in the
general election, in which two Republicans and a Populist
brought up the rear.

Probably as a result of exclusive emphasis placed upon
the lottery issue by Foster himself in 1892, historians have
remained totally unaware of Foster's simultaneous aversion
to the James lease, which the senator had actively opposed
since 1884. Consequently, no previous historical account of
Foster's career deals with the lease in any manner whatsoever. Equally ignored by historians has been the role of black
Republican legislators in sustaining the James lease and in
renewing both the lease and the lottery in 1890. Each of
these important and interrelated aspects of Louisiana history
has been rediscovered and placed into context with one another only within this present study.

The Fosterite General Assembly of 1892 lost no time clos-
ing in on their two remaining enemies—Negro voters and

[25] *Ibid.*, 224–25. Two years later, in 1894, the lottery company left
Louisiana for Central America, where it continued to operate for several
more years.

Major James. A committee of the assembly was appointed and instructed to prepare drafts of constitutional amendments to accomplish, among other things, reduction of the electorate (by means of property and literacy tests) and termination of the convict lease system. The committee was to have the draft amendments completed and ready for presentation to the assembly at the next (1894) biennial session. Thus the decision to discontinue the leasing of convicts was made in 1892 by the Foster administration, as soon as it came to power, for reasons of political security and retaliation. The Prison Reform Association must have had little influence in this matter, either in 1892 or at any later time, as ensuing developments all too clearly indicate.

Two years later, in 1894, the committee reported back to the assembly. A joint resolution, embodying the recommendations of the committee with reference to the lease, was introduced by Senator Charles Gauthreaux of New Orleans. The resolution passed the senate by a vote of 31–0 and the house by a vote of 69–0, with no debate recorded in either chamber.[26] Governor Foster had recommended passage of the proposal earlier in the session. (The General Assembly also passed the suffrage restriction amendment, among others, which would go before the electorate for their approval in the forthcoming 1896 election.) The text of the lease resolution follows:

> Section 1. First, no penitentiary convict shall ever be leased or hired to any person or persons, or corporation, private or public, or quasi public, or board, save as authorized in the next section, *provided that this article shall take effect upon the extinguishment of the lease made pursuant to Act 114, approved July 10, 1890.*
>
> Section 2. The General Assembly may authorize the employment under State supervison and the proper officials and employees of the State, of convicts on public roads or other public works, *or on convict farms or in manufactories owned or controlled by the State* or by any levee

[26] *Senate Journal* (1894), 328; *House Journal* (1894), Calendar, 162.

board or any public levee under such provisions and restrictions as may be imposed by law.[27]

While both the Parlange bill of 1884, which Foster had energetically supported, and the Downing bill of 1886 had called for immediate abolition of the lease system, this "reform" measure of the Foster administration did not propose to evict the lessee at all. James would remain in charge of Louisiana's penal system for the duration of his contract, which had seven additional years to run. It should also be noted again that the state was just as eager to make money from farm and plantation work as the lessee had been, and was no more concerned than he about convict competition with free black labor.

Eventual restoration of state control was all the 1894 measure embodied. While this "reform" would certainly be desirable, and the sooner the better, no further modifications in penal policy were indicated. There was no state commitment to rehabilitation of convicts and no implication that Louisiana's penal system would become in fact anything other than a state-operated business enterprise rather than a lessee-operated business enterprise.

Within a decade Foster had gone from condemnation of the lessee on humanitarian grounds to emulation of the lessee on economic grounds. In the interim he and his supporters decided to end the convict lease system, as they had also decided to kill the lottery. Unlike the lottery, however, which had been made the public foil of Fosterian wrath, the James lease was left unmentioned and relatively undisturbed. And while the lottery was subjected to a quick and widely celebrated demise, the lease was permitted to fade quietly away, sipping its hemlock in moderate doses over a seven-year period.

On July 26, 1894, three weeks after passage of the anti-lease resolution, the major "was sitting on the gallery [at Angola] conversing with his family when he was taken with

27 *Senate Journal* (1894), 328. Italics added.

a smothering sensation." He went to the railing and "attempted to vomit," but instead "blood gushed from his mouth and
nose." Within twenty minutes Samuel Lawrence James was
dead.[28] His passing was sudden and unexpected, for, despite
his age and girth, James was thought to be in good health
at the time. On July 28 in New Orleans, as the lessee's body
lay in a rosewood casket, the Reverend A. J. Tardy consoled
grieving friends and relatives by reminding them that James
had been "happiest when making others happy." Such a man
as James "never dies," intoned Tardy, because "a good name
is never erased from the records of time."[29] The New Orleans
Times-Democrat, Burke's pro-lottery organ in former days,
offered its measure of whitewash by stating that James had
lived in a "world generally returning hard knocks for deeds
of kindness and bestowing censure where praise should have
been the reward."[30]

James was comfortably wealthy at the time of his fatal
attack: between 1895 and 1899 the executors of his personal
estate collected and disbursed more than 2.3 million dollars,
a fortune even by today's standards and a monumental sum
in economically depressed Louisiana during the 1890s.[31] James
also died in personal and complete control of the Louisiana
penal system, a status he had enjoyed for many years, but
which political circumstances had already begun to erode.
His death did not alter the established anti-lease policy of
Foster's administration: S. L. James and Company, taken
over by the major's executors and by his son, Samuel, Jr.,
was not given a reprieve from the proposal of 1894.

Murphy J. Foster was, if anything, a loyal Bourbon Democrat from head to toe. He valued the security and solidarity
of the Louisiana Democratic Party above everything else,
evidently including himself. Defending his past administrations in 1900, Foster would admit that he might have made

28 New Orleans *Times-Democrat*, July 28, 1894.
29 New Orleans *Daily Picayune*, July 29, 1894.
30 New Orleans *Times-Democrat*, July 28, 1894.
31 Succession of Samuel Lawrence James, Sr., Probate Box #52, Office
of the Clerk of Court, West Feliciana Parish, St. Francisville, Louisiana.

some mistakes. But, he would add, "because I have sinned don't destroy the Democratic party; strike down the sinner. If I have been recreant in my duty, strike me down, but for God's sake don't destroy the Democratic party."[32] According to his biographer, "every appointment and every political move" of Governor Foster "had as its ultimate objective the unification of the Democratic party in Louisiana."[33] If the "reform" proposal of 1894 stands bereft of any genuine ingredients of penal reform, the omission is probably best explained by the absence of any reform motivation therein. In 1894, with the lottery already dead, only two of Foster's enemies remained with any life in them—black political influence in Louisiana and the James lease. The suffrage restriction amendment, passed by the General Assembly in 1894, was designed to remove the former menace. Most blacks, as well as many rebellious poor whites, could be easily disfranchised by the literacy and property tests which the amendment embodied. And once deprived of black support in the assembly, S. L. James and Company would not have its way with the Democratic Party in the future as it had in the past. Thus reduced to political harmlessness, the lessees need not be feared any longer and could be left alone to pay the $350,000 they owed the state for the last seven years of their contract. This was in effect what Foster's administration provided for in 1894, and not penal reform. For their part, the major's successors reciprocated with unprecedented liberality. Between January 1, 1895, and January 1, 1901, the lessees submitted $278,688.96 to the state treasurer. This amount, while considerably short of the $350,000 anticipated by the state during this same period—and which the company was legally obliged to pay—nonetheless exceeded by more than $100,000 the entire revenue collected by Louisiana from the convict lease between 1870 and 1891. The convict death toll also reached an all-time high after 1894: 216 during 1896 alone and prob-

---

[32] Quoted in Sidney J. Romero, Jr., "The Political Career of Murphy J. Foster," *Louisiana Historical Quarterly*, XXVIII (1945), 1193.
[33] *Ibid.*, 1167.

ably close to 800 altogether for the last seven years of the lease.[34] These circumstances further diminish whatever claim might be made for Governor Foster as a penal reformer.

Seeking a second term in 1896, the repressive and unpopular Foster had to be "counted in" over his Populist-Republican opponent by former Governor McEnery's henchmen in the heavily Negro cotton parishes of North Louisiana.[35] Fraudulent returns from the cotton belt gave Foster an undeserved total of 116,116 votes to 87,698 for John N. Pharr.[36] All the proposed amendments of 1894 failed, however, in this election, which was highly charged with emotion, class conflict, fraud, and racial obsessions.[37] Thus, when the General Assembly of Foster's second administration convened in the spring of 1896, there was unfinished business to be taken care of.

To compensate for the defeated suffrage amendment, the assembly passed a new registration and election law, to take effect the following year. The purpose of this law was "to

[34] State of Louisiana, *Annual Report of the State Treasurer* (New Orleans, 1870–80), *passim; Biennial Report of the State Treasurer to the Governor of Louisiana* (Baton Rouge, 1882–1902), *passim; Biennial Report of the Board of Control of the Louisiana State Penitentiary to His Excellency Murphy J. Foster, Governor of Louisiana* (Baton Rouge, 1898), 160. Published biennial reports of the board are hereinafter cited as *Biennial Report, Board of Control*, with appropriate year indicated. The death rate rose from 6 percent in 1895 to 20 percent in 1896, declining to an average of about 10 percent for the remaining years of the lease.

[35] After 1892, with the lottery issue settled, the Foster and McEnery wings of the Louisiana Democratic Party merged in the face of a growing mutual threat, Populism. McEnery was rewarded in 1896 with a seat in the United States Senate, which he occupied until his death in 1910. For conflicting views of the 1896 election, see Hair, *Bourbonism and Agrarian Protest*, 259–67; and Romero, "The Political Career of Murphy J. Foster, 1180–83.

[36] Hair, *Bourbonism and Agrarian Protest*, 262. Ironically, both Foster and Pharr were sugar planters from St. Mary Parish, in which Foster received 1,102 votes in 1896 to Pharr's 3,483. *Senate Journal* (1896), 22.

[37] For an editorial expressing dismay concerning the fate of the amendments, see New Orleans *Times-Democrat*, May 1, 1896.

reduce the votes of the uneducated of both races."[38] Another administration bill, also passed in 1896, provided for an election early in 1898 to determine the question of holding a state constitutional convention. By 1898, of course, "mostly because of the registration law, at least 90 per cent of the blacks were to be off the rolls, along with tens of thousands of poor whites."[39] The convention, once authorized and its delegates elected, could then proceed to make disfranchisement of unreliable electors permanent and unassailable, because the result of the convention's efforts would not be submitted for popular ratification.

In January, 1898, the prescribed election took place, the convention was approved, and delegates chosen. Later in the spring, they convened in New Orleans. This gathering of the elite, described by its own presiding officer as "little more than a family meeting of the Democratic party of the State of Louisiana,"[40] drafted a new organic law requiring prospective voters thenceforth to own property worth at least $300 or be able to read and write. Louisiana was by then the most illiterate state in the nation. It was also the home of many people who owned little or no property. As was intended, the number of voters outside the "family" was reduced dramatically.[41]

Reduction of the electorate was the principal mission of the constitutional convention of 1898. But other matters had to be settled also, one of which was the status of the penal system. On April 15, 1898, by a vote of 104–0–30 (with no recorded discussion), the "family meeting" consummated the political decision made six years earlier, by placing in the constitution a prohibition against the leasing of convicts "to private firms or individuals" after 1901.[42] While the Prison Reform Association of Louisiana may well have lobbied enthusiastically within the convention, it is highly doubtful

[38] Hair, *Bourbonism and Agrarian Protest*, 268.
[39] *Ibid.*   [40] Quoted in *ibid.*, 275.   [41] *Ibid.*, 276–77.
[42] State of Louisiana, *Official Journal of the Proceedings of the Constitutional Convention of 1898* (New Orleans, 1898), 222–23.

that its influence alone contributed in any way to ending the convict lease system in Louisiana, either in 1898 or at any other time.[43] Nor did Populism, a vocal critic of convict lessees elsewhere,[44] play an important role in terminating the lease system in Louisiana. Engaged in mortal combat with the Democrats over control of the state government, Louisiana Populists omitted the convict lease from their platforms and ignored it otherwise as well. And on the two occasions in 1894 and 1898 when official votes were taken concerning the lease, only one Populist was present each time—not enough to have made any difference one way or the other.[45]

Considerable adjustments were necessary before the state could resume control of the penal system. Buildings had to be constructed, land purchased, employees recruited and trained, and a state board of administration organized, all of which, lamented Governor Foster in 1900, would require that "grave financial questions must be met and solved."[46] Act 70 of that year provided for these requirements and authorized the new State Board of Control "also [to] enact rules for the grading and classifying of the convicts according to

[43] The assumption that termination of the convict lease system in Louisiana resulted exclusively from efforts of the Prison Reform Association was given scholarly credence a generation ago in Elizabeth Wisner, *Public Welfare Administration in Louisiana* (Chicago, 1930), 162–63. Wisner's only evidence, however, was the word of F. S. Shields, an official of the association. All subsequent studies, nonetheless, have accepted the Wisner-Shields thesis. The most recent of these is Mark T. Carleton, "The Politics of the Convict Lease System in Louisiana: 1868–1901," *Louisiana History*, VII (Winter, 1967), 22–23.

[44] Woodward, *Origins of the New South*, 85, 257, 425; Hilda Jane Zimmerman, "Penal Systems and Penal Reforms in the South since the Civil War" (Ph.D. dissertation, University of North Carolina, 1947), 278.

[45] New Orleans *Times-Democrat*, February 19, 1892; Natchitoches (La.) *Louisiana Populist*, March 27, 1896. The only Populist in the General Assembly of 1894 was Senator B. F. Brian of Grant Parish. Brian was among the 31 senators who voted to discontinue leasing convicts after 1901. B. W. Bailey of Winn Parish was the sole Populist delegate to the constitutional convention of 1898. Although he was among the 103 delegates voting to terminate the lease system after 1901, Bailey refused to sign the final draft of the Constitution of 1898.

[46] *Senate Journal* (1900), 6.

the most modern and enlightened system of reformation, the assignment of work and the character of the same, the prohibition of harsh or cruel punishment, the right of a convict to communicate directly with the Board without interference . . . the purpose being to restore and reform the individual to a better man, physically, intellectually, and morally."[47] A section requiring the separation of convicts between the ages of seven and seventeen from older prisoners was also included. This act, for what it proved to be worth, had been drafted in consultation with the Prison Reform Association.

On January 9, 1901, shortly after reestablishment of state management, a jubilant New Orleans *Daily Picayune* remarked that "since the penitentiary was first leased out the world has progressed . . . no longer are [convicts] looked upon in well-regulated communities as being beyond the pale of humanity. They are no longer treated as animals, but as human beings, in whom there yet remains some good which might be developed, and the convict [may] yet become a good and useful citizen."[48]

The world might indeed have progressed since 1844, but in Louisiana the new penitentiary management included living legacies from the past. A member of the three-man Board of Control was Edward White, one of the major's executors and last manager of the penal system under the lease. Chief Warden W. M. Reynaud had also held the same position under James.[49] The two plantation managers were carryovers

---

[47] *Acts of Louisiana* (1900), 118.

[48] New Orleans *Daily Picayune*, January 9, 1901.

[49] The prison physician for many years, Reynaud was made state warden by Act 127 of 1896, the year in which the death toll under James reached its zenith. Reynaud's duties prior to 1901 consisted of investigating the convict camps and suggesting improvements which he thought could reduce convict mortality. Between 1896 and 1900, the number of reported convict deaths per year was 216 (1896), 68 (1897), 102 (1898), 115 (1899), and 72 (1900). Supposedly the state's man and apparently effective in fulfilling his purpose, Reynaud nonetheless made this interesting statement in 1898: "While, as a principle, I do not favor the lease system, I do not think that the State, under like conditions, could take better care of prisoners than do the present lessees." After 1901 Reynaud was for several years the chief administrative officer of

from the previous regime. One of them was the lessee's son, S. L. James, Jr.[50]

Was it not strange that such men had been retained to manage a prison designed to "restore and reform the individual"? The Baton Rouge *Daily Advocate,* still Louisiana's official journal, resolved this puzzle with vivid clarity in an editorial several days later.

> There is no doubt that from every point of view, the lease system is a bad one and the sentiment for a change was practically unanimous. . . . The records show that . . . before the [Civil] War, State control was an expensive luxury. . . . But conditions have changed, and with new avenues of employment and modern business methods, the convicts under the charge of the present management will . . . not only be self-sustaining, but yield a revenue to the State. Of course in inaugurating a system of such . . . import, it may require some time to place things on a paying basis, but we confidently believe that with the present scrupulously careful business methods and the earnest, conscientious, and intelligent attention that the Board is giving the management of the convicts, the result will be, from every standpoint, financially and all, entirely satisfactory.[51]

The convict lease system in Louisiana was supported by almost everyone in an official position from its beginning down to at least 1883. Not until 1894, however, did an abolition proposal pass the General Assembly. Not until 1898 was leasing of convicts actually made illegal. And not until 1901 did lessees vacate the penal system. During this period of hypocrisy and procrastination, Bourbon Democracy in Louisiana, whether pro-lease or anti-lease, continued to expect every bloody penny of promised revenue. And when the lease did at last expire, the profit motive, by which it had hypnotized several generations of Louisiana public officials, survived

---

Louisiana's penal system, which under his supervision remained financially sound. See *Biennial Report, Board of Control* (1898) , 5.

[50] Baton Rouge *Daily Advocate,* January 1, 1901.

[51] *Ibid.,* January 13, 1901.

for many years as the dominant principle in the state's philosophy of prison management.

Abolishing the convict lease system throughout the South took forty-three years, from Mississippi's constitutional prohibition in 1890 to the disappearance, by 1933, of the system's lingering vestiges in North Carolina.[52] Louisiana was the fourth southern state to prohibit convict leasing and the last to do so during the nineteenth century.[53] But the apparent virtue of Louisiana's having been in the forefront of the reform movement was somewhat compromised by the nominal commitment to penal reform on the part of those who abolished the lease and by the limited reforms which were effected following resumption of state control.

There is a fitting epilogue to the history of the convict lease system in Louisiana. By 1911 Murphy J. Foster had been a United States senator for eleven years. An old man, he was seeking reelection, had lost contact with many of his constituents, and was running scared. Foster opened his campaign in New Orleans on October 3 with a speech that proved to be his political valedictory. (He was to be defeated by Joseph Ransdell, who in turn lost to Huey P. Long in 1930.) Like a Confederate brigadier, the venerable Foster reviewed his irrelevant victories on the battlefields of the past. For two hours and forty minutes he elaborated upon

[52] Zimmerman, "Penal Systems and Penal Reforms," 218, 417–20. Mississippi retained for several years a system whereby private plantations were leased by the state penitentiary Board of Control, which permitted plantation owners to continue utilizing convict labor. In 1906 Governor James K. Vardaman urged abolition of these neo-lease arrangements and their replacement by state penal farms. The legislature complied and convict leasing in Mississippi was finally dispensed with. See Albert D. Kirwan, *Revolt of the Rednecks, Mississippi Politics, 1876–1925* (Lexington, 1951), 168–69, 174–75.

[53] Tennessee's legislature in 1893 prohibited further leasing after 1896; South Carolina's contract system was replaced by state farms in 1897. See A. C. Hutson, Jr., "The Overthrow of the Convict Lease System in Tennessee," *Publications of the East Tennessee Historical Society*, No. 8 (1936), 82–103, and William J. Cooper, Jr., *The Conservative Regime: South Carolina, 1877–1890* (Baltimore, 1968), 114.

his services to Louisiana, rendered over a period of thirty-two years in public office.[54]

Not once did the man who had led the fight against the convict lease system in Louisiana make the vaguest reference to any of his experiences during that struggle. No word was uttered concerning the motives behind eventual destruction of the lease by the man who had destroyed it. If Foster himself chose not to include penal reform among his many accomplishments, it must have been because he did not wish to be remembered as a "penal reformer." His own silence on the subject was well considered, for he had nothing of which to be proud.

[54] Romero, "The Political Career of Murphy J. Foster," 1226–27; New Orleans *Times-Democrat*, October 4, 1911.

CHAPTER IV

"Judicious" State Administration 1901-1920

B Y 1900 A MONOLITHIC Democratic Party had acquired complete control of Louisiana's government and political life. The disfranchising provisions written into the state constitution by the "family meeting" in New Orleans two years before had accomplished their objectives. The vast majority of black voters was stricken from the rolls. Rural whites in many cases were no longer voting either, and not necessarily because they had failed, or would fail, to qualify under the new laws. Hardy Brian, editor of the *Populist*, lamented after the 1898 congressional elections that "the great bulk" of former Populists "stayed at home in sullen despair," convinced that "it was no use, the Democrats would count them out."[1] Two years later another Populist leader, A. A. Gunby, observed that "apathy [has] seized the majority and they are willing that the minority should rule."[2]

And the minority ruled—without interruption and without any serious challenge to their authority—until the emergence of Huey P. Long as a gubernatorial candidate in 1924. Until then the once stormy waters of Louisiana politics re-

[1] Natchitoches (La.) *Populist*, November 11, 1898, quoted in William Ivy Hair, *Bourbonism and Agrarian Protest: Louisiana Politics, 1877–1900* (Baton Rouge, 1969), 278.   [2] Quoted in *ibid.*

mained a tranquil pond, mildly agitated now and then by internecine squabbles between impermanent factions of the triumphant and genteel conservative Democracy. Only white Democrats, almost all of whom were conservatives were elected to public office. This homogeneity of membership gave Louisiana's administration the appearance of a social fraternity. Journals of the General Assembly ceased to record debates, votes were rarely close, and absenteeism became common.

On the surface, therefore, Louisiana's leadership during the early twentieth century would seem to have been complacent, uninspired, and devoid of positive achievements. Such was not altogether the case, for while second-generation Bourbon Democrats of the Pelican State continued to believe in some of the ideas and to share some of the fears of Samuel D. McEnery and Murphy J. Foster, they did not behave in office altogether like carbon copies of these elder statesmen.[3] A new reform movement was abroad in the nation, and the diverse progressive impulses which inspired people outside the South attracted southern disciples, too. Throughout the region, during the Progressive Era, schools and colleges were given more money with which to raise standards and expand curricula, more and better roads were built, corporations were more effectively regulated, much attention was devoted to improving public health, and institutions—including prisons —were in many cases elevated above the horrible levels of maintenance which had been allowed to prevail during the latter nineteenth century.

These and other accomplishments—even to some extent in Louisiana—would comprise by the twenties a record of unprecedented achievement by southern governments in the fields of public service and social responsibility. But there was a limit to how far southern progressives would go in these directions. If, as a perceptive scholar has concluded, the movement did have "its day in the South," southern progressivism

[3] Between 1900 and 1910 McEnery, who probably stole the 1888 election for Nicholls, and Foster, who (with McEnery's help) stole the 1896 election for himself, served together as Louisiana's "progressive" United States senators.

nonetheless "no more fulfilled the political aspirations and deeper needs of the mass of people than did the first New Deal administration."[4]

Southern progressivism was "for whites only." It did not cross the barriers of disfranchisement and proscription to which, in many cases, southern progressives had themselves made additions. Thus, the status of black people received little amelioration during the Progressive Era. And while willing to spend more money than their predecessors, many southern progressives continued to cherish low taxes and to frown upon extensive borrowing.[5] Therefore, what they spent was often not enough. A corollary to this policy was the assumption that certain institutions, prisons especially, should pay their own way and thus require no appropriations at all. In Louisiana this notion had had its adherents from the very beginning, and "self-support" continued to be the objective of the state's penal policy during the early decades of the twentieth century. Not far behind was another guiding principle of overriding importance, the belief that because most convicts were blacks, little more than agricultural work and Sunday preaching needed to be provided to effect rehabilitation of the inmates.

The resumption of state control and supervision of Louisiana's penal system led to immediate and positive changes in treatment of convicts. Much more could have been accomplished, however, if official policy had not been crippled by two traditional considerations, which limited Louisiana progressives as much as their predecessors—considerations of race and of cost.

Of the two, race was the more important in determining

[4] C. Vann Woodward, *Origins of the New South, 1877–1913* (Baton Rouge, 1951), 395. For a recent and comprehensive treatment of southern Progressivism in the 1920s see George B. Tindall, *Emergence of the New South, 1913–1945* (Baton Rouge, 1967), 219–84.

[5] This was particularly the case in Louisiana, where Riley J. Wilson, Huey P. Long's conservative opponent for the governorship in 1928, "thought [Long's] program to pave roads was preposterous—it would cost too much money." T. Harry Williams, *Huey Long: A Biography* (New York, 1969), 250.

what manner of penal system Louisiana would adopt in the
wake of Major James's departure. When James took charge
of the penitentiary in 1869, Negroes already comprised a
majority of the convicts. Their proportionate number increased steadily through the years, so that by 1900 approxi-
mately 84 percent of Louisiana's prison population was black.[6]

James had never employed convicts exclusively at manufacturing within the penitentiary. That system had originated prior to the Civil War when most convicts were white,
and neither the lessee after 1869 nor the state after 1900 ever
fully revived it. Finding himself in possession, as it were, of
many black prisoners, James set them to work at "black"
jobs—levee work primarily, plus farm or plantation labor
when such employment was available. While each of these
activities paid handsomely, levee work was the more lucrative. It was also the more arduous and deadly. Because the
major drew no distinctions between convicts on the basis of
physical condition, and because "it is manifest that out of the
total number of prisoners more than half were not physically
able to perform this work," life on the levees was short for
less robust prisoners.[7] Overwork and brutal treatment in the
levee camps were responsible for most of the recorded deaths
among the inmates between 1890 and 1900.

But the state was not prepared to abandon levee work,
which had provided the major with ample remuneration and
was expected similarly to enrich the Louisiana penal system.
Levees along both sides of the Lower Mississippi River demanded careful maintenance in order to prevent extensive
flood damage at high-water time each spring. In pre-bulldozer
days, the immense quantities of earth and sand required to

[6] In 1900 there were 840 black convicts to 149 whites within the
Louisiana penal system. State of Louisiana, *Official Journal of the Proceedings of the Senate of the General Assembly, 1900* (Baton Rouge,
1900), 6. Published proceedings of the senate are hereinafter cited as
Senate Journal, with appropriate year indicated.

[7] State of Louisiana, *Board of Control, State Penitentiary, Annual
Report—Calendar Year 1901* (New Orleans, 1902), 28. Published reports
of the board are hereinafter cited as *Biennial Report, Board of Control*,
with appropriate year indicated.

construct or shore up a levee section had to be broken up and moved by plows, mules, men, and wheelbarrows. The work was slow, backbreaking, and expensive, but utterly necessary in the several states of the low-lying Delta. Thus, Louisiana could not have neglected her levees in any event, and to employ convicts upon them reduced considerably the costs involved, both in money and in "free" human lives which would otherwise have been risked. Shortly after the state resumed control of the penal system, Governor W. W. Heard confessed that, while agricultural work would be emphasized, "a portion of the [convict] forces physically adapted" would continue to construct and maintain levees. As late as 1912 the portion remained sizable—625 prisoners out of a total of 1,955 males. Of the former number, 616 were Negroes.[8]

The other suitably "Negro" occupation, farm and plantation work, would also be maintained and in fact became the keystone of the state's "new" penal system. Here again the lucrative example of Major James provided an incentive, as the lessee had also made substantial sums of money from having prisoners cut sugar cane and pick cotton. In addition, other southern states (Mississippi, especially) which had recently ended the lease system were demonstrating that "a very large percentage of the prison population [could] be most profitably employed in agricultural work."[9] A sympathetic northern penologist, who in 1906 had just completed an inspection tour of Louisiana's recently acquired plantations, offered further reasons for the emphasis placed upon agricultural work within southern prisons. Addressing the annual

[8] State of Louisiana, *Journal of the Proceedings of the House of Representatives of the General Assembly, 1902* (Baton Rouge, 1902), 24. Published proceedings of the house are hereinafter cited as *House Journal*, with appropriate year indicated. *Biennial Report, Board of Control* (1912), 108.

[9] *House Journal* (1902), 23–24. Profits from agricultural work within Mississippi's penal system amounted to $98,000 in 1900. Hilda Jane Zimmerman, "Penal System and Penal Reforms in the South since the Civil War" (Ph.D. dissertation, University of North Carolina, 1947), 334.

congress of the National Prison Association, Frederick H. Wines remarked that

> the negro [*sic*] is not fitted for indoor life. He is not wanted as an industrial rival to the white man, and there is no possibility (and perhaps it is not desirable) of introducing into Southern prisons those forms of carrying on industries by machinery common in our [Northern] prisons. . . . [Louisiana's prisons] are agricultural prisons such as we know nothing about, and I can not imagine, except for the question of reformation *(and they are not reformatory)*, anything more ideally suited to the conditions which exist down there than the large plantations on which the convict population is assembled, properly cared for, and governed.[10]

Insofar as convict labor and rehabilitation were concerned, the transition in Louisiana from lessee control to state control was much less dramatic than state officials proclaimed or reformers would have preferred. Plantations and levee camps continued to be the abode of Louisiana's convicts long after 1900. The only difference between the two systems would be one of emphasis. James had concentrated upon levee work, the state would rely principally upon agricultural work. In each case, black convicts performed most of the labor, and in neither case was reform or rehabilitation of prisoners given much serious consideration.

Act 70 of 1900 created a Board of Control of the State Penitentiary, to be composed of three gubernatorial appointees serving staggered six-year terms. Though identical in name to its forerunner during the lease period, the new agency possessed substantially greater power, for it was invested with complete responsibility for reorganizing and administering Louisiana's penal system. A warden, appointed by the board, acted as chief operations officer and was responsible for both convict management and business matters. The board was authorized to purchase land, livestock, and tools,

---

[10] Frederick H. Wines, "The Prisons of Louisiana," National Prison Association of the United States, *Proceedings of the Annual Congress of 1906* (Indianapolis, 1906), 156. Italics added.

supervise financial operations, make rules for the employment and treatment of convicts, and "bid for [levee and road construction] as a private contractor."[11] Neither the board members nor the warden was required to be an experienced prison administrator, although one of the initial members, Edward White, and the first state-appointed warden, W. M. Reynaud, had both served under the lessee.

Indicative of the board's discomfiture, soon after it assumed control of the system in 1901, was its report of the condition in which it found the old penitentiary building in Baton Rouge. The report points out that: "as it stands today [it] is simply a relic of the past. When we took charge the large Factory Building was filled with rusting and decaying machinery, spindles and looms of obsolete type that have not been operated for a quarter of a century. It was absolutely worthless except for junk. . . . The power plant, a large and valuable one, which the State turned over to the lessee had disappeared."[12]

Given the board's immediate problem—having to organize a penal system with nothing of value upon which to build— and bearing in mind the traditional attitude of official Louisiana regarding the costs of public institutions, the objective which the group set for itself in its initial report was both conventional and familiar. Because "organizing and training and building" took priority, reform or rehabilitation of convicts would have to wait. The report concluded: "After so many years of lessee management, reformation is difficult and slow. . . . The improvement in physical conditions had to precede the moral upbuilding. . . . There is yet much to do [before] we can take hold of the individual and deal with him."[13]

[11] State of Louisiana, *Acts of the General Assembly, Regular Session, 1900* (Baton Rouge, 1900), 120. Published legislative actions of the General Assembly are hereinafter cited as *Acts of Louisiana*, with the appropriate year indicated.

[12] *Annual Report, Board of Control* (1902), 37. The old "walls" served as a receiving station, clothing factory, and place of execution until 1918 when the property was purchased by the city of Baton Rouge.

[13] *Ibid.*, 14.

And, considering the pressures under which the board had to operate, the fact that it was able, within four years, to construct a penal system and to make it self-supporting must be acknowledged as its greatest achievement between 1901 and 1916, the year in which the board was abolished.

The state of Louisiana owned no land suitable for use by her penal system. Nor did she possess any buildings (other than the old penal factory in Baton Rouge), livestock, or implements. Finally, there was no prison staff on the payroll, ready to go to work. All of these essentials had to be purchased or built, recruited and trained. Initial appropriations by the General Assembly were necessary for the board to proceed with its task.

Between 1900 and 1904 the following sums were appropriated for use by the board. In each case the money went to the state treasurer for credit to the Penitentiary Fund, from which it could be drawn on the board's warrant:

1900	$100,000.00
1901	200,000.00
1902	115,285.57
1903	73,608.42
1904	42,080.85

$530,974.84[14]

In addition, loans were obtained amounting to about one-quarter of the total appropriation, with expected earnings from the penal system pledged as security. Angola, where James himself had lived and died, was purchased from the lessee's heirs.[15] Located on the east bank of the Mississippi River some sixty miles north of Baton Rouge, Angola pos-

[14] State of Louisiana, *Biennial Report of the Treasurer to the Governor, 1900–1901* (Baton Rouge, 1902), 13, 40–41; (1902–1903), 43, 47, 60–61, 120; (1904–1905), 75. Biennial reports of the treasurer are hereinafter cited as *Biennial Report, State Treasurer*, with the appropriate years indicated.

[15] Further purchases of adjacent land in 1922 increased Angola's 8,000 acres to 18,000.

sessed rich bottomland and extensive stands of timber. Cotton was the principal crop grown until 1912 when, as a result of a boll weevil invasion, sugar cane was substituted. (The transition from cotton to sugar cane, which required construction of a large sugar refinery, cost the penal system and the state more than $500,000.) Three smaller plantations were also acquired, Hope, Monticello, and Oakley, all sugar cane producers located in parishes of South-Central Louisiana. Four levee camps completed the state's acquisitions.

By 1902 the farms and levee camps were able to report initial earnings of $120,525.64. The following year was even better—despite a flood which had inundated Angola—as the board turned in $125,580.37 to the Penitentiary Fund. In 1904, the last year during the transition period in which an external appropriation was required from the General Assembly, the penal system earned $197,905.95. Earnings of $239,488.81 for 1905 amply justified the assembly's confidence and expectations.[16] On December 31, 1905, the Penitentiary Fund contained a surplus of $2,975.66.[17] In 1906 the board proudly summarized the scope of its labors over the past five years:

> We have adhered to the general policy of employing the prison labor on farms owned and operated by the State, and in the construction of public levees . . . and have not deemed it advisable to enter upon manufacturing of any kind beyond the making of shoes and clothing for the prisoners [by a small force consisting largely of white convicts within the old "walls" at Baton Rouge], and the sawing up of timber felled in clearing our own lands. . . . It has been demonstrated that on these lines [the penal system] can be made self-supporting and at the same time afford some surplus to build up and improve the properties, buildings and equipment without calling upon the taxpayer for assistance.[18]

Apparently as an afterthought, the board hastened to add,

[16] *Biennial Report, State Treasurer* (1902–1903), 60, 120; (1904–1905), 76, 162.   [17] *Ibid.* (1904–1905), 163.
[18] *Biennial Report, Board of Control* (1906), 3.

"while according humane and proper treatment to the prisoners"! The board, in the words of Governor Heard, was engaged not only in "the handling of a large prison as such, but in the establishment of a great industrial and business enterprise."[19] Spectacular achievements along business lines, however impressive by 1906, would be of limited duration. When state officials decided to commit Louisiana's penal system to an agricultural base, they made the system vulnerable to the same hazards which frequently afflicted other cotton and sugar cane producers—acts of God and acts of man. Between 1903 and 1916 the system was first troubled and finally disrupted by one or another of these.

If the "great industrial and business enterprise" was ultimately destined for hard times, the cause of penal reform foundered almost immediately upon the rocks of hostility, indifference, and procrastination. Because penal reform was not the foremost objective of those who had abolished the convict lease system in Louisiana, so reform remained without priority among those who took over management of the penal system for the state in 1901. Although Louisiana, by 1920, would have adopted the indeterminate sentence, expanded application of commutation laws, and established a parole system, the net result of these provisions was simply to release well-behaved convicts from day-to-day custody. The extent to which a prisoner actually returned to society "a better man, physically, intellectually, and morally," better able to find acceptance as a person, secure a good job, and remain on the safe side of the law was neither furthered by the operation of these laws nor guaranteed by them.

Treatment of convicts within the system remained purely custodial. Even though the more brutal methods of the lessee were abandoned, there was no accompanying policy aimed at rehabilitation. Convicts who were illiterate when admitted were illiterate when discharged. Officials were slow to separate juvenile offenders from older and confirmed criminals, and separation of first from subsequent offenders was not implemented for decades.

19 *House Journal* (1902), 24.

Underlying this state of affairs were both of the traditional taboos, race and cost. Louisiana, declared the president of the board in 1914, was a state "where the vices and defects of the [N]egro race [were] well known." It would be foolish to apply in Louisiana "what are called the advanced systems of treatment in use in some other wealthier states, where only white men are dealt with."[20] The Negro offender, once convicted, was viewed (even by some reformers) as incorrigible. Money spent attempting to rehabilitate him was thought to be money wasted.

Nothing so vividly demonstrates the race-cost consciousness of Louisiana progressives as the manner in which they dealt with juvenile offenders who, like older convicts, were predominantly black. But the policies applied to black juveniles influenced the treatment meted out to white youths as well.

The General Assembly session of 1900 was visited by lobbyists of the Prison Reform Association of Louisiana. These sincere men, believing their day had come at last, were anxious to be heard and consulted while foundations of the new state penal system were being laid. They hoped to secure a system dedicated to rehabilitation and were certain that whatever they could write into law would have immediate and permanent consequences. They were soon to be disappointed in both of these expectations.

Near the top of their list of recommendations was the separation of juvenile offenders from older criminals. "A State Reformatory is an absolute necessity and will tend to decrease crime, for in such an institution the 'germ' of crime will be killed," read a portion of the *Memorial* which they circulated among legislators.[21] A section of the bill which became Act 70 directed the Board of Control to establish a reformatory as soon as "possible." During house consideration of the measure, this section was amended by deleting "pos-

[20] *Biennial Report, Board of Control* (1914), 17–18.
[21] Prison Reform Association of Louisiana, *Memorial to the Senate and House of Representatives on Prison Reform and on the Necessity of a State Reformatory with the Opinions of Judges, District Attorneys, and Sheriffs* (New Orleans, 1900), 1–2.

sible" and substituting "practicable."[22] The final version, which became law, reads as follows: "That the Board of Control shall, as soon as practicable, and the moneys on hand in the Penitentiary fund will permit, establish a reformatory branch of the Penitentiary in which all convicts who are between the ages of seven (7) and seventeen (17) years of age shall be separated from the other convicts."[23] Separation of children from hardened criminals, even at the outset of state control, was thus indefinitely postponed.

In 1904, with no reformatory as yet under construction, the board stated that "reduced income from crops" because of the flood of 1903 had prevented action from being initiated. Anticipating increased revenues in the future, the board promised that "later on the matter will be brought up and steps taken to carry [the] law into execution."[24]

"Later on" was not soon enough for the administration of Governor Newton C. Blanchard. In the same year, prodded by the governor, the assembly passed an enabling act authorizing construction of a reformatory in which "all male persons eighteen years of age or less who shall be convicted of crime, except that of murder, manslaughter or rape, shall be confined."[25] (It should be noted that this statute narrowed the original application of Act 70, which had made no exceptions for crimes committed.) No appropriation was provided, however, until 1906 and construction did not begin until 1908. Not until 1910 was the reformatory completed and ready for use.[26] Even then, it was much too small to accommodate the number of eligible juveniles who remained in custody on the penal farms and at Baton Rouge. In 1912 six white and nineteen black youths, all between twelve and sixteen years of age, could still be found among the adult

---

22 *House Journal* (Regular Session, 1900), 291.
23 *Acts of Louisiana* (Regular Session, 1900), 121.
24 *Biennial Report, Board of Control* (1904), 10.
25 *Acts of Louisiana* (1904), 353.
26 *Ibid.* (1906), 289; Elizabeth Wisner, *Public Welfare Administration in Louisiana* (Chicago, 1930), 175. The genuine reforms of the Blanchard administration were probably in the field of public education.

offenders.[27] Chaplain J. P. O'Slattery indignantly protested this situation: "There is one thing that to my mind is a disgrace to the State. . . . The sending of youngsters, fourteen, fifteen and sixteen years of age to the Penitentiary [which is] a funny place for the State to send a boy to make him a good citizen. . . . If there's any chance for a youngster's reformation, that chance seems to be taken away . . . when he is placed with a crowd of criminals who are guilty of every crime on the calendar practically."[28] Chaplain H. S. Johns urgently requested that the General Assembly take steps to enlarge the reformatory so as "to prevent so many white and colored youths from being sent to the penitentiary."[29]

Two years later the General Assembly took action, although not along precisely the same lines recommended by Chaplain Johns. Senator L. R. Smith of Caddo Parish introduced a bill directing the board to set aside a portion of the penal farms as a reformatory for offenders between the ages of eighteen and twenty-one. There were many of these youths within the system and they were not eligible for transfer to the already overcrowded reformatory at Monroe, because there the maximum age for admission was eighteen. While this measure would not help the youngest inmates, about whom the chaplains were most concerned, it did possess the merit of proposing to separate older juveniles, most of whom were also first offenders, from adult convicts.

The senate passed the Smith bill by a vote of 33 in favor, one opposed, and seven absent. In the house, the measure passed by a vote of 72 for, none opposed, and 45 absent.[30] The bill was promptly vetoed by Governor Luther E. Hall, who had been elected in 1912 as the candidate of the Good Government League, a slogan of which was, "Let's make government more businesslike."[31] Hall's veto message was very "businesslike" indeed:

[27] *Biennial Report, Board of Control* (1912), 106.
[28] *Ibid.*, 125.   [29] *Ibid.*, 123.
[30] *Senate Journal* (1914), 348; *House Journal* (1914), 938.
[31] Perry H. Howard, *Political Tendencies in Louisiana, 1812–1952* (Baton Rouge, 1957), 111.

While there is much in this bill to commend it, the Penitentiary Board of Control is not, at this time, in such financial condition [as] to enable it to make the outlay necessary to render effective and useful the provisions of the bill . . . the Board of Control has sustained very heavy losses through [recent] overflows and other causes. . . .[It] has become necessary to borrow large sums in order to carry forward the work of the Board. Under these circumstances it is not deemed advisable to require the Board to undertake untried and unfamiliar plans of administration.[32]

The house and senate of the General Assembly were no less aware than Governor Hall of the extensive damage and financial loss suffered by the penal system from the disastrous flood of 1912. It was in consideration of these circumstances that the Smith bill had not sought to expand the reformatory at Monroe, as any proposed improvement on that level would require a specific appropriation from the Penitentiary Fund, which the governor could be expected to veto. It was thought that the bill as proposed, which carried no appropriation, would impose no unreasonable task upon the board and could accomplish the desired objective of further isolating young offenders. For its pains, the assembly was rewarded with a gubernatorial veto anyway. Nineteen senators voted not to sustain the governor's action, a number only nine short of the required twenty-eight.[33]

During an extra session in 1915, concerned legislators attempted to achieve their previous objective by less forceful means. Representative F. J. Heintz of St. Tammany Parish introduced a house concurrent resolution noting that "a number of boys, delinquent juveniles, who morally belong at the Louisiana Training Institute at Monroe" were still confined within the penal system. The resolution further requested that Governor Hall confer with the attorney general to devise legal means for the transfer of these youths to the reforma-

[32] *Senate Journal* (1914) , 896–97.   [33] *Ibid.*, 933.

tory.[34] Although both houses concurred in the resolution, Hall again did nothing.

In 1910 one of Louisiana's foremost penal reformers had declared that "a [N]egro male of sixteen years is a mature man, and to say that when he commits a felony he is merely a 'delinquent,' and shall not be treated and punished as a criminal is to expose society to very grave dangers."[35] A Negro of any age, it would appear, upon conviction of a felony, was likely to be "treated and punished as a criminal" in Louisiana. As late as 1917, the last year during this period for which penal data are available, there were still a number of younger juveniles (all but one of them black) confined within the walls or on the farms—one white and thirty-one blacks between the ages of twelve and sixteen, plus two little Negroes under age twelve.[36] None of these boys had yet been born when the General Assembly, in 1900, initially authorized construction of a reformatory. It was left to a later age, indeed a much later age, to provide and maintain acceptable facilities and correctional therapy for juvenile offenders, especially black offenders, in Louisiana.

During these first decades of state control, even less progress was made in the direction of separating first offenders from confirmed criminals. In this area, as with juvenile offenders, the gap between statutory provision and enforcement was a wide one.

Act 70 of 1900 had instructed the board to "enact rules for the grading and classifying of convicts according to the

[34] *Ibid.* (Extra Session, 1915), Calendar, p. 18.

[35] State of Louisiana, Commission Authorized to Draft Criminal and Penal Codes, *Code Letter to his Excellency Jared Y. Sanders, Governor of the State of Louisiana* (n.p., 1910), 18. The chairman of this commission, Robert H. Marr, was the state's foremost scholar of criminal jurisprudence, a prominent criminal lawyer, judge, and longtime member of the Prison Reform Association of Louisiana. The codes prepared by the commission were not adopted.

[36] State of Louisiana, *Report made by Hy. L. Fuqua, General Manager of the State Penitentiary to the Governor and General Assembly for the Regular Session of 1918 Covering the Biennial Period of 1916 and 1917* (Baton Rouge, 1918), 41, hereinafter cited as *Fuqua Report, 1918.*

most modern and enlightened system of reformation."[37] Lob-byists of the Prison Reform Association had influenced the drafting of this provision, the intent of which was to separate first from repeat offenders. But the same provision further directed the board to grade prisoners according to "the assignment of work and the character of same."[38] Penal officials implemented the latter part of the directive but ignored the rest of it. All male convicts were divided into four classes, with little regard for age or intelligence and with no regard for number or nature of offenses: "First-class men are . . . sound in every respect and accustomed to manual work. These men are sent to the levee camps where the work is the most severe. Second-class men are . . . of moderate strength and capabilities, and are assigned to the sugar plantations. . . . Third-class men are assigned to the cotton plantation [Angola], and fourth-class men are assigned to the hospital."[39]

Such a division of labor was motivated entirely by "practical" considerations, and had not the slightest correctional or rehabilitative value, except that physical wrecks were allowed the privilege of hospitalization. Antebellum slaveowners had divided their work force along similar lines. So had postbellum lessees in states other than Louisiana.[40] In the first instance, all of the laborers were Negroes; in the second, almost all were Negroes. And as the convicts of "progressive" Louisiana were also predominantly black, the classifications enumerated above were applied "almost exclusively to the colored men. All white men, with a few exceptions, and all females . . . are eventually assigned to Angola. The few exceptions in the case of the white men are those sent to the other plantations and the levee camps for commissary clerks, or similar mental services."[41] On January 1, 1908, for example,

---

[37] *Acts of Louisiana* (Regular Session, 1900) , 118.   [38] *Ibid.*

[39] State of Louisiana, *Second Biennial Report of the State Board of Charities and Corrections: December 1907* (Baton Rouge, 1908) , 11.

[40] Dan T. Carter, "Prisons, Politics and Business: The Convict Lease System in the Post-Civil War South" (M.A. thesis, University of Wisconsin, 1964) , 63.

[41] *Second Biennial Report, Board of Charities and Corrections,* (De-

the ratio of black males to white males in the levee camps was 99 to 1, on the sugar plantations, 55 to 1, but at Angola only 1.4 to 1.[42] The nearest the board had come to devising a "modern and enlightened" system of classification was merely to reapply the traditional race-job distinctions of the biracial South, which ensured that blacks received the more onerous assignments, whites (if any) the easier ones.

Despite frequent official boasts that Louisiana since 1900 had made "drastic and radical changes in handling the penitentiary system," several informed persons branded the claim as excessive.[43] The state, however, persisted in merchandising the illusion that sweeping humanitarian reforms had been inaugurated. Penal officials repeatedly called attention to reduced convict mortality rates, which—while certainly a commendable achievement—comprised only one aspect of convict treatment and penal reform. Members of the Prison Reform Association, however, were not seduced by official rhetoric. F. S. Shields observed in 1906 that the board "has had a big work upon its shoulders and if it has accomplished little so far in reformatory methods, it has, as shown by the death rate index, made great strides in the physical betterment of the conditions of the convicts."[44] Having put the system on a paying basis and having solved the "sanitary" problem, the board could be "expected" to "take up reformatory measures."[45]

Even earlier, in 1902, Robert H. Marr had expressed a

---

cember 1907), 10–11. White and black females were all sent to Angola, where they worked as cooks, laundresses, and seamstresses. Italics added.

[42] *Ibid.* Exact numbers were as follows: levee camps, 6 whites, 591 blacks; sugar plantations, 11 whites, 550 blacks; Angola, 208 whites, 283 blacks.

[43] *Biennial Report, Board of Control* (1910), 4. Quoted is former Governor W. W. Heard, who by 1910 had returned to the public payroll as president of the Board of Control.

[44] F. S. Shields, *Prison Reform: Its Principles and Purposes—What It Has Accomplished—The Work Yet to Be Done* (New Orleans, 1906), 18. Reduction of convict mortality after 1901 should be credited largely to the efforts of Warden W. M. Reynaud, who had been a prison physician under the lessee.   [45] *Ibid.*

more critical view: "Good financial returns, [and] a lowered death rate among the convicts are matters that appeal to everyone, that even the dullest can comprehend . . . but the appraisement of the worth [of these matters] to the reformed convicts . . . must be largely speculative."[46]

Repeated criticism in this vein, along with continued official disinclination to "take up reformatory measures," brought forth a candid admission from W. W. Heard in 1910 that nothing more had been achieved in the area of reform and rehabilitation than the reduction of the mortality rate.[47]

But even this sole official claim for penal reform cannot be demonstrated with exactness, because official figures released by the penal system itself were imprecise and therefore unreliable. In 1918 Henry L. Fuqua, chief administrative officer of the Louisiana penal system, submitted to the General Assembly a report containing comprehensive statistical data on prisoners who had entered and left the system between 1893 and 1917. Information furnished included the numbers of convicts annually admitted, discharged, commuted, pardoned, and (after 1914) paroled. Also given were the numbers of convicts who had annually escaped, who had been recaptured, and who had died. (Causes of death were not specified.) For each of the inclusive twenty-five years an "average" number of convicts within the system was additionally furnished.

Fuqua's report is the only official state document combining figures covering the last eight years of lessee control (1893–1900) with figures from identical categories covering the first seventeen years of state control (1901–17). For this reason, the Fuqua report would appear, at first glance, to be an invaluable source of official information.

Actually, a portion of Fuqua's tables are worthless, because the "average" number of convicts annually on hand for each reported year varies too widely from totals of the other data for there to be any meaningful correlations. (In fact, how

46 Robert H. Marr, "The Institutions of Louisiana," National Prison Association of the United States, *Proceedings of the Annual Congress of 1902* (Pittsburgh, 1903), 267.

47 *Biennial Report, Board of Control* (1910), 4.

Fuqua had arrived at the average totals for each year was unexplained.) Consequently, as there is no precise record of the number of convicts actually imprisoned in Louisiana at any specified time between 1893 and 1917, no reliable rates of increase or decrease can be computed for any of the separate categories, such as admissions, discharges—or deaths. By releasing muddled figures in 1918 (after which no information of any kind was released by the penal system until 1932), Fuqua made it as difficult then as it remains now to determine actual progress achieved in penal reform during the crucial transition in Louisiana from lessee to state control. And if Louisiana's data are themselves imprecise, the task of drawing valid comparisons with contemporary penal systems is rendered futile.

For what it may be worth, Fuqua's data do furnish evidence of an impressive decline in the death toll between the last eight years of lessee control and the first seventeen years of state control. According to Fuqua, an average of 100.6 convicts perished annually between 1893 and 1900 as against 35.3 per year between 1901 and 1917.[48] But while demonstrated trends generally endorse claims made by state officials for reduced mortality, the impossibility of computing exact death rates (or any other rates) leaves a number of questions largely unresolved.

Other aspects of official behavior and policy further illustrate the erratic course of penal reform which characteristically became evident following resumption of state control. Article 395 of the Constitution of 1898 instructed the General Assembly to create a state Board of Charities and Corrections. Like Article 196, providing for abolition of the lease, this

[48] *Fuqua Report, 1918*, p. 42. Pre-1901 death figures may be accepted as valid, because the same totals appear in reports of the Board of Control released while James was still in business. Post-1901 deaths also match Fuqua's totals—at least until 1913, when the last report of the Board of Control was prepared. But totals for "average" numbers of convicts on hand for 1901–13 (as reported by the board) do not always jibe with Fuqua's totals. This only adds to the confusion and suggests that perhaps no Louisiana penal official during the early years of this century ever learned to count correctly.

provision was supported by lobbyists of the Prison Reform Association. The board was to have no executive powers but was authorized to visit all jails, penal farms, asylums, hospitals, and reformatories. Should the board discover that conditions within these institutions were unsatisfactory, they could recommend improvements to the governor and to the assembly. Six years elapsed before the assembly got around to creating this impotent visitorial body, and only then at the urging of Governor Blanchard, who during the same session of 1904 had also insisted upon creation of a reformatory. Several causes for procrastination seem to have existed. F. S. Shields summarized them in 1906 as follows: "This delay [in creating the board] was largely due to the active opposition of some of the large institutions in the State, and possibly to the indisposition of many of the parish officials to have their crude and uncivilized methods of caring for their prisoners criticized and laid bare, and was partly due to claim of poverty on the part of the State as it would require a few thousand dollars to pay the expenses of the Board."[49]

Quite understandably, neither sheriffs nor penal officials wanted do-gooders, however powerless, snooping around their establishments. In order to forestall embarrassing publicity, which was certain to result from the presence of troublemakers, the sensitive bugaboo of cost was invoked as a means of discouraging the whole idea. While this tactic failed to prevent creation of the board, its enemies within the assembly were able to restrict its activities by providing niggardly appropriations for the next six years. In 1910 no appropriation at all was voted, and the board sank into a decade of limbo.

If the prospect of reformers visiting state institutions repelled most Louisiana officials, the idea that experts or professional personnel should operate the institutions was equally offensive. There were two reasons for this point of view, one sheerly political and the other subtly connected with the considerations of cost and race.

[49] Shields, *Prison Reform*, 19.

When the state resumed control of its penal system, a major source of patronage was created. "Not one of our penal institutions is under expert management," complained Robert H. Marr in 1902, for "throughout the state there is no office, high or low which is not looked upon as the absolute property of the successful faction of the dominant political party, and which is not bestowed as a reward for partisan service."[50]

Rewarding party stalwarts was not the only purpose served by filling Louisiana's penal system with political hacks. "One of the greatest obstacles to be overcome in judiciously handling a penal institution," warned W. W. Heard in 1912, "is to guard against indiscretion and unbridled zeal on the part of those whose intentions are good."[51] The enemies of a judiciously handled penal system, in less euphemistic terms, were penologists and reformers. Such people entertained silly ideas—that criminal behavior was a kind of disease, and that most criminals (even Negro criminals) could be cured if treated soon enough. This was harebrained theory to the generation of Louisiana politicians who were schoolboys during "Black Reconstruction." They did not believe the theory for a moment, but they believed that those whose intentions were good—if catered to altogether—could bankrupt and discredit the penal system in their "indiscreet" attempts to prove it.

It was not only good politics, therefore, to appoint reliable party men to positions within the penal system, but also a matter of "judicious" administration. As far as official Louisiana was concerned, the best penal system, as always, was one that restricted its operations to the confinement of criminals and the making of money; and political appointees could be trusted to accept and implement these objectives more readily than others, to whom a penal system might mean something else.

Frequently, however, this policy defeated at least one of its own purposes—sound financial administration. Well before

[50] Marr, "The Institutions of Louisiana," 272.
[51] *Biennial Report, Board of Control* (1912), 8–9.

Josef Stalin discovered that politically reliable marshals could be ineffective on the battlefield, Louisiana found out that politically reliable penal officials could disrupt its penal system. Even a man like Heard, himself a party stalwart of the first rank, had to recognize the "considerations of a political nature" which made his job as president of the Board of Control a difficult one. In the same report quoted above, Heard stated: "The importance of administering the penal system, together with the magnitude and volume of the financial interests involved, makes it such that only special qualifications for the work to be performed should be considered."[52]

While holding firm against "those whose intentions were good," Heard, in 1912, was also concerned about those whose abilities were nominal—political appointees whom he obviously did not believe were necessarily the best appointees. Reformers, of course, had criticized patronage appointments from the beginning.[53] Generally, the state ignored their complaints, but in 1914 Governor Hall's "businesslike" administration took a firm step toward "reform" by dispensing with Heard's services. With the penal system sinking deeper into economic chaos as a result of the 1912 floods, it was decided not to renew Heard's appointment as president of the Board of Control.

The state reinstalled C. Harrison Parker, the man who had accomplished financial miracles as first president of the board following resumption of state control. (Parker died, however, later in 1914.) W. M. Reynaud, former warden under both the lessee and the state, was also given his old position again. This time, however, miracles were not forthcoming. In 1916, with the Penitentiary Fund overdrawn in the amount of $99,330.30, the entire Board of Control joined

[52] *Ibid.*, 8. Heard's own "special qualifications" for penal administration seem to have been eight years' prior service as a state legislator, followed by eight more as state auditor and four more as governor, all of which had been rendered for and within the "successful faction of the dominant political party" in Louisiana.

[53] See note 50; and Shields, *Prison Reforms*, 25.

Heard in the administrative dustbin.[54] The board was abolished and in its place was substituted the office of general manager of the state penitentiary. The first general manager, who served from 1916 to 1923, was Henry L. Fuqua, successful Baton Rouge hardware merchant. Fuqua's father-in-law had been the lessee's clerk, a coincidence which may have given Fuqua some knowledge of penal administration.

Neither the removal of Heard, nor of Reynaud, nor the abolition of the board derived in the slightest measure from inadequate programs of reform or rehabilitation. What was really at stake is spelled out in an editorial from the Baton Rouge *State-Times* on the occasion of Fuqua's appointment as general manager:

> . . . There is a great opportunity before Mr. Fuqua. The man who can make good in the management of the state penitentiary, and place that property on a sound basis will make a name for himself over the State. . . .
> . . . There is, of course, no reason why large profits should not be made out of the penitentiary system if it is run along sound business lines and not made a place for soft berths for political appointees. If there is not big money in farming, under the conditions which [exist at] the state farms—with large plantations, no taxes, an abundance of labor in dependable quantities, over which the manager has absolute control, and this labor free at that—then civilization itself has been wrong, and money simply can't be made at farming.[55]

The state journal, along with the rest of official Louisiana, had come to regard the penal system simply as a farming operation. Farming, however, was only one of the activities carried on within the system. Levee work, lumbering, sugar refining, and manufacturing had either been engaged in since 1901 or added along the way. The penal system had, in fact,

[54] *Biennial Report, State Treasurer* (1916–1917), 11.

[55] Baton Rouge *State-Times*, July 8, 1916. In 1924 Fuqua was elected to the governorship, having defeated in the process a young man from Winnfield named Huey P. Long.

developed into the "great industrial and business enterprise" envisioned by Heard in 1902.

Agricultural work remained, nonetheless, the major occupation of most of the convicts who, in turn, were mostly black. And while free in the sense that their forebears had not been—most slaves had initially to be purchased—black convicts in 1916 were as abundant and as much under absolute control as chattels had been sixty years before. They were also, as noted above, classified for work purposes along similar lines. Finally, black convicts in Louisiana during the early twentieth century were treated very much like black slaves had been treated on any large, "well-run" antebellum plantation, as the testimony of Frederick H. Wines indicates:

> [The life of the Negro convict] on the State farms is almost identical with that he would lead if working for wages. It is indeed more moral, more regular and more sanitary. He is well housed, well fed and well cared for in sickness and in health. He is not overworked. . . . He is easily controlled, but is liable to punishment by strapping for insubordination or persistent laziness. He will not often run from an armed overseer, and if he does . . . he runs but a short distance before he is treed by the dogs.[56]

The state established a parole system in 1914.[57] And she commuted sentences more frequently after 1900 than before. In addition, the death toll was substantially reduced. These were all creditable achievements in the field of penal reform. And they were also the only achievements made in Louisiana between 1900 and 1920, the value of which was reduced by other developments which took place simultaneously. Treatment of convicts, especially black convicts, within the penal system still left much to be desired with reference to reha-

[56] Frederick H. Wines, *Detailed Report upon the Penal and other State Institutions and Upon Thirty-Nine Parish Jails, for the Prison Reform Association of Louisiana* (New Orleans, 1906) , 7–8.

[57] The state thus was behind Alabama and Arkansas, which established some form of parole between 1900 and 1910, but ahead of most other southern states, in which parole systems were not created until after 1930. Zimmerman, "Penal Systems and Penal Reforms," 526–28.

bilitation, for if the state had largely abandoned the unacceptable methods of the lessee, the sum of her reforms had been to raise the level of treatment to the idealized standards of antebellum days. In reality, therefore, the "largest slaveholder of post-bellum Louisiana" was not Samuel L. James in the late nineteenth century, but Henry L. Fuqua in the early twentieth.[58]

Fuqua's only report as general manager of the Penitentiary was submitted in 1918. Twenty-four pages of financial data precede the conclusion, demonstrating that the first two decades of state control were about to end largely as they had begun: "We have thus far discussed purely the business or economic side of our administration of Penitentiary affairs, not that we are placing the dollar above the man, but because we recognize that the first thing necessary to improve the general living conditions of the prisoners is to have the money with which to do it."[59] Substantial commitment to reform and rehabilitation within Louisiana's penal system had been postponed, as usual, again.

[58] When Fuqua died in 1926, it was reported that convicts at Angola grieved for "Marse Henry." Baton Rouge *State-Times*, October 12, 1926. There is no record of any convict voluntarily referring to S. L. James as "Marse Sam."

[59] *Fuqua Report, 1918*, p. 24. This statement should be compared with the first report of the Board of Control, submitted in 1902. In 1917, imitating the example set by Mississippi's penal system, Fuqua fired most of the professional guards and gave their jobs to "trusty" convicts. Money saved, needless to say, was considerable.

CHAPTER V

Years of Erosion
1920-1940

MOST ASPECTS of life in Louisiana acquired twentieth century dimensions between World Wars I and II. By 1940 the state possessed a network of modern highways, one of the strongest universities in the South, a much improved public school system, better medical services for the poor, a promising social welfare program, and a robust (if recently tarnished) bifactionalism within her ruling political party. The state penal system, however, was conspicuously successful in resisting the currents of change. By 1940, as a result of adverse circumstances and continued brutality and mismanagement by state officials, the Louisiana State Penitentiary had marched backward toward the age of lessee James.

Some of the positive achievements noted above were helped along by New Deal largesse. But for the most part, progress in Louisiana had been initiated and developed at home, years before Franklin Roosevelt was either willing or able to propose a national system of social security or to provide federal aid to sharecroppers. John M. Parker, a progressive of the genteel and conservative stripe, launched the state toward maturity during his gubernatorial administration from 1920 to 1924. Among Parker's major contributions were the State Constitution of 1921 (a flexible document when drafted, which has since been amended into ossification), a broader tax base, the removal of Louisiana State University to a vast tract of land south of Baton Rouge—thus ensuring room for future expansion—and the construction of numerous gravel roads. Neither a liberal in the modern sense nor a charismatic leader, Parker nonetheless was the transitional figure between his aloof and relatively do-nothing predecessors and an aggressive neo-Populism which soon followed.

Henry L. Fuqua, formerly general manager of the state penitentiary, and gubernatorial candidate of the New Orleans machine, succeeded Parker in 1924. "Marse Henry," as Negro convicts allegedly called him, died in office two years later. Neither he nor O. H. Simpson, who completed Fuqua's term, were impressive or creative chief executives.

The penal system under these three governors seems to have lurched along, guided by the benign and disappointingly mortal precepts of "Marse Henry." Rarely visited, officially mute, and seldom discussed, Louisiana's penal farms made headlines only when inundated by adjacent rivers or when someone managed to discover that the system was "financially unsound," as it rapidly became during the 1920s. Official interest in treatment or rehabilitation of convicts remained modest in the extreme.

Far from modest in any category was the man who dominated Louisiana's political scene from 1928 to 1935, and who even in death has continued to influence the state's destiny— Governor and United States Senator Huey Pierce Long, Jr. A lengthy summary of Long's origins, rise to political prominence, and controversial career is beyond the limits of this study.[1] That Long and his associates exerted a negative in-

[1] Scholarly analyses of Huey P. Long are numerous and vary considerably in approach, interpretation, and merit. A recent, extensive, and well-written study is T. Harry Williams' Pulitzer prize-winning *Huey Long: A Biography* (New York, 1969). More concerned with the mechanics of his political environment than with Long personally is Allan P. Sindler, *Huey Long's Louisiana, State Politics 1920–1952* (Baltimore, 1956). A comprehensive and useful collection of interpretive readings is Hugh Davis Graham, *Great Lives Observed: Huey Long* (Englewood Cliffs, 1970). All possess excellent bibliographies, though Sindler's is the most inclusive.

fluence upon penal reform in Louisiana is both relevant and fairly indisputable.

However dramatically Long may have broken with the past in transforming the frustrations of Louisiana's "little people" into the tangible realities of paved roads, schools, and hospitals, his views concerning the penal system were frankly and utterly conventional: the "Kingfish" looked upon the penitentiary simply as a state-operated business enterprise, the sound management of which was required to save the taxpayers unnecessary expenditures and to protect his administration from embarrassment. Appraised on this level alone, Long emerges no better than William Pitt Kellogg, Murphy J. Foster, or W. W. Heard.

The goal of a self-supporting penal system remained as elusive as ever during the depressed 1930s. With money universally hard to come by, it is understandable why Long's administration was especially loath to appropriate any amount of state funds to such a low priority item as the penitentiary. As a result, his prison appointees continued the traditional practices of flogging and long convict work-hours in their determination to make the system self-supporting. An examination of prison records in 1941 revealed that Longite guard captains had inflicted ten thousand admitted floggings—sometimes consisting of as many as fifty lashes each—between 1928 and 1940. And only "official punishments" were recorded. An indeterminate but probably much larger number of beatings was inflicted upon convicts working in the cane fields, vegetable patches, and elsewhere.[2] One result was a higher number of deaths (if not an actually higher death rate) between 1931 and 1935: under the general managership of Long's appointee, R. L. Himes, an average of forty-one convicts perished annually,[3] the highest toll officially on record

[2] New Orleans *Times-Picayune*, May 11, 1941. Longite guard captains recorded each flogging administered in the file of the individual convict. Some convicts received several beatings over the years, thus the total of ten thousand floggings inflicted between 1928 and 1940 represents the total number of beatings recorded and not the number of different convicts punished.

[3] State of Louisiana, *Biennial Report of the Louisiana State Peni-*

since termination of the convict lease system a generation before.[4]

Despite the continued use of flogging, self-support was never fully realized at the penitentiary during the tenure of Long and his followers. In 1934 prison expenditures exceeded revenues by $10,000; Longite legislatures had to appropriate more than $700,000 from the General Fund between 1928 and 1939 to help pay operating expenses and to retire bonded indebtedness; in 1938 General Manager Theophile Landry, successor to Himes and himself an appointee of the Long organization, accused his fellow Longite of having permitted "the physical plant and working equipment which cost hundreds of thousands of dollars" to become "badly depreciated and run down."[5] Evidence of venality and corruption within the system was subsequently brought to light. While prison officials had "diverted" money designated for "feeding, clothing and housing prisoners," the latter had to subsist on "the dietary deficiencies of a daily table fare of grits, greens, sweet potatoes and black strap," none of which cost the system anything, as it

tentiary: 1938–1940 (Baton Rouge, 1940), 19. Biennial reports of the penitentiary are hereinafter cited as Biennial Report, State Penitentiary, with appropriate years indicated.

[4] The average number of annual convict deaths during the last eight years of the James lease was 100.6. During the first seventeen years of renewed state control (1901–18), an average of 35.3 convicts died each year. State of Louisiana, Report made by Hy. L. Fuqua, General Manager of the State Penitentiary to the Governor and General Assembly for the Regular Session of 1918 Covering the Biennial Period of 1916 and 1917 (Baton Rouge, 1918), 42, hereinafter cited as Fuqua Report, 1918. As no penitentiary reports were issued between 1918 and 1932, neither the total number nor the annual average of convict deaths is known for that period. Available evidence, together with lack of evidence to the contrary, indicates that the 1920s were not an especially brutal decade for Louisiana's convicts.

[5] State of Louisiana, Biennial Report of the State Treasurer to the Governor, 1928–1929 (Baton Rouge, 1930), 20, 50; (1930–31), 44; (1934–35), 3, 12, 23; (1936–37), 7, 29; (1938–39), 7, 29, 36. Biennial reports of the treasurer are hereinafter cited as Biennial Report, State Treasurer with appropriate year indicated. Biennial Report, State Penitentiary, 1936–1938, p. 6. Just prior to the remark quoted, Landry stated that the penitentiary under Himes "had been paying its own way for several years, and was free of floating debt with a substantial sum of money in the bank." Himes, as will be shown, was less successful than Landry believed.

was produced on the farm.[6] The result by the end of the era of Huey Long in 1940, was a penal system in a condition of physical wreckage and moral collapse similar to that handed over to Governor Heard by the James regime in 1901.

During the 1920s so far as any documented record is concerned, the Louisiana penal system might as well have ceased to exist. Until General Manager Himes resumed the practice of issuing biennial reports in 1932, no official information whatever was released concerning procedures or conditions within the system after 1918. Only in the state treasurer's reports and in scattered legislative acts and journals is there any official indication of how the system was being managed. The James-dominated Board of Control had likewise remained silent during the 1880s. But unlike this earlier period, when the lessee had been under constant attack within the General Assembly, exposed by some of the state press, and criticized by the Prison Reform Association of Louisiana, no outside agitation developed between 1918 and 1940 comparable to what had produced the vehement debates concerning the merits and shortcomings of the convict lease system.

There does not seem to have been any reason, indeed, why such agitation should have materialized, at least prior to 1928. If excessive brutality had been in vogue, certainly one of several agencies would have exposed it, as had been done in the past and would be done again in the future. The Prison Reform Association of Louisiana, discouraged by a minimum of progressive legislation since 1901, had become in its last years, during the 1920s, more concerned with New Orleans jails than with the penitentiary. Still, it is difficult to imagine that this organization, though greatly reduced in influence, would have failed to criticize the state penal system if there had been reason to do so. Nor did the state Board of Charities and Corrections make any charges of brutal treatment of convicts. Newspaper comment regarding the penal system was entirely limited to financial matters. Brutality and mismanagement were carried on by Longite officials between 1928

[6] *Angola Argus* quoted in New Orleans *Times-Picayune*, May 11, 1941.

and 1940. But few people cared (or knew) about it at the time, for not until an anti-Long administration came to power in 1940 were Angola's records and the farm itself, both generally removed since 1930 from public scrutiny, reopened to investigation by the press.

Even though infrequent references to brutality were made prior to the Long era by outside commentators,[7] and while state officials remained traditionally disinclined to implement worthwhile rehabilitative programs, the Louisiana penal system appears to have been no less humanely administered overall during the 1920s than it had been since the state resumed control in 1901. Much credit for this state of affairs should go to "Marse Henry" Fuqua, who seems to have supervised his charges in the paternalistic manner of a kindly antebellum slaveowner. Those who followed Fuqua at Angola, up to the middle of the Long administration, generally followed his method also, which was to economize and streamline internal operations rather than to achieve solvency at the expense of convict welfare, the standard practice of some other Louisiana penal officials, whether lessee or state.[8] Some degree of brutality no doubt existed under the regime of Fuqua and his immediate successors. Flogging, for example, remained as the standard method of discipline long after termination of the lease in 1901. But Fuqua's associates appear to have held brutality to a minimum. Longite officials, on the other hand, squeezed between a depression and their own venality, may well have resorted more often to brutality in order to make the penal system self-supporting. They were not ultimately successful, and as the system had to be continuously subsidized

[7] Frank Tannenbaum, *Darker Phases of the South* (New York, 1924), 93, 105–106. Neither of the instances of brutality cited by Tannenbaum took place within the penal system, but occurred instead at a facility of the state mental hospital at Jackson. Tannenbaum, however, believed Jackson was a penal institution.

[8] For two generally favorable outside comments on the Louisiana penal system during the 1920s see "Honor System at Sing-Sing and Louisiana State Prison," *Social Service Review*, I (September, 1927), 499–500; and "Life in a Prison De Luxe in Louisiana," *Literary Digest*, LXXVII (April 21, 1923), 50–52.

by the General Fund, Angola became a heavier burden upon the state's resources.

Henry L. Fuqua, general manager of the penal system from 1916 to 1923, was no "softie." He approached his financial responsibilities with a seriousness equal to that of any of his predecessors. His objective was the same as theirs had been: to make the penal system self-supporting at the least and to provide an annual surplus if possible. Fuqua's philosophy was most dramatically illustrated by his decision, in 1917, to get rid of most paid guards and to replace them with "trusty" convicts. The convict-guard system (currently being phased out at Angola—at last) was subsequently, and justly, criticized in later years. At the time of its inauguration by Fuqua, however, the convict-guard system was envisioned as a sensible money-saving innovation and as a means by which better-behaved prisoners could be more effectively rehabilitated through the exercise of responsibility.

During the first six years of Fuqua's tenure as general manager, the penal system was effectively rescued from the morass into which it had sunk as a combined result of the 1912 flood and administrative inadequacy. But the respite was to be only temporary. In 1922 the Father of Waters again smashed through the levees, drowning Angola, killing livestock, ruining the 1923 crops, and precipitating a series of financial reverses with which three gubernatorial administrations and as many general managers were unable to cope effectively.

The legislature of 1922 was forced to authorize the state Board of Liquidation to borrow $1,500,000 to repair flood damage within the penal system over the subsequent biennium.[9]

9 State of Louisiana, *Official Journal of the Proceedings of the House of Representatives of the Legislature, 1922* (Baton Rouge, 1922), HCR No. 34, p. 316. Published proceedings of the house are hereinafter cited as *House Journal*, with appropriate year indicated. Only $1,045,250 was appropriated specifically for 1922, leaving a balance of $454,750 for the following year. *Biennial Report, State Treasurer, 1922–1923*, Statement "B" facing p. 6.

An Angola camp in 1902. These buildings remained in use for more than a half-century.

View of the original state penitentiary in Baton Rouge, 1907. Completed in 1835, the buildings were at last demolished in 1918.

Sleeping quarters at a levee camp in 1907.
The crowded bunks are typical of such camps.

A camp dining hall at Angola in 1939. The meal consists of "heaping plates holding four vegetables, with stacks of corn

In 1923 receipts from sale of produce brought in only $20,846.56, a twentieth of what had been collected the previous year. The balance of penitentiary revenues for 1923 consisted of $8,415.87 in "interest paid by banks and other sources," the balance of the loan authorized above, a sum of $454,750, and a balance in the Penitentiary Fund, carried over from 1922, of $75,000.[10] Adding these four amounts, the state treasurer arrived at the sum of $740,012.43, representing total penitentiary revenues for 1923. As penitentiary expenditures came to $739,512.43, there remained a "balance" of $500 in the Penitentiary Fund at the end of 1923.

Perhaps as the result of a clerical error, a sizable overdraft had been hidden, for when $8,415.87, $20,846.56, $75,000, $454,750 are added, the actual sum is $559,012.43, an amount $181,000 less than what was claimed for total revenues and $180,500 short of total expenditures.

Juggling figures did not relieve the financial woes of the penal system. While sale of produce zoomed upward to $556,437.97 in 1924 (the year in which Fuqua was elected governor), the legislature had to transfer $585,000 from the General Fund in order to meet penitentiary expenditures.[11]

In 1925 the penal system sold produce worth $719,323.11. But because expenses came to $1,441,323.11, the legislature had to dip into the General Fund for $722,000 with which to cover the tab. One reason for these consistently high expenditures was that loans secured to assist the penal system were made obligations of the system, to be repaid from its earnings. When this was not possible, the legislature had to appropriate funds from other state resources. On this occasion, however, the fund was raided a second time, for $193,000, which together with the conventional balance of $500 carried over from 1924, left an impressive balance of $193,500 in the Penitentiary Fund at the conclusion of the year.[12] It would appear that the $180,500 "error" of 1923, having been at last

[10] *Biennial Report, State Treasurer, 1922–1923,* Statement "F" following p. 35.   [11] *Ibid.* (1924–25), Statement "B" following p. 7.
[12] *Ibid.,* Statement "B" following p. 36.

"discovered," was being adjusted two years later by yet another large donation from the General Fund.

Sale of produce in 1926 dropped to $290,083.04. The "balance" of $193,500 boosted total penitentiary revenue for the year to $483,583.04, while expenses amounted to $1,441,630.96. But the legislature of 1926, the last over which Fuqua governed before his death in October, declined to bail the system out this time and an overdraft of $958,047.92 resulted.[13] Possibly realizing, as a contemporary observed, that "the depression in all agricultural pursuits [had] been widespread throughout the state as elsewhere, and [that] successive crop failures and overflows [had] brought [the penal system's] farming operations to the verge of bankruptcy,"[14] the legislature resolved to put the convicts to work at other and more reliable tasks. Act 290 of 1926 authorized the highway commission to contract with the general manager for convict labor "to such an extent as may be necessary to keep the penitentiary forces of the State continuously occupied."[15]

In the year preceding Huey Long's inauguration as governor of Louisiana, the state's penal system reached a most embarrassing financial condition. No earnings whatever were reported. Penitentiary revenues for 1927, totalling $1,387,566.36, came entirely from outside sources: $429,518.44 from interest on the severance license tax, and $958,047.92 from the General Fund.[16] This amount was just in excess of expendi-

[13] *Ibid.* (1926–27), Statement "B" following p. 6.

[14] Elizabeth Wisner, *Public Welfare Administration in Louisiana* (Chicago, 1930), 167–68.

[15] State of Louisiana, *Acts of the Legislature of 1926* (Baton Rouge, 1926), 523. Published legislative actions are hereinafter cited as *Acts of Louisiana*, with appropriate year indicated. Employment of convicts on highway construction had been initially authorized on a practical basis on 1921, but without the feeling of urgency apparent five years later. See *Acts of Louisiana, Extra Session of 1921*, p. 196. Road work ceased to be a major undertaking of the penal system in 1933. See *Biennial Report, State Penitentiary, 1934–1936*, p. 18.

[16] *Biennial Report, State Treasurer* (1926–27), Statement "B" following p. 36. Angola's levees held during the record-breaking flood of 1927, but the necessity of employing convicts on levees elsewhere probably was responsible for the penal system's making no money from sale of produce.

tures, leaving the customary $500 balance in the Penitentiary Fund.

Two points of significance should be noted concerning the administration of Louisiana's penal system on the eve of Long's governorship. As recalled a decade later, the penitentiary had become "a perennial grief . . . a place of big appropriations [and] continuous annual deficits."[17] It was also, under Fuqua and his associates, an institution in which convicts were not subjected to extraordinary brutality, because officials, apparently, did not wish to impose that kind of discipline, even in the face of constant financial difficulties. And while the penal system's fiscal problems were uppermost in the minds of legislators—when they thought about the penal system at all—some attention was paid during the 1920s (more than during the ensuing decade) to matters within the area of penal reform. In 1926, a financially disastrous year for the penal system, the legislature appropriated $50,000 for the creation of a State Industrial School for delinquent white girls between the ages of twelve and nineteen, most of whom were currently kept in city or parish jails and, occasionally, at Angola.[18] The sponsor of this measure was the venerable Representative S. O. Shattuck of Calcasieu Parish, who in 1890 had also sponsored the lottery amendment—and had voted to renew the James lease that same year. The legislature of 1926, in addition, updated the laws relating to commutation of sentence, indeterminate sentence, and parole; reduced the maximum age for juveniles at Louisiana Training Institute from eighteen to seventeen; and authorized the state's judicial districts to set up "district prison farms" for prisoners convicted of violations "not necessarily punishable by hard labor." The intent of the last two measures was primarily to reduce the convict population at Angola, but also

[17] New Orleans *Item*, June 11, 1937.
[18] *Acts of Louisiana* (1926), 280–82. Legislation to establish such an institution had passed in 1918 and again in 1920, but each time without an appropriation. *Acts of Louisiana* (1918), 248, 250; *Acts of Louisiana* (1920), 476–81.

made possible was the separation of additional younger offenders and petty offenders from hardened criminals.[19]

Thus the record of the 1920s, so far as Louisiana's penal
system was concerned, was not altogether discreditable. Although the decade ended with the system in financial disorder, this condition was neither unprecedented nor was it
due to human failure alone. Since the purchase of Angola
by the state in 1901, repeated overflows of the adjacent
Mississippi River had been the major cause of penitentiary
expenditure and indebtedness. The staggering amount (for
the 1920s) of $3,350,000, which legislatures under Governors
Parker, Fuqua, and Simpson had to appropriate to maintain
the penal system between 1923 and 1927 alone, was tied
initially to the massive flood damage suffered in 1922. During
the 1930s the federal government, through the Army Corps of
Engineers, expanded its work on the river's levee system.
Stronger embankments were added, spillways constructed, and
although Angola's own levees remained inadequate, the farm
was not flooded during the Long era. Had these improvements been made two decades earlier, perhaps the Louisiana
penal system under Parker, Fuqua, and Simpson would have
been less oppressed financially; Angola, after all, was the only
state penitentiary in the nation whose greatest annual concern
was to avoid being inundated and ruined by the mightiest
river in North America. In any event, the progressive taming
of "Old Man River" by Washington proved a benefit to prison
officials under the Long regime.

[19] *Acts of Louisiana* (1926), 331–34, 355–56, 512–14, 591–93, 640–43.
Act 127 of 1938 authorized district judges, within their "sound discretion,"
to send to the district prison farms persons sentenced "to imprisonment at
hard labor . . . notwithstanding said person is convicted of an offense requiring imprisonment in the penitentiary." *Acts of Louisiana* (1938), 306.
If acted upon, this provision would have reversed the intent of its predecessor by placing major offenders among petty offenders. The act seems
to have been motivated, however, by the desire to separate "youthful first-
offenders," excepting those convicted of really serious crimes, from the
more hardened criminals at Angola. See State of Louisiana, *Biennial Report of the State Board of Charities and Corrections to the Governor and
State Legislature 1936–1937* (New Orleans, 1938), 13. A separate institution for first offenders within the penal system itself was not completed
and ready for occupancy until 1958.

But this was not the only factor which would enable Long-ite legislatures to appropriate, over an eleven-year period, less than a fourth of the amount spent by their predecessors for penitentiary support, as noted above. Sound business management was the critical reason for the relative success achieved by the Long administration in reducing penitentiary expenditures, if not eliminating them altogether (as was frequently claimed). And Longite officials at least maintained, even though they did not accelerate, the traditional methods of deriving a "full day's work" from the convicts: long hours and application of the lash.

General managers during the 1920s, faced with monumental financial problems, no doubt also employed these methods but apparently did not do so excessively. It might be asked, Why not? The latter-day Bourbons of the 1920s were not indifferent to the necessarily large appropriations and the continuous annual deficits which the penal system inflicted upon them. But they had all been young adults during the last, and most brutal, years of the convict lease system in Louisiana. They were well aware of the methods James had employed in order to pay his rentals and to secure his profits. (It should be remembered that Fuqua himself was a son-in-law of the lessee's clerk. From his father-in-law, the general manager-governor doubtless accquired some knowledge of the major's system.) The lessee's methods were universally known and widely deplored well before the turn of the century. They were not soon forgotten and continued to be deplored for many years afterward. However conventional Louisiana's neo-Bourbon governors and prison officials may have been in their skepticism concerning prison reform and prison reformers—the "indiscreet" and "zealous" whose "intentions are good," as W. W. Heard had characterized them—state officials nevertheless wanted to avoid a reversion to the practices of Major James and seem to have resisted the utmost pressure to revert.

Between 1901 and 1918 treatment of convicts improved and the death toll dropped significantly. While these were the only signal achievements in penal reform during this period, they were achievements of which the state could be rightfully proud. No data relative to convict deaths are available for the years between 1918 and 1932. In all likelihood, the death rate remained low during the period, and treatment of convicts, as has been suggested, was generally humane. Had the case been otherwise, someone would certainly have exposed the facts, officially or unofficially. When security tightened up and the number of deaths rose under the Long regime, sufficient evidence, both official and unofficial, was ultimately forthcoming.

Finally, Parker, Fuqua (especially), and probably Simpson as well were among the last of their kind in Louisiana: men born and reared in the paternalistic world of the Old South, in the best sense of that term; men who might whip a "darkey" (or a convict) if he "deserved it," but who would find it difficult to utilize or to condone brutality as a legitimate means of making money.

Huey Long was not a product of the Old South, having been born in upland Winn parish in 1893 at the commencement of the Populist movement, which represented the political thinking of most of his neighbors and was an essential ingredient of his own subsequent political outlook. Neither was young Huey given a classical education, nor did he have inculcated into him the tradition of "noblesse oblige." Neither did he have the leisure time in which to reflect upon pleasant abstractions, as "respectable" boys still did in New Orleans, Baton Rouge, and the plantation districts. Part-time student, traveling salesman, small-town lawyer, member of the state's railroad commission, and once-unsuccessful gubernatorial candidate, Huey Long, by 1928, was an ambitious hard-driving example of the new southern middle class. More important, he was an uncommonly perceptive and equally pragmatic twentieth century politician, the very first of his kind in Louisiana.

As governor and as United States senator, Long virtually ran the state singlehandedly. But neither his political machine nor his successes as a wheeler-dealer comprised the "secret of Long's power," which, as T. Harry Williams has concluded, derived from Long's record—"he delivered something."[20] Highways, bridges, hospitals, and free school books were among the more needed, and hitherto neglected, services delivered by Long to Louisiana's voting masses, who winked at the negative characteristics of the Kingfish while continuously reelecting Long and his retinue to high office throughout the 1930s.

Convicts at Angola were not, however, among the state's voting masses, and popularity among those who supported Long at the polls could be jeopardized by lavishing "their" tax money upon the "perennial grief." Long was not the first politician from Winn Parish to regard the penal system as a burden upon taxpayers. State Senator George A. Kelly had opposed abolition of the convict lease system in 1884 on the grounds that state control would require extra taxation. The "Winn philosophy of prison management" had helped sustain Major James, and the lash, during the 1880s. Reapplied fifty years later by another native of Winn—who, as a child of seven when the lease system ended, could not have known or cared much about it—the "Winn philosophy" maintained use of the lash, this time under state auspices. Thus, while brutality may not have increased at Angola after 1928—as implied by anti-Long investigators during the 1940s—Longite officials resorted to it and showed themselves, at the very least, to be just as ready to utilize the lash to maintain discipline and to ensure penal self-sufficiency as any other regime since 1901.

The first legislature of Long's administration dealt with penal reform in the established manner of well-intentioned ineffectiveness. An act was passed "to provide for the creation, maintenance, and government of a State Industrial School for colored male youths of the age of seventeen years and under." Failure to include an appropriation, however, ren-

[20] T. Harry Williams, "The Gentleman from Louisiana: Demagogue or Democrat," in George B. Tindall (ed.), *The Pursuit of Southern History: Presidential Addresses of the Southern Historical Association, 1935–1963* (Baton Rouge, 1964), 407.

dered the act meaningless.[21] But in order to have some place where Negro juveniles might be sent, "until a State Reformatory for colored juveniles is built," the legislature in a subsequent statute directed that such offenders be commited to the district prison farms. Each farm was to provide "a special department where colored juveniles may be held." To complete their new function as warehouses for castoffs and undesirables, the farms were additionally empowered "to create and maintain . . . a work house, or home, for the paupers."[22] For each of the years 1928 and 1929 a penitentiary appropriation from the General Fund of $75,000 was also necessarily provided.[23]

In 1929 the penal system and everything else receded into the background because of Governor Long's impeachment by the lower house of the legislature. Proceedings in the upper house came to an abrupt end on May 16 when fifteen senators, "constituting more than one-third of the membership of this senate, sitting as a court of impeachment," collectively announced that they would "not vote to convict."[24] Long had survived the first, and potentially most serious, threat to his power.

One year later the governor was again the target of legislative harassment. On this occasion the administration was the defendant in the first major investigation of the penal system since 1915. (Only two such investigations by either house of the legislature had been conducted since the beginning of Reconstruction. The first was in 1878.) Long had been quoted "as stating that the Penitentiary is on a paying basis" while "others" believed that it was not.[25] The senate

[21] *Acts of Louisiana* (1928), 200–203.

[22] *Ibid.*, 251. A reformatory for Negro juveniles was finally constructed and "opened for inmates" twenty years later during an administration of Huey's younger brother, Earl K. Long. See Robert G. Pugh, *Juvenile Laws of Louisiana: History and Development* (Baton Rouge, 1957), 400.

[23] *Biennial Report, State Treasurer* (1928–29), 20, 50.

[24] Huey P. Long, *Every Man a King* (New Orleans, 1933), 133–82, 170–71. Long's account of his own impeachment, though one-sided, is lively and interesting. For a complete and more objective analysis, see Williams, *Huey Long*, 355–405.

[25] State of Louisiana, *Official Journal of the Proceedings of the Senate of the Legislature of 1930* (Baton Rouge, 1930), SR No. 16, Calendar, p.

committee on the penitentiary was directed to resolve the question by making "a thorough and complete investigation of the status and condition of the State Penitentiary, financially and otherwise."[26] The committee visited Angola soon afterward and submitted its report on July 9, 1930.

General Manager Clay J. Dugas, who had received his appointment from Long as a political reward, did not, in the committee's judgment, "possess the necessary ability to administer the affairs" of the penal system.[27] In addition to having permitted the "financial affairs of the penitentiary" to fall into a "deplorable condition," Dugas was found to be leasing convicts to a private rice grower, who had agreed to divide the crop evenly with the penitentiary. The committee condemned this transaction as "violative of both the letter and the spirit of the constitution" in which was embodied the 1898 provision against leasing convicts to private firms or persons.[28]

It was discoverd, in addition, that salaries of penitentiary employees had been "indiscriminately raised," and that the warden at Angola was a twenty-seven-year-old law student at Louisiana State University. This "excellent gentleman," the committee stated, was "devoting but little time or attention to the duties of the office."[29] By far the most distressing revelation was that "the penitentiary is not self-sustaining." The senators gloomily concluded, "As far as we know or have been able to ascertain, the penitentiary has never been self-sustaining."[30] This last observation was, for the recent past, a sound one, but should hardly have been news to anybody.

Only three of the committee's eleven members could be de-

---

126. Published proceedings of the senate are hereinafter cited as *Senate Journal*, with appropriate year indicated.   [26] *Ibid.*

[27] Committee report quoted in Baton Rouge *State-Times*, July 9, 1930.

[28] *Ibid.* This episode was probably the basis for Allan Sindler's conclusion that "in 1930 [Long] revived the practice of farming out state prisoners at Angola to private contractors." It is not certain, however, whether the "lease" was in fact initiated by Long, or by Dugas with or without Long's knowledge. Sindler, *Huey Long's Louisiana*, 105.

[29] Quoted in Baton Rouge *State-Times*, July 9, 1930.   [30] *Ibid.*

scribed as administration stalwarts.[31] Whatever the bias of its majority, the committee's report produced tremors violent enough to elicit the resignations, nine days later, of General Manager Dugas (for reasons of ill health) and of Warden A. P. Steckler (for reasons he kept to himself.)[32]

Although the resignation of Dugas was officially accepted, it was understood that he would remain at his post ad interim until the governor was able to appoint a suitable replacement. Long was occupied at the time with moving his campaign for the United States Senate into gear. He would face in the 1930 primary Senator Joseph E. Ransdell—"Feather Duster," as Long himself described him—an elderly relic who had replaced Murphy J. Foster in 1911. The Baton Rouge *State-Times*, Louisiana's official journal in spite of a viscerally anti-Long point of view, editorialized on July 19 that Dugas "will probably remain until after the primary in order that Governor Long can promise the job to a least 40 different political leaders over the state."[33] For whatever reason, Long waited until April 18, 1931 to appoint a successor to Dugas. The senator-elect's choice was R. L. Himes, business manager of Louisiana State University.

Huey Long's penal policy, insofar as he officially had one, was clearly articulated at the time he appointed Himes to be general manager: "I have directed Mr. Himes to operate the penitentiary 100 per cent on the basis of efficiency. . . . He can fire and hire anybody he chooses and I will help him do it. I have appointed him because of the close manner in which he has guarded every fund and every property of the University. . . . His careful manner of handling the university business has given him the name of 'tighty' on the campus and that is the kind of a man we need at the penitentiary."[34]

[31] Chairman Wingate and Senators Larcade and Knott were among the fifteen "round-robineers" of 1929.

[32] Baton Rouge *State-Times*, July 18, 1930.

[33] *Ibid.*, July 19, 1930.

[34] Quoted in Baton Rouge *Morning Advocate*, May 16, 1932. A building named after Himes on Louisiana State University's Baton Rouge campus presently houses the University's College of Business Administration.

Within twenty years, three occasions of financial crisis in the penal system had provoked three Louisiana governors, Hall, Pleasant, and Long, to make top level changes in penal administration. In 1914 Board President (and former Governor) W. W. Heard was replaced by former Board President C. Harrison Parker. The Board of Control itself was thrown out two years later. Centralization of responsibility was embodied in the new position of general manager, which was conferred initially upon Henry L. Fuqua. And in 1930–1931, one unsuccessful and embarrassing Longite general manager was being replaced by another, presumably more qualified and competent, Longite general manager. The mission of each replacement was the same: miraculous achievements in business management, to be initiated immediately and maintained indefinitely.

A reorganized Board of Control had been unable to liquidate debts incurred from the 1912 flood and was abolished altogether. Fuqua, also victimized by a major inundation, was kicked up rather than out, becoming governor of Louisiana. And both Himes and Long were soon to discover, probably to their mutual disillusionment, that managing the finances of a university, which was not required to support itself, was a less complex and far less frustrating responsbility than managing the finances of a penal system during a time of national economic depression.

"Tighty" Himes got off to a good start. (So had Fuqua in 1916.) Shortly before the former academician assumed his duties at Angola, the legislature had found it necessary to make another transfer from the General Fund to the Penitentiary Fund, probably to pay for the lingering debts of the Dugas regime. The amount involved was $41,125.[35] By the end of the following year, 1932, Himes could show the conventional $500 balance in the Penitentiary Fund without benefit of legislative assistance, while Governor Alvin O. King had been able to inform the lawmakers in May that "the penitentiary has at last reached the point where it seems to be self-

[35] *Biennial Report, State Treasurer* (1930–1931), 44.

sustaining. Within the past year it not only has been able to pay its operating expenses but has paid off about $25,000 of the old indebtedness. This can be continued by proper management."[36]

The Himes magic, however, was already beginning to fade. In February, 1933, while Senator Long bragged in Washington that the Louisiana State Penitentiary was not only "on a self-sustaining basis," but "perhaps" on a "paying and profitable basis" as well,[37] the system was inexorably reverting to "normal": expenditures and revenues for 1933 cancelled out at $227,075.85.[38] And even though there was no overdraft and no need to bleed the General Fund, the balance in the Penitentiary Fund at the conclusion of the year was precisely zero. There was a $10,000 overdraft the following year, together with $129,312.50 worth of ransom taken from the General Fund.[39] In 1935 expenditures were again equalled by revenues, but again the General Fund had to be called to the rescue—for $84,124.98.[40] Himes died in office on October 31, 1936, a little more than a year after Long himself had died of an assassin's bullet in Baton Rouge. During "Tighty's" last year as general manager the penal system broke even, but required for payment of debts yet another transfusion from the General Fund, an amount of $69,875.[41]

It would be as unfair to blame all of this on Himes alone as to hold the Board of Control or Fuqua entirely responsible for the financial chaos produced by the floods of 1912 and 1922. The Louisiana penal system succeeded in defeating almost everyone who had tried to manage it since 1901. The Mississippi River, the elements, and the boll weevil had been the particular nemeses of general managers prior to 1930. After that, the elements were joined by other factors, over which no general manager could exercise effective control. General Manager Theophile Landry, appointed to succeed

[36] House Journal (1932) , 8.
[37] Quoted in Henry C. Dethloff (ed.) , Huey P. Long: Southern Demagogue or American Democrat? (Boston, 1967) , 26.
[38] Biennial Report, State Treasurer (1932–33) , 57.
[39] Ibid. (1934–35) , 3, 12.   [40] Ibid., 23.
[41] Ibid. (1936–1937) , 7, 13.

Himes by Longite Governor Richard W. Leche, summarized his four years' experience in 1940: "In an economic or financial sense, the most efficient operation of our farms and of the prison can be absolutely nullified by such elements as the weather, the markets for our products, the policies of the administration in power, the restrictions imposed by state and federal laws upon our operations, and the complaints of pressure groups who feel that in our efforts to make a living for the institution we are competing with them improperly."[42]

Successful management of the penal system, in Landry's view, depended in large measure upon "hoping always that the elements, the markets, the lawmakers, and the Almighty will, somehow, permit us to sell the finished product for enough to live on."[43] Rarely, if ever, did all these factors combine to make possible a sufficiently desirable result, as Louisiana penal officials over the past generation could have testified.

The miracle of self-support had not been forthcoming. C. Harrison Parker, Henry L. Fuqua, Clay J. Dugas, and R. L. Himes were unable to deal permanently or even very effectively with the complex causes of the penal system's being a truly "perennial grief." Theophile Landry, for that matter, was no more fortunate than his predecessors. Between 1937 and 1939 more than $245,000 had to be drawn from the General Fund to help operate the penitentiary and/or to pay its debts.[44]

<hr>

[42] *Biennial Report, State Penitentiary* (1938–40), 4. Act 169 of 1936 had prohibited the sale in Louisiana of "goods, wares or merchandise manufactured, in whole or in part, out of leather, iron, textiles, lumber or vegetable fibre, by convicts or prisoners." *Acts of Louisiana* (1936), 494. This law virtually eliminated the sale of anything other than farm produce by the penal system. And by 1940 the principal source of revenue, sugar cane, had become "hedged about with a bewildering multiplicity of Federal laws, regulations and restrictions, which are not infrequently changed . . . in the middle of the crop." Landry anticipated having to "plow up 600 acres of growing cane" during 1940. Along with floods, weather, insects, market conditions, politics and pressure groups, the New Deal had become an obstacle to Angola's financial stability.

[43] *Biennial Report, State Penitentiary* (1938–1940), 5.

[44] *Biennial Report, State Treasurer* (1936–37), 29, 35; (1938–39), 7, 14, 29, 36.

Both Himes and Landry failed to transcend completely
the various circumstances which had made life hectic for all
state penal officials. Financially speaking, the Louisiana penitentiary was no more intrinsically sound by 1940 than it had
been a decade or two decades earlier. In their determination
to make it so, however, the two Longite general managers had
permitted, perhaps even encouraged, their captains to drive
and to mistreat the convicts to an extent that had not been
documented within the penal system since 1901.

The scandalous disclosures of 1930 convinced many legislators that operations of the penal system should no longer be
veiled from either official or public scrutiny. In the senate a
bill was introduced which, if enacted, would have compelled
the general manager to issue biennial reports, a practice dis-
continued in 1918.[45] The measure passed the upper house
by a vote of 35–0, but got no further.[46] Nonetheless, there
appeared in 1932 the first public document released by the
penal system in fourteen years.[47] Perhaps General Manager
Himes considered it good public relations to report goings-on
at Angola, even though not required by law to do so.

Accepted at face value (as it was doubtless intended they
should be) the reports of Himes read like an academic course
in modern prison administration. They describe a system that
was meticulously and conscientiously managed along business
lines and tell of convicts whose lives were "made as happy as
possible."[48] Himes the academician is at his best when he
elaborates upon the frailties of human nature, and especially

[45] *Senate Journal* (1930), Calendar, 90.

[46] The House Penitentiary Committee failed to report it, probably
because the bill was introduced too late in the session. *House Journal*
(1930), Calendar, 306–307. There is no indication of such a measure in
the *Acts of 1930*.

[47] *Louisiana State Penitentiary Report to His Excellency, The Honorable O. K. Allen, Governor of Louisiana, and to the Honorable Senators
and Representatives of the General Assembly of the State of Louisiana*
(Baton Rouge, 1932), hereinafter cited as *Louisiana State Penitentiary
Report, 1932*. Someone had forgotten that the "General Assembly" had
become the "Legislature" with the Constitution of 1921. Subsequent
penal reports were more accurately and less bombastically titled.

[48] *Ibid.*, 16.

when describing the educational and training programs which he himself apparently initiated, on his own and without directives from higher authority.[49]   Rarely was mention made of the darker side of prison life, except to remind the reader that the "physical problem" of separating convicts from society "involves iron fences, bars of steel, leather straps, clubs, and guns."[50] In none of his reports did Himes furnish any specific details concerning how many convicts were punished, the reason for the punishments, or how punishment was administered.   Several years later a study of prison records revealed that 1,547 floggings "with 23,889 recorded blows of the double lash" were administered during 1933 alone.[51]   While crediting Himes with putting "Angola on a paying basis" (which he really did not do) and admitting that while he "aided many convicts [and] shortened prison terms," the same source passed what seems to be a fair judgment upon Himes, which concluded that "he could not be persuaded that flogging in itself was harmful or brutalizing. Like many persons who defend corporal punishment in the abstract, it is doubtful if [Himes] ever witnessed a flogging. . . . If unusually severe punishments for apparently trivial offenses showed up in the daily reports he either didn't see them or he failed to realize their significance."[52]

[49] Ibid., 17–18; Biennial Report, State Penitentiary (1934–36), 12–13. Writing of the Louisiana penal system in 1930, Wisner noted that "facilities for any type of education" did not then exist at Angola. Public Welfare Administration in Louisiana, 176. As it is highly doubtful that Dugas launched any educational programs, the credit for doing so most likely should go to Himes, a professional educator after all. Considering how the penal system was being managed in other respects, however, the conduct of these courses during the 1930s must have been uneven and their value to the inmates nominal. Educational and vocational rehabilitation was not meaningfully implemented at Angola until the late 1950s, under professional penologists.

[50] Louisiana State Penitentiary Report, 1932, p. 15. For a long anecdote told by Himes to justify a nasty beating received by a convict, see Biennial Report, State Penitentiary (1934–36), 9–10. The story itself, and the enthusiastic manner in which Himes related it, both vividly exemplify what George Tindall describes as the "South and the savage ideal."

[51] New Orleans Times-Picayune, May 11, 1941.   [52] Ibid.

Himes, like W. W. Heard before him, despaired of those who seemed to believe "that the state should spend tax money lavishly in reformatory programs worked out by 'brain-trusters' who have never really done anything practical."[53] Always practical, "Tighty" Himes had been given the job of making the penal system self-supporting, and so it was probably natural for him to envision "practical" reformation as putting all convicts to useful work "according to the creative law that man should eat bread in the sweat of his face."[54]

Between 1931 and 1936 a number of convicts, 194 in all, registered their extreme displeasure at having to sweat for Himes and to being flogged by his captains—they escaped.[55] Apparently, it was easy for them to do so under the Himes regime. Neither Warden Wade Long, a relative of Huey's, nor Warden W. L. Whitman, who succeeded Long in 1934, was overly concerned with security of confinement.[56] Warden L. A. Jones, who replaced Whitman in 1936 just before Himes died, recalled in 1940 that when he took office

> there was little system to the safety and protective meas-
> ures, which were slipshod in the extreme; guards were care-
> lessly selected and untrained; they were armed with old
> worn-out, undependable shotguns . . . ammunition was
> scanty and in poor condition: there were no rifles; men
> were taken to the fields before daylight and often brought
> in after dark; there was no outer line of guard towers on
> the levee around [Angola]; supervision was poor or non-
> existent; when an escape occurred there was a lack of organi-

[53] *Biennial Report, State Penitentiary* (1934–36), 25.

[54] *Ibid.*, 26.

[55] *Ibid.* (1938–40), 14. In his earlier days at Angola, Himes liked to believe that convicts did not want to escape. He imagined them as saying, "I made a mistake. Let me pay for the debt and be free, really free!" Quoted in Baton Rouge *Morning Advocate*, May 16, 1932.

[56] Between 1901 and 1918, while the penal system comprised four major farms and several levee camps, the average number of escapes was 67.3 per year. During Himes's tenure, by which time most operations were centralized at Angola, the average number of escapes annually was 36.8. Under the last seven years of lessee control, an average of 37 convicts a year managed to escape. See *Fuqua Report, 1918*, p. 42; *Biennial Report, State Penitentiary* (1938–40), 14.

zation and cooperation in the pursuit and search undertaken.[57]

Jones also listed as causes of escapes "lack of discipline and low morale of the inmates," "a certain amount of actual brutality," soft jobs given to some inmates," poor food, and poor recreational facilities.[58]

By August, 1936, a number of "improved safety measures" had been taken. Twenty-five guard towers had been erected along an outer guard line around Angola, guards armed with high-powered rifles and trained in marksmanship had been added, more and better bloodhounds were acquired, and a substation of the state police established on the premises. As an extra precaution, Jones stated (unofficially) that "we work [the convicts] hard. . . . We give them all they can eat. And we hope they're so tired they'll sleep all night."[59] After 1936, in addition, "there was a change in policy as to the reporting of punishments. . . . The number officially recorded dropped sharply; but the same old crowd was in charge and floggings actually reported showed no lessening of severity."[60]

No reasonable person can question the wisdom of securely confining felons until their time of release or parole arrives. Security of confinement had become an obsession, however, within Louisiana's penal system by 1940, quite possibly because the Jones measures, supported by General Manager Landry, had proved to be totally successful: between August, 1936, and May, 1940, no one escaped from Angola, although "eight men were shot and killed" attempting to do so.[61] Angola, in the words of Harnett T. Kane, had become the "Alcatraz of the South."[62] In his report submitted in 1940, General Manager Landry gave as the "first and more important duty" of the penal system the responsibility "to keep the prisoners safely." Relegated to second place, for the first time officially

[57] *Biennial Report, State Penitentiary* (1938–40) , 14.   [58] *Ibid.*
[59] Quoted in New Orleans *Sunday Item-Tribune*, June 4, 1939.
[60] New Orleans *Times-Picayune*, May 11, 1941.
[61] *Biennial Report, State Penitentiary* (1938–40) , 15–16.
[62] Quoted in New Orleans *Sunday Item-Tribune*, June 4, 1939.

in history, was the duty to "use [convict] labor so as to make the [penal system] as light a burden on the tax-payer as possible."[63] Reform or rehabilitation received no mention whatever as duties of the penal system.

Even more ominous from the standpoint of prospective change for the better was a statement made by Himes just prior to his death: "We have frequent occasion to point out that the penitentiary belongs to the people. In fact, we have tried to impress on the public the importance of studying the penitentiary and studying the whole subject of criminality, police, sheriffs, courts, and prisons. We have made no progress."[64] The limited penal reforms effected in Louisiana by 1920 had undergone serious erosion by 1940. Still a financial burden upon taxpayers, Louisiana's penal system had little to show for itself in return, because it was demoralized within by brutality and corruption, uncertain as to what its proper objectives should be, and ignored or misunderstood by the public. Nor were these conditions soon alleviated. Angola continued to deteriorate until, in 1951, the worst prison scandal in the state's modern history erupted.

[63] *Biennial Report, State Penitentiary* (1938–40) , 3.
[64] *Ibid.* (1934–36) , 29.

CHAPTER VI

"America's Worst Prison"
1940-1956

I N THE PRIME of his political life Huey P. Long is said to have predicted that if "those fellows [referring to his underlings] ever try to use the powers I've given them without me to hold them down, they'll all land in the penitentiary."[1] Less than five years after the Kingfish had been laid to rest, his prophecy was partially fulfilled. The Longite administration of Richard Webster Leche, "conduct[ing] the affairs of government as a plunderbund,"[2] exploded in the widely publicized "Louisiana Scandals" of 1939. Governor Leche, Louisiana State University President James M. Smith, and several lesser officials were convicted of diverse offenses including violation of the Connally "hot oil" Act, income tax evasion, embezzlement, and using the mails to defraud.[3] "Dick" Leche was hustled away to the federal prison in Atlanta. "Doc" Smith, however, whose conviction was the "sole major successful state prosecution,"[4] was obliged to don the familiar black-and-white-striped attire of an Angola convict.[5]

[1] Quoted in Allan P. Sindler, *Huey Long's Louisiana: State Politics, 1920–1952* (Baltimore, 1956), 128.   [2] *Ibid.,* 139.
[3] The best account of the scandals is still Harnett T. Kane, *Louisiana Hayride* (New York, 1941).
[4] Sindler, *Huey Long's Louisiana,* 139.
[5] For a photograph of Smith in Angola garb, see *Life,* December 11,

Shocked, embarrassed, and distracted by these sordid developments, Louisianians in the early 1940s tended to lose sight of Angola's problems and shortcomings. If any connection was made in the public mind between the penitentiary and scandal, it was because a prominent "emeritus" of Louisiana's oligarchy had been deservedly imprisoned at Angola. World War II, of course, was itself a major distraction until 1945, as was the proliferation afterward of state agencies on the executive level (very much in the federal pattern), each lobbying and grasping for its share of the public's attention and the tax dollar. Not until 1951 were the terms "penitentiary" and "scandal" again closely associated—so closely, in fact, as to become interchangeable. In that year thirty-seven convicts at Angola slashed their heel tendons in protest against "the system"—overwork, brutality, control by political appointees, and lack of recreation, rehabilitation, decent housing, and edible food. This time Louisianians took notice, particularly when a detailed and well-documented article in *Collier's* magazine described Angola as "America's Worst Prison."[6] How this condition came about and was brought to light, as well as what was done to correct it, forms the substance of this chapter.

By 1940 the confinement of Louisiana's prisoners had been centralized in three locations, all within eighty miles of each other—a small farm camp worked by Negro convicts at St. Gabriel, just south of Baton Rouge; a stock farm north of Baton Rouge in East Feliciana Parish; and the center of the penal system, Angola, a cluster of farm and timber camps spread over an 18,000-acre domain along the Mississippi River about sixty miles northwest of Baton Rouge.

"Some industry" was part of the system in 1940.[7] But with

1939, p. 31. A recent issue of the same magazine, April 10, 1970, portends yet another Louisiana "scandal," this time involving high officials of the McKeithen administration and alleged New Orleans mobster Carlos Marcello.

[6] John Lear and E. W. Stagg, "America's Worst Prison," *Collier's*, CXXX (November 22, 1952), 13–16.

[7] James Wayne Allgood, "A Sociological Analysis of the Transition of the Louisiana Penal System" (M.A. thesis, Louisiana State University, 1956), 58.

the exception of a plant manufacturing automobile license plates, Louisiana's prison industries—a sugar mill, a cannery, and an abbatoir—existed for the purpose of processing the system's farm products, which required the labor of most of the convicts to cultivate and which continued to be the major source of income.[8] As Louisiana became increasingly urban and acquired a more diversified economy, her penal system remained nonetheless remote, rural, and based almost entirely upon the cultivation and sale of agricultural products. Such a system was obviously unsound, viewed from the standpoint either of economics or of rehabilitation.

Despite pious affirmations concerning training and rehabilitating the convicts, a rhetoric which continued to emanate on occasion from wardens, general managers, and other officials, the "main emphasis in the prison's operations," as a professional penologist has observed, "was on keeping the prisoner, working him and making as much money as possible for the institution."[9] This objective had been pursued without spectacular brutality (or success) by Henry L. Fuqua and his followers during the 1920s. Flogging was maintained by Longite penal officials during the next decade and was continued under "reform" Governors Sam Jones and Jimmie Davis (1940–48). The practice increased disgracefully under another Long administration, that of Huey's younger brother, Earl, from 1948 to 1952.

That brutality was never wholly eliminated, that in fact brutal methods of coercing prisoners to work harder comprised the standard rather than the exceptional procedure at Angola before 1952, was a perennial and direct consequence of the kind of personnel whom the system employed. Well into the 1950s the bulk of Angola's employed custodial force was composed of the same elements that had been with the system since the days of lessee James—"prejudiced 'red-

[8] Joseph Clarence Mouledous, "Sociological Perspectives on a Prison Social System," (M.A. thesis, Louisiana State University, 1962), 84.

[9] Allgood, "Sociological Analysis," 78. Allgood became Angola's warden for a brief period during the 1960s.

neck' farmers and French speaking 'cajuns.' "[10] This unprofessional custodial staff, recruited from the lower class of
Louisiana's rural dwellers, was probably the most decisive
factor in the perpetuation of traditional brutality at Angola,
especially against black convicts.

General Manager "Marse" Fuqua, a kindly man in his own
way, had fired large numbers of these people in 1917, primarily in order to save money, but also because he viewed
them as "riff-raff" and "brutal bullies with large whips."[11]
Only eleven employed guards remained by 1923; and between
that year and 1952 no more than eight others were added.[12]
It would seem absurd to expect nineteen guards to maintain
control over more than two thousand convicts. They were
not unassisted. Since 1917 most guards at Angola have in
fact been convicts themselves, as many as six hundred at one
time. Armed with rifles and shotguns, these trusties have
guarded the periphery of the camps, under orders to shoot
anyone attempting to escape. While the use of convict-guards
has saved money, it has also contributed in large measure to
the brutality and low morale of prisoners at Angola over the
years.[13]

Bossing the lower-class whites and the convict-guards, who
in turn rode herd over the mass of other convicts, were captains, one in charge of each camp.[14] These "semi-literate"
officials "were permitted to administer punishment as they
saw fit and with little or no interference" from wardens or

10 Mouledous, "Sociological Perspectives," 136. Also an Angola staff
member at one time, Mouledous served from 1957 to 1961 as a classification officer and assistant director of the Division of Probation and
Parole.

11 Quoted in *ibid.*, 77.

12 Allgood, "Sociological Analysis," 63.

13 For an excellent discussion of the convict-guard system at Angola,
see Mouledous, "Sociological Perspectives," 99–117.

14 A reliable authority has stated that "prior to 1953 some of the
large prison camps at Angola were operated without a single paid employee on duty during the night. Inmate guards were in charge of counts
and of any other matters that would need attention. If an emergency
did arise an employee could be called, but fights and sexual perversion
were seldom considered emergencies." Allgood, "Sociological Analysis," 67.

general managers.[15] During the furor over the 1951 heel-slashings, columnist Westbrook Pegler stated, with characteristic bluntness, that "most of the white trash who infest the [Louisiana] penal service are no better than their victims."[16] Much evidence had been revealed to substantiate such a verdict, even before Pegler rendered it.

Principal causes of nonprofessionalism at Angola were the unattractively remote location of the farm, political patronage, a total lack of systematic training in penology, and low salaries. In 1945, for example, the general manager (invariably a political appointee) could earn as much as $625 per month. But the guards received only $130–$180 and the captains $200–$275. As recently as 1963 the average monthly salary for all personnel at Angola was no more than $365.[17]

The state penal system was, as the director of institutions described it in 1946, "one of the largest businesses in Louisiana."[18] But it was an agricultural business in an area undergoing rapid economic diversification. It was administered by sheriffs, businessmen, and farmers with political connections at a time when the best penal systems in the nation were being taken over by professional penologists. And despite the fact that most of Angola's convicts had begun to arrive from urban areas, to which they would presumably return upon release, the penitentiary remained in a rural area where it was operated along rural lines by a small, unenlightened, and occasionally vicious group of rural Louisianians. Angola was an economic and sociological anachro-

[15] *Ibid.*, 63; Mouledous, "Sociological Perspectives," 80.

[16] Westbrook Pegler, "Fair Enough," Baton Rouge *State-Times*, July 5, 1951.

[17] State of Louisiana, *Report of the Department of State Civil Service, 1943–1944* (Baton Rouge, 1945), 57; *Department of Civil Service, Annual Report 1962–1963* (Baton Rouge, 1963), 20.

[18] State of Louisiana, *Annual Report of the Department of Institutions, May 15, 1946* (Baton Rouge, 1946), 47. However, the Director, R. L. Pettit, went on to state that Angola "*should* be operated *primarily* for the rehabilitation of the inmates and *secondarily* as a business enterprise." Italics added.

nism, its proper functions repressed by a long history of political conservatism, myopia, and patronage. All of this became undeniably evident in the aftermath of the 1951 heel-slashings.

This debacle should never have happened. Three times during the 1940s Angola was given a thorough going-over by outside experts and other observers. On each occasion opinions ranging from mildly favorable to uniformly unfavorable were expressed. A number of suggestions and specific recommendations were also submitted. The point is that by 1948 (the year in which Earl Long took office as governor) Angola's few strengths and many weaknesses were matters of common and official knowledge. But the ample warnings given were to be largely ignored, as had happened in the past.

Former Warden Lewis E. Lawes of New York's Sing Sing prison inspected Angola in 1943 as an advisor to the War Production Board. While judging Louisiana's penal system as "pretty good" compared with some others he had known, Lawes was concerned about the lack of "rehabilitation" and "vocational" reforms and was "very much impressed" by the fact that the "only men . . . carrying arms" at Angola were the convict-guards. "If we had ever tried that at Sing-Sing," Lawes remarked, "we would probably have had a general break within a few hours." The reasons why the convict-guard system appeared to work well enough at Angola, as Lawes observed it, were that the prisoners chosen to carry weapons exhibited the best "morale" and because the "old-time gangster" element, so large a part of Sing Sing's inmate population, was not to be found in southern agricultural prisons. The former warden concluded his evaluation, however, by recommending nominal incentive pay for prisoners, more trained personnel, and a "better system of prisoner classification" at Angola.[19] In these areas Lawes identified

[19] Quoted in New Orleans *Times-Picayune*, December 11, 1943. At this time, remarkably enough, "none of the [few] paid guards" at Angola carried "pistols or other weapons." Only the trusties were armed. New Orleans *Times-Picayune*, February 15, 1942.

three of the penitentiary's most glaring deficiencies, as it was considered heresy to pay convicts any amount of money for any reason, because Angola's few civilian personnel had received virtually no training at all, and because the classification system that prevailed still concentrated almost exclusively upon levels of physical strength and failed to consider the convict's background, intelligence, or rehabilitative potential. (But why worry about a convict's rehabilitative potential when there was no rehabilitative program to develop it?)

Much more severe in its appraisal of Angola was a committee of Louisianians who visited the penal farm in 1944 at the request and by the authority of Governor Sam H. Jones. They reported that sanitary conditions were "decidedly inadequate," gambling was Angola's only "organized" recreation, flogging on a scale just "short of rank torture" was practiced, "vice conditions" were "almost universal" and separation of convicts according to nature of offense and length of sentence was "practically nonexistent."[20] It was recommended that these conditions be corrected immediately.

Governor Jones, a Lake Charles attorney, left office soon thereafter and was succeeded by another "reform" governor, James H. "Jimmie" Davis, a member of the State Public Service Commission but "doubtless more widely known as 'Singing Jimmie' Davis, composer of the popular song, 'You Are My Sunshine.' "[21]

"We are well aware of the need for improvements at the state penitentiary," admitted Davis in 1945.[22] As proof of his interest in prison reform, the governor had in the meantime asked two federal penologists to conduct exhaustive studies of Louisiana's penal facilities and to make necessary recommendations.[23] The two experts were Joseph W. Sanford, warden of the federal penitentiary in Atlanta, and Charles V. Jenkinson, an engineer with Federal Prison Industries, Inc., of Washington, D.C. Their report, when released

[20] Report of Jones committee, quoted in *ibid.*, May 2, 1944.
[21] Sindler, *Huey Long's Louisiana*, 182.
[22] Quoted in Baton Rouge *State-Times*, August 4, 1945.
[23] New Orleans *Times-Picayune*, May 4, 1946.

in 1946, pointedly indicted "decades of inefficient prison administration" in Louisiana. In terms of personnel standards and procurement the federal penologists found "the present organization of the Louisiana State Penitentiary . . . so inadequate, and in most instances, so unqualified to develop and administer the numerous activities [of an acceptable penal system] that its presence has, of necessity, been discounted in [the report's] discussion of personnel requirements."[24]

Most severely condemned was the thirty-year-old practice of using convict-guards which all Louisiana administrations since that of Governor Pleasant had found to be a wonderful salary-saver. "No prisoner," it was asserted, "can be trusted with weapons, keys or with any authority over the custody and control of others." The employment of convict-guards resulted in the formation of cliques among prisoners, imposed a "brutalizing effect on the morale of the institution," and caused tremendous waste of money and supplies.[25] Sanford and Jenkinson also reported that prison housing facilities were "unsafe, unsanitary, and inadequate," that the water supply was also "inadequate," that "sanitary facilities" were "practically useless," and that educational rehabilitation was "practically non-existent."[26]

Precisely because conditions within Louisiana's penal system were just as bad as the federal penologists had described them, the Davis administration proposed a massive rebuilding and reorientation program, the first major proposals in penal reform since Louisiana had abolished the lease system.

In a communication to the legislature of 1946, the governor suggested that members consider and approve "a far-reaching, long-range program to reform and modernize Louisiana's penitentiary system at a minimum cost of $6,745,000.00 spread

24 State of Louisiana, *Recommendations for Reorganization of the Penitentiary System: A Survey Report by the United States Department of Justice, Bureau of Prisons, and Federal Prison Industries, Inc.* (n.p., n.d.) , 147–48.
25 *Ibid.*, 160.
26 *Ibid.*, 1–3.

over a five-year period."[27] Implementation would have to be "gradual" as "sources of funds [were] not sufficient" to underwrite any accelerated modifications.[28] Davis recommended the following, however, as urgent priority objectives: (1) construction of a modern receiving station and classification center; (2) construction of a new hospital; (3) conversion of the stock farm into "an industrial center to accommodate first offenders"; (4) "removal of women prisoners from Angola"; and (5) diversification of prison industries.[29] All of these improvements had also been given priority status by Sanford and Jenkinson. One other priority recommendation which was not endorsed by Davis was the hiring of 620 qualified civilian employees, to include 285 civilian guards. In 1942 Angola's civilian employees had numbered 84, only 14 of whom had "purely custodial" duties.[30] It is unlikely that many more had been hired by 1946. In these circumstances Davis probably considered it inadvisable to recommend to the legislature that Angola's staff be expanded by 700 percent and converted overnight into a nonpolitical corps of trained professionals. So he suggested instead that civilian guards could be used "on an experimental basis" as soon as the institution for first offenders was completed.[31]

Such were the findings and recommendations of three outside penologists and a number of competent citizens, all of whom visited Angola within a three-year period and during two separate "reform" administrations. By 1948 implementation of the various recommendations, while not negligible, had been far from complete, which had much to do with the shocking status of the penal system exposed by the convict heel-slashings three years later.

Blame for inaction and delay should be placed less upon

[27] Baton Rouge *State-Times*, May 6, 1946.
[28] *Ibid.*
[29] *Ibid.*, also May 8, 1946.
[30] State of Louisiana, *Department of Institutions, Biennium* [sic] *Report for the Period Ending June 30, 1942* (n.p., n.d.), 237.
[31] Quoted in Baton Rouge *State-Times*, May 6, 1946. In effect, Davis had indefinitely postponed reform of Angola's fundamental liability—a staff of unprofessional appointees.

Governor Jones and Governor Davis than upon the penal establishment itself and the legislature, the latter reflecting views of both the political establishment and, to a lesser extent, public opinion. Although the distance from the governor's desk in Baton Rouge to Angola is only sixty miles, this distance might just as well have been measured in light-years insofar as executive orders relating to prison administration were concerned. Two examples may suffice to illustrate the communications gap which separated governors from camp captains during the 1940s.

Quite early in his administration, as a result of the newspaper publicity given to floggings inflicted by Longite officials, Governor Jones ordered an end to the practice "under any conditions whatever."[32] Three years later his own committee discovered that flogging was still carried on, which prompted Governor Davis late in 1944 again to announce that this brutal form of punishment "would not be condoned."[33] But Sanford and Jenkinson discovered evidence in 1946 of recent floggings, and the practice continued into the next decade. A civil service hearing held in 1944 revealed that Angola officials had not bothered to pass the executive orders along to several of their subordinates.[34] (It might have made no difference if they had.)

Opposition to change was not restricted to general managers and wardens, who as political creatures had risen within the status quo and were disposed to retain it. The poor white captains, guards, and other prison employees had "lived an idyllic life" with their families for over a generation along Angola's fertile bottoms and rolling hills. Provided with quarters, supplies, status, and Negro convicts to cook and clean for them, these people enjoyed an existence which "mimicked that of the passing plantation aristocracy."[35] They, too, were opposed to any outside interference which might deprive

[32] Quoted in New Orleans *Times-Picayune*, June 30, 1941.
[33] Quoted in *ibid.*, December 2, 1944.
[34] See "Prison Beatings Aired at Hearing," *ibid.*, October 20, 1944.
[35] Mouledous, "Sociological Perspectives," 80.

them of the physical security and sense of importance afforded them by Angola as they knew it.

It was bad enough that reforms applicable to the penal system, such as the provision in 1900 for a reformatory, might remain unenforced or fail to be implemented over a number of years because of inertia in Baton Rouge. But penal reform could be additionally frustrated in Louisiana simply by failure of the system to "digest" it, because of the threat which reform posed, or seemed to pose, to those within the conservative Angola community.

Enemies of penal reform in Louisiana before 1940 generally clustered near the top, among the governors and legislators. The James concern succeeded in remaining in business for thirty-one years primarily because it was able, through one means or another, to keep enough highly placed political leaders on its side. And although the lessees finally were evicted by other highly placed leaders who opposed them, many of these same officials, in turn, opposed further penal reform in the belief that abolition of the lease, reduction of convict mortality, and establishment of parole were basically sufficient; and that further endeavors toward rehabilitation of convicts and professionalization of the penal staff would be financially disruptive and politically undesirable.

After 1940, however, the center of opposition moved down toward the grass roots level. Most governors, most legislators, and many administrators increasingly favored penal reform (at least to the extent that advocating it would not hurt them in other ways). Legislators and administrators who continued to oppose penal reform, either because reform cost too much or because an unprofessionalized Angola was a better vehicle of patronage, acquired valuable allies among personnel within the penal system itself, residents of the area surrounding and servicing Angola, and any others whose interests would be served best by keeping Angola as it was. Among the last have been taxpayers who, in spite of the shocking conditions revealed within the penal system during the 1940s and 1950s, have continued to grumble about lavishing on convicts money which could be utilized to better advantage on roads, schools, welfare, or some other preferable service.

By 1948 those in favor of reform had managed to obtain enough money to construct a $1,400,000 prison hospital, a $100,000 camp for female prisoners, and some minor repairs.[36] But in all other areas reform was blunted. Educational and other rehabilitative programs were not instituted. Separation and classification of convicts were not modernized. Revenue continued to be derived chiefly from farm products cultivated and processed by obsolete methods. Worst of all, the old personnel remained in charge at Angola. Camp captains and their odious retinues went on brutalizing convicts until the worst prison scandal in modern Louisiana history erupted.

Earl Kemp Long had been elected lieutenant governor in 1936 on the Leche ticket. Rising to the governorship following Leche's resignation in 1939, Long attempted to secure a full term in his own right at the 1940 election, but was defeated by Sam Jones.[37] The Long faction denied Earl the nomination in 1944—perhaps unwisely, because the relative unknown whom they selected lost to Jimmie Davis. Four years later, however, "Ole Earl" roared out of retirement to bury his enemy, former Governor Jones, under 66 percent of the vote.[38] The success of Long's campaign, according to a per-

[36] State of Louisiana, *Biennial Report of the Department of Institutions, July 1, 1945 to June 30, 1947 (Partly supplemented to March 15, 1948)* (Baton Rouge, 1948), 16; Baton Rouge *State-Times*, December 30, 1947.

[37] During the campaign Long described Jones as "High Hat Sam, the High Society Kid, the High-Kicking, High and Mighty Snide Sam, the guy that pumps perfume under his arms." Quoted in V. O. Key, *Southern Politics in State and Nation* (New York, 1949), 167. This is a choice example of the platform rhetoric that endeared Long to many, if not all, of Louisiana's voters from 1940 to 1960.

[38] Sindler, *Huey Long's Louisiana*, 205. A satisfactory biography of Earl Long has yet to be written. Richard McCaughan, *Socks on a Rooster: Louisiana's Earl K. Long* (Baton Rouge, 1967), is recent enough but is too narrowly documented and lacks sufficient analysis. Stan Opotowsky, *The Longs of Louisiana* (New York, 1960), and Thomas Martin, *Dynasty: The Longs of Louisiana* (New York, 1960), provide interesting reading. A. J. Liebling, *The Earl of Louisiana* (New York, 1961) is a

ceptive authority, was achieved by condemning "the Jones-Davis administrations as 'do-nothing,' " and by promising "pie in the sky for all."[39] Once in office Long proceeded to build more roads and schools, raise teachers' salaries, old-age pensions, and homestead exemptions, pay bonuses to veterans—and increase overall state taxes by 50 percent.[40]

The penal system was not to be denied its slice, however thin compared with chunks received by other agencies, of Long's abundant pie. Angola's general appropriation for 1948–1949 was almost $500,000 more than the last preceding appropriation under Davis,[41] while an additional sum of $2,000,000 for the biennium 1948–1950 was dedicated to construction of staff housing facilities and improvement of drainage, sewerage, and the power and water systems.[42] In 1950 another separate appropriation of $332,000 was earmarked for construction, improvements, and levee repair. Act 350 of this same year established the "state use" system in Louisiana, which made it illegal for the penitentiary to sell on the open market any products, except its abundant sugar crop and surplus vegetables. On the other hand, state agencies were required to purchase as many of their supplies as possible from the penal system. This worthy statute hushed the last protests of organized labor against competition with convicts, provided the penal system with guaranteed customers, and stimulated further diversification of prison industries.[43]

Nor was the convict himself altogether forgotten. For a

shrewd yet sympathetic treatment of Long by one of America's great journalists of the mid-twentieth century.

[39] Sindler, *Huey Long's Louisiana*, 200.   [40] *Ibid.*, 200, 214.

[41] State of Louisiana, *Executive Budget for the biennium 1948–1950, submitted to the Legislature by Earl K. Long, Governor of Louisiana* (Baton Rouge, 1948), 154; *Executive Budget* (July 1, 1950 to June 30, 1952), 101. Much of this money was used to pay the many followers whom Long put on Angola's staff during his administration. See Baton Rouge *State-Times*, March 14, 1951; and New Orleans *Times-Picayune*, March 15, 1951.

[42] State of Louisiana, *Acts Passed by the Legislature at the Regular Session, 1948* (Baton Rouge, 1949), 573. Published legislative actions are hereinafter cited as *Acts of Louisiana*, with appropriate year indicated.

[43] *Acts of Louisiana* (1950), 457–58; 584–87.

brief period of about two years, Angola actually attempted to establish a rehabilitation program. This effort seems to have been initiated, however, without Long's blessing and possibly even without his knowledge.

Long's first superintendent at Angola was Rollo C. Lawrence, former mayor of Pineville, a small town in Central Louisiana not far from the governor's "pea-patch" at Winnfield.[44] Like all of his predecessors at Angola in that he was a politician rather than a penologist, Lawrence nonetheless was different in one crucial respect—he viewed rehabilitation of convicts as Angola's most important obligation, and by 1949 he was making a "small dent" in what had been Angola's "mountainous problem" for decades.[45] Working under the superintendent as director of rehabilitation was none other than Angola's best-educated former inmate, James M. Smith. Lawrence and Smith both believed that Angola should make "an honest effort" to "fit prisoners, particularly first offenders" into a legitimate and remunerative occupation that could be pursued following release from prison. The "great weakness" of southern penal farms, as seen by these two exceptional men, was that "incarcerating offenders" and using them "merely to labor" all too often comprised the only objectives and purposes of the institutions.[46] Both men were determined to make Angola do more than that.

But several formidable obstacles lay in the path of making rehabilitation at Angola a productive reality. In addition to

[44] Act 252 of 1944 (Davis) abolished the positions of general manager and warden which had coexisted, with increased friction between the occupants, since Fuqua's time. Both positions were combined, in the interests of efficiency, under the single title, "Superintendent." But in 1950 Long's legislature (for patronage reasons) re-created the position of warden, and thus restored the squabbles and confusion of divided authority to Angola.

[45] Margaret Dixon, "Behind the Big Gates," Baton Rouge *Morning Advocate*, February 6, 1949. Late managing editor of the *Morning Advocate*, a former member of the Board of Supervisors of Louisiana State University and of Governor Earl K. Long's Citizens' Committee which investigated Angola in 1951, Mrs. Dixon was among Louisiana's most dedicated and influential penal reformers in recent years.   [46] *Ibid.*

cost and official disfavor from above, there was the sacrosanct sugar cane crop, which demanded all year long the "time and energies of most of the . . . prisoners as well as . . . the [prison] authorities.'" Lawrence and Smith would have liked to deemphasize cane cultivation enough to release some of the convicts for other forms of more rehabilitative work: even by 1949 the need for cane-cutters in the labor market was nominal. Nonetheless, at Angola "the cane crop [was] traditional," and "breaking tradition" at Angola was, to say the least, "sometimes a hard job."[47]

But the superintendent and the rehabilitation director did what they could without breaking tradition altogether. "Doc" Smith served as a one-man classification department, interviewing each new convict regarding background, family life, and level of schooling. Lawrence took as many men as could be spared from the cane fields and put them on construction projects where they could acquire a "working knowledge of carpentry and ditch-digging." Any convict with an "aptitude for office work" was thus utilized; before long "practically all of Angola's book work" was performed by inmates.[48] As the prison population increased, and as bureaucratic procedures correspondingly multiplied, additional convicts were added to the administrative staff. During and after the heel-slashing scandals, it was frequently charged that between the convict-guards and the "convict-clerks," Angola was in fact being operated entirely by convicts.

The more positive of these meager efforts at rehabilitation began to evaporate following the death of Smith (who was not replaced) in June of 1949.[49] In 1950 Governor Long's appointee to the newly re-created position of warden was Rudolf Easterly, a state senator from rural Livingston Parish.[50] Easterly, who was selected because Long considered him

47 *Ibid.*

48 *Ibid.* Some of Angola's "white collar" convicts later embarrassed the penal system when they were caught selling early releases to fellow inmates. This "service" was performed by altering inmate records. See Baton Rouge *Morning Advocate*, August 4, 1955.

49 For an editorial praising Smith's efforts, see *ibid.*, June 22, 1949.

50 See note 43 above.

to be "a most thoroughly capable farmer, business man and
law enforcement officer," seems to have been the exact opposite in temperament to Superintendent Lawrence, his
superior at Angola, who was described (also by Long) as
being "at times, too kind and too considerate."[51] Lawrence
and Easterly did not work well together.[52] Six months after
the latter assumed his duties, the heel-slashings commenced.

During the latter half of February, 1951, a released prisoner
disclosed to newsmen that a number of convicts at Angola
had each cut one of their heel tendons "to avoid hard work
in the fields and further punishment by guards and other
prison personnel."[53] When asked to clarify the situation,
prison officials admitted that thirty-one convicts had slashed
their heel tendons with razor blades, but denied that brutal
treatment had taken place. Soon afterward ten of the heel-
slashers cut their other tendon as well. All of these men
were from Camp "E," the barracks for "un-cooperative" white
convicts. On February 27 six men from an area set aside for
white first offenders, Camp "H," mutilated themselves in the
same manner.[54] By that time, Angola was swarming with
reporters while across the state editors of major newspapers
were demanding that Governor Long authorize a full and
immediate official inquiry.[55] Not since the 1880s, when the
deserved target of their criticism was lessee James, had Louisiana's press been so concerned with operation of the penal
system.

Governor Long was not in tune with this movement nor
with the torrent of public opinion it was mobilizing. However progressive, up-to-date, or even liberal he may have been
in terms of political acumen and public services, Long's assessment of Angola's troubles was twenty years behind the times.

[51] Quoted in New Orleans *Time-Picayune*, February 27, 1951; see also
Baton Rouge *State-Times*, March 7, 1951.

[52] During an investigation of the heel-slashings, Easterly was asked
about the division of authority between Superintendent Lawrence and
himself. He replied "not even the Lord can straighten it out the way it
is." Quoted in New Orleans *Times-Picayune*, March 9, 1951.

[53] *Ibid.*, February 26, 1951.   [54] *Ibid.*, February 28, 1951.

[55] *Ibid.*, February 27, 1951.

Among the first to be informed of the heel-slashings, "Ole Earl" went to the penal farm immediately and personally conducted his own investigation, some time, in fact, before the self-mutilations became public knowledge. Thus, when the storm broke, Long was ready, on February 26, with a prepared statement demonstrating his loss of contact with reality. "If the present efficient leadership at Angola is left alone," he maintained, "Angola will be on a paying basis before I leave office or shortly afterwards, instead of a cancer or headache on state finances as it has been in the past."[56] He was virtually echoing brother Huey's assurances, uttered in 1930, on the occasion of the discovery of fiscal mismanagement at Angola by a committee of the state senate. Like his elder brother, he dreaded a scandal at the penal farm. And, for both Longs, scandal meant publicized financial chaos. But it was no longer 1930. The depression had long since vanished. A wartime boom had lifted Louisiana, and much of the South, from the mire of economic stagnation. Angola's occasional deficits had lost much, if not all, of their traditional sting. In any event, putting Angola on a paying basis was certainly not the issue posed by the convict heel-slashings. The unprecedented barbarism of Hitler's "prison camps" had only recently been exposed in horrifying detail; it had become much more difficult for an informed public to condone brutalization of people behind walls or fences, even if these people were convicted felons. When the thirty-seven Angola convicts focused public attention on themselves by self-mutilation, enough Louisianians, in and out of public life, were ready to inaugurate the most revolutionary and ambitious program of penal reform in the state's history. Governor Long had no choice, for the moment, but to swim with the tide.

Bowing to pressure from press and public, Long quickly appointed a thirty-four-member Citizens' Committee to investigate Angola.[57] During his address to the group at its

[56] Quoted in *ibid.*
[57] Two members were Negroes. The rest were judges, law enforcement

organization meeting in Baton Rouge, the governor promised
that he would try to carry out the committee's recommendations, "provided, of course, the money and materials are
available."[58] When questioned about his own fiscal objectives
for the penal system, Long emphasized that he did not want
to "make money at Angola," but desired only to place the
system on "a self-sustaining basis."[59] Both General Manager
Lawrence and Warden Easterly were present in Baton Rouge
to meet the committee. Easterly urged that the group disre-
gard his feelings, make an honest investigation, and recommend a new warden if they believed the step necessary since
"I (Easterly) really don't want this job."[60] Lawrence stated
that his own investigations had revealed only two cases of
"striking or whipping" and that in both episodes prison personnel had "acted in self-defense."[61]

A member of the committee, E. W. Stagg, Baton Rouge
correspondent for the New Orleans *Item,* suggested that the
group refrain from making "any detailed study" of the penal
system, as several had been recently conducted during the
1940s, the findings and recommendations of which were "just
as good [in 1951] as when they were made." Instead, the
committee should seek to answer the following specific questions: "(1) Was there mistreatment? (2) What [was] the overall treatment? (3) What [was] the philosophy for handling
prisoners at Angola? (4) How well [did] administration operate—with two officials (warden and superintendent) both
seeming to have general authority?"[62] Before embarking by
car for Angola, the committee heard Warden Easterly caution
them against viewing the convicts with "tender hearts." He
urged, "Please look at them with firm minds, because some of
them are hardened criminals and must be dealt with with a
firm hand."[63]

Among the hardened criminals at Angola in 1951 was Wil-

officers, and members of the press. A partial list of committee members
may be found in he Baton Rouge *State-Times,* March 7, 1951.

[58] Quoted in *ibid.*   [59] Quoted in *ibid.*
[60] Quoted in *ibid.*   [61] Quoted in *ibid.*
[62] Quoted in *ibid.*   [63] Quoted in *ibid.*

bur "Blackie" Comeaux, twenty-eight, a fourth offender whose activities had included car theft, narcotics peddling, and murder. Interviewed by reporters shortly before Long's committee arrived at the penal farm, Comeaux gave a lengthy résumé of the prison's ills. He blamed Warden Easterly for turning Angola into a place that "ain't fit for hogs." Sexual perverts were not segregated, according to Comeaux, but were mixed indiscriminately with other prisoners. Captains and other employees ate the inmates' meat ration, leaving only "bones and scraps for the cons." Beatings were administered often and frequently without sufficient reason. Comeaux himself claimed to have been whipped with a wet rope once simply because he "laughed at another prisoner." The prison was a "mad house," in its worst condition since 1940, except that in former days "the food was okay and there was a clean place to sleep."[64]

The most comprehensive, authoritative, and lacerating denunciation of Louisiana's penal system heard in many years came on March 8, when Long's committee interviewed at Angola Mrs. Mary M. Daugherty, an outspoken native of Ireland who had been the penal farm's registered nurse for almost eight years. Angola was a "sewer of degradation," she declared, where "sex offenders, stool pigeons, homosexuals," and "degenerates of every type" were "huddled in bedside companionship with the new arrivals."[65] Whippings and beatings were common, she went on to state, but the "real brutality" at Angola was the "complete lack of rehabilitation." Mrs. Daugherty had seen almost seven thousand men discharged from Angola during her tenure, and not one of them was

[64] Quoted in New Orleans *Time-Picayune*, February 28, 1951. The heel-slashers and prisoners such as Comeaux, according to Warden Easterly, would "do anything to get their names in the [news]paper." Quoted in New Orleans *Times-Picayune*, February 27, 1951.

[65] Quoted in *ibid.*, March 9, 1951. Several days earlier Easterly himself had testified that "lack of facilities" was a grave problem at Angola. "We don't have any place to segregate [troublemakers]. We just have to put them in there with the others and hope for the best," he said. Quoted in New Orleans *Times-Picayune*, February 27, 1951.

"as qualified to enter society as he was the day he was admitted."[66]

Politics was the underlying cause of Angola's demoralization, according to the nurse. Brutality of all kinds would continue so long as Angola remained a "political football and dumping grounds for the state of Louisiana." Patronage was rife at Angola. "Very few . . . employees," Mrs. Daugherty charged, "are qualified for their positions; the remainder are small-time politicians to whom a political position is owed and who for the most part are unable to hold any other legitimate job for the state."[67]

One week later *Times-Picayune* reporters gained access to Angola's personnel files where they found much to substantiate Mrs. Daugherty's allegations. Two letters of recommendation for individuals employed by the penal system contained the following remarks: One letter requested, "Please see that this man gets a few days off because there are some people I want him to contact in behalf of [United States Senator] Russell Long." The other stated, "This has been Earl Long's man for many years and has been a consistent worker to help return the Long government to Louisiana."[68]

Authors of these letters were, for the most part, legislators, but included sheriffs, other officials, and Governor Long himself. Political patronage had always been present at Angola, and Earl Long's administration was neither the first (nor the last) to utilize the penal system as a dumping ground for those to whom governors were obligated—or wished to exile. But not until 1951—a full half-century after resumption of state control from lessee James—were the deleterious effects

---

[66] Quoted in *ibid.*, March 9, 1951. Well in advance of her testimony, Warden Easterly had asked the governor to fire Mrs. Daugherty. Long refused, stating "that would be the worst thing to do at [this] time." Quoted in New Orleans *Times-Picayune*, March 15, 1951.

[67] Quoted in *ibid.* In order to avoid giving Warden Easterly "the pleasure of firing" her, Mrs. Daugherty resigned from the Angola staff on April 3, 1951. She described Easterly in her letter of resignation as an "arrogant, uncouth, narrow-minded, unprincipled bigot." Quoted in Baton Rouge *State-Times*, April 3, 1951.

[68] Quoted in New Orleans *Times-Picayune*, March 13, 1951.

of patronage on Louisiana's penal system so bluntly indicted and widely advertised. Even Warden Easterly felt compelled to join the chorus of critics. On March 16 he admitted "when some of the free personnel are sent to us by outsiders—politicians—you don't know who you'll get."[69]

The Citizens' Committee devoted a full month to a thorough investigation of Angola, spending most of this time at the penal farm itself inspecting facilities, camps, and barracks and interviewing administrators, captains, guards, and convicts. On April 20, 1951, the committee released its report to the press.

Stating that it "appeared conclusively that the 'heel slashing' was the result of physical brutality" inflicted upon convicts, the report observed that "the practice of brutality was established beyond question" on several levels—"physical, mental, emotional, and moral."[70] Significantly, the committee expressed its belief that "human lives and law enforcement can not be measured in dollars and cents," a long-overdue, but nonetheless revolutionary, conception of penal policy in Louisiana.

It was generally recommended that the Sanford-Jenkinson survey of 1946 be followed as a guideline for reorganizing the system; among the twenty recommendations of the committee, the following six reiterated most of the priorities of the earlier report: (1) establishment of a comprehensive program of convict rehabilitation to include "classification for vocational training, educational opportunities and post-penal supervision"; (2) a "qualified penologist free from political influence" to be in complete charge of the penal system; (3) abolition of corporal punishment and solitary incarcerations in "dungeons"; (4) a merit system for hired personnel; (5) segregation of first offenders, "incorrigibles, perverts, and

[69] Quoted in Baton Rouge *State-Times*, March 16, 1951. The director of the Federal Bureau of Prisons, James V. Bennett, remarked during a New Orleans address that Angola's "basic trouble" arose from "political appointees to the prison staff." Quoted in Baton Rouge *State-Times*, May 25, 1951.

[70] Report of Citizens' Committee, quoted in New Orleans *Times-Picayune*, April 20, 1951.

other abnormal inmates" from the general prison population, and (6) removal of the woman's camp from Angola.[71]

Two members of the committee vocally dissented from the majority view. D. D. Bazer had been Angola's warden from 1940 to 1948 during both the Jones and Davis administrations. Having somehow ingratiated himself with Governor Long, Bazer would be returned to Angola as Easterly's deputy in May, 1951. Bazer indentified himself as a thorough traditionalist when he stated as his prognosis for the committee's recommendations, "You don't expect the governor [Long] to accept all of this?"[72] The other dissident was Colonel E. P. Roy, head of the state police, who together with Bazer emphatically opposed a recommendation to substitute paid guards for convict-guards. Both men thought the expense involved would be too great and Roy added that the change would "never be carried out."[73]

Twice within five years the Louisiana penal system had been rigorously examined and found seriously deficient in the areas of personnel procurement, treatment, and rehabilitation. "Outsiders" made the first appraisal, a fact that rendered its conclusions more vulnerable than those of the second, which followed in the wake of an embarrassing scandal and was rendered by prominent and influential Louisianians. That a sizable portion of Governor Long's Citizens' Committee consisted of journalists was also important. These individuals imposed their influence on subsequent developments by keeping Angola on the front page until major reforms were initiated.[74]

[71] *Ibid.* Female prisoners were eventually transferred in 1961 to the St. Gabriel camp, where they remain in overcrowded and uniformly unsatisfactory quarters at this writing. See Baton Rouge *State-Times*, June 20, 1961.

[72] Quoted in New Orleans *Times-Picayune*, April 20, 1951. Perhaps Long was comforted by Bazer's loyalty to the old ways and hoped that the latter's presence on the committee and later on the prison staff itself would exert a stabilizing influence.   [73] Quoted in *ibid.*

[74] The power of the press was vividly credited, in a negative way, when Associate Warden Bazer barred newsmen from Angola on May 30, 1951. This ban remained in effect until the following year, after a change

But no major reforms took place under the Long administration, which had less than a year to run. Superintendent Rollo Lawrence resigned (possibly under pressure), effective May 31. This would have been an opportune time for Governor Long to demonstrate his commitment to penal reform by appointing a "qualified penologist free from political influence" to supervise Angola. Long thought otherwise. Professing his conviction that "Louisiana citizens would never stand for an out-of-state prison head," the governor instead appointed Warden Rudolph Easterly to succeed Lawrence "in full charge" of the penal system.[75] (Under the circumstances, this nomination was akin to rewarding a company president who had run the enterprise into bankruptcy, with the board chairmanship.) As a "successful businessman and former sheriff," however, Easterly evidently continued to retain Long's approval and confidence.[76] Six months later Easterly himself resigned to assume management of a Ford dealership in the town of Denham Springs. He was succeeded by L. H. Mulina, ex-sheriff of rural Washington Parish and a former parole officer.[77]

Continuity of administrative personnel was reflected in piecemeal legislation during the last months of Long's administration. While the legislature of 1951 provided $695,000 for construction and repairs at Angola, nothing was done to implement the fundamental reorientation of penal policy recommended by the governor's committee.[78]

Each individual or group critical of the penal system after 1940 took care not to condemn the incumbent administration. Sanford and Jenkinson spoke of "decades" of mismanagement

in administration had taken place. See Baton Rouge *State-Times*, May 30, 1951; and Baton Rouge *Morning Advocate*, July 17, 1952.

[75] Quoted in Baton Rouge *State-Times*, May 21, 1951.

[76] Quoted in *ibid.*

[77] New Orleans *Times-Picayune*, November 14, 1951.

[78] *Ibid.*, June 29, 1951. A "20-point program" for improving Angola was proposed on October 16, 1951, by Long's attorney general, Bolivar E. Kemp. Governor Long had not authorized the survey on which the proposals were based and thus nothing came of them. Long and Kemp were politically at odds at the time.

in their report submitted to Governor Davis in 1946. Long's committee of 1951 blamed nothing less than the "people of Louisiana"[79] for conditions at Angola, while Earl himself has since been virtually absolved of responsibility by a scholar who viewed him as "no more guilty of poor prison direction than . . . his predecessors."[80] The faults of Angola were indeed cumulative, perpetrated or extended as they were by every gubernatorial administration since the time of W. W. Heard. And behind official indifference, avarice, and neglect lay a vast reservoir of public ignorance and apathy. But between 1901 and 1952 there were relatively good times and relatively bad times at Angola. And available evidence strongly indicates that times were worse while Longite administrations were in power.

Both Longs, Huey and Earl, arose from and spoke for what might be characterized today as the "lower-white-middle-class-law-and-order" element. Such people are, apparently, more disposed to have convicted criminals punished than to have them "rehabilitated," a term which can be easily and erroneously translated into "coddled." And as recipients of modest, hard-earned incomes, those who spoke and responded to the Long idiom during the 1930s and 1940s could have resented the use of their tax money for suspected schemes of convict coddling especially when large numbers of Negroes might be involved. And, finally, whether led in combat by Huey or Earl, the Longite rank and file maintained a voracious appetite for public employment which demanded, and received, satiation following every victory at the polls.[81]

While fiscally "liberal," therefore, when supporting programs benefiting law abiding Louisianians, Longites were

[79] Committee report, quoted in *ibid.*, April 20, 1951. Perhaps this communal indictment was what inspired Westbrook Pegler to brand the committee as "gutless" and "timid," and its report "pallid" and "quavering." See "Fair Enough," Baton Rouge *State-Times*, July 4, 1951.

[80] Sindler, *Huey Long's Louisiana*, 236.

[81] State civil service was alternately opposed and undermined by the Longites up until it became a fairly viable fact of life in the 1950s.

ultra-conservative, fiscally and politically, in terms of convict rehabilitation and professionalization of the penal service. And if patronage had always affected Angola for the worse under any administration, Longite administrations with their patronage excesses, prior to 1952, produced Louisiana's most inept and brutal penal regimes since the turn of the century.

Angola, the "sewer of degradation," figured prominently in the 1952 gubernatorial campaign. Each of the eight principal candidates promised to appoint a "trained penologist to revamp the administration of Louisiana's penal system."[82] (Among these was the Longite candidate, Judge Carlos G. Spaht of Baton Rouge.) Not since the 1880s had penal reform been such a hot political issue in Louisiana, and not since 1901 had the old ways—patronage, fiscal conservatism, and brutality—seemed to be up against such adverse circumstances.

Conditions at Angola, however, exposed only one aspect of Long's vulnerable and increasingly unpopular regime. While few Louisianians disparaged the comprehensive benefits provided by "Ole Earl," the higher taxes enacted to pay for them soon became a source of widespread resentment. In addition, both the honesty and efficiency of Longite administrators was, by 1951, open to serious question—especially at Angola.[83] Consequently, a popular desire for reform was again in the air; the beneficiary of this sentiment in 1952 was Robert F. Kennon of Minden, also a judge, who was elected governor of Louisiana over the Longite judge, Spaht.[84]

Angola stood high on Kennon's priority list. Immediately following his inauguration he informed the state's hospital board, under whose supervision Angola was then administered, that "the employment of a competent penologist . . . is your No. 1 job." Suspending patronage, the governor further in-

[82] Sindler, *Huey Long's Louisiana*, 236.

[83] In later years Long stated his belief that "the Angola situation was one reason for Spaht's poor showing in the [1952] governor's race." Quoted in New Orleans *Times-Picayune*, March 5, 1958.

[84] Kennon was no political neophyte, having run unsuccessfully in 1948 for both the governorship and the United States Senate.

formed the group that there had not been "a single commitment made regarding jobs at Angola." The board was to receive the penal system "free of strings."[85]

Early in May, 1952, a professional penologist from out of
state was invited to inspect Louisiana's penal system. This
man was Reed Cozart, at that time director of the United
States Correctional Institute at Seagoville, Texas. Cozart went
to Angola, surveyed its operations, and submitted to the governor a "12-point program of sweeping reforms for the oft-
troubled prison."[86] Shortly thereafter, Cozart was appointed
superintendent of Angola on a leave-of-absence basis from
the federal prison service, to which he would soon return after
having initiated basic and much-needed reforms in Louisiana.
Cozart, who took over on June 17, brought to Angola during
his tenure a team of federal penologists who, as successive
wardens, continued to operate Louisiana's penal system for
more than a decade.

In the meantime, Governor Kennon had taken the case
for penal reform before the 1952 legislature, which responded
with unprecedented financial generosity. Angola's operating
budget for 1952-1953 was increased by $700,000 over the pre-
ceding Longite appropriation. A separate sum of $250,000
was provided to pay additional civilian guards. Most significantly, a $4,000,000 bond issue was authorized to finance
construction and improvements at Angola.[87] During this same
session, the penal system, together with the various correctional facilities for juveniles, was placed under a newly
created Board of Institutions, the membership of which,
though appointed by the governor, was conceived to be non-
political. In 1953 the board received another $4,000,000 for
capital outlay and equipment.[88] Most of this money was
subsequently spent on Angola. In 1954, midway through Ken-

[85] Quoted in New Orleans *Times-Picayune*, May 28, 1952.
[86] *Ibid.*   [87] *Acts of Louisiana* (1952), 684, 837.
[88] *Ibid.*, 362; *Acts of Louisiana* (1954, with extra sessions of 1953), 15.

non's term, a separate correctional institution for first offenders was at last authorized.[89]

Within two years the penal system had received almost
$8,000,000 with which to rebuild and reorganize itself, and
a definite commitment had been made to curtail the use
of convict-guards. Separation of first offenders was on its way
toward becoming a meaningful reality in Louisiana—more
than fifty years after this basic ingredient of penal reform
had initially been urged by the Prison Reform Association.
Finally, those in direct charge of implementing these massive
building programs and innovations would not be sheriffs,
planters, businessmen, or politicians, but penologists—the first
to operate Louisiana's penal system since 1835.

Among the initial steps taken by Cozart and Warden Sam
Anderson was to readmit the press to Angola, thus lifting the
"iron curtain" imposed by Associate Warden Bazer one year
earlier.[90] Nothing remained to be hidden at Angola, according to a *Times-Picayune* reporter, "except the wreckage of
years of brutality, misrule, and neglect."[91] Cozart and Anderson envisioned a new Angola in which flogging as punishment would be replaced by deprivation of privileges, convict-
guards by trained civilians, political appointees by an expanded professional staff, and money-making for its own sake
by rehabilitation. In order for any of these objectives to be
realized, the "principle of segregation" would have to be
applied as soon as possible, the convicts divided accordingly
into three categories: (1) incorrigibles; (2) those "occasionally
but not continuously turbulent and obstructive"; and (3) the
"majority" who would "conform to the rules, serve a minimum sentence . . . and get out on parole at the earliest pos-

[89] *Acts of Louisiana* (1954), 1278. This facility, located at DeQuincy
in western Louisiana, was not ready for occupancy until 1958.
[90] New Orleans *Times-Picayune*, July 20, 1952; Baton Rouge *Morning
Advocate*, July 17, 1952. Members of the Cozart team continued to cultivate, and to receive, favorable treatment from the press.
[91] New Orleans *Times-Picayune*, July 20, 1952.

sible moment."[92] Grouping of inmates along these lines neces-
sitated, in turn, the early establishment of a sound system
of prisoner classification, so that each new arrival could be
examined, categorized, and placed in an appropriate job and
residence.

Warden Anderson saw nothing "novel" in the "procedures
and routines" he and Cozart planned to implement at Angola.
They were "in effect in well managed penal institutions
everywhere" and there was no reason, in Anderson's opinion,
why they should be "unworkable in Louisiana."[93] No reason
except, perhaps, that many Louisianians had long been accustomed to a prison operated along entirely different lines,
with different relations between staff and inmates, and with
different objectives in mind. Speaking of the Cozart team
in terms of the difficulties they encountered in Louisiana,
a reliable authority recently observed that "these Federal
men had been trained in a highly bureaucratic system in
which relations between prison officials and inmates were
formal and impersonal. They were accustomed to rules and
regulations which covered virtually every possible situation."[94]

Such a background, closely resembling the military, ill-
equipped Cozart and his colleagues to adjust readily to
Angola's traditional patterns which were "characterized by
familiarity and mutual cooperation between selected inmates
and officials, brutality, a dominant goal of profit based on the
widely accepted virtue of hard labor . . . and close ties with
citizens and elected officials in the immediate area [of
Angola]."[95] The "procedures and routines" of the federal men
did not prove to be totally unworkable in Louisiana. But
neither were they accepted undiluted nor without criticism
or opposition. To have expected an immediate and thorough

[92] *Ibid.*

[93] Quoted in *ibid.* Anderson resigned in December of 1952 to return
to federal service. He was succeeded as warden by Maurice Sigler, another of Cozart's out-of-state professionals. Baton Rouge *State-Times*,
December 26, 1952.

[94] Mouledous, "Sociological Perspectives," 119–20.   [95] *Ibid.*

revolution in Louisiana's penal policy would have been optimistic in the extreme. Warden Anderson himself remarked soon after his arrival that Angola "didn't get this way overnight" and could not "be cleaned up in a day."[96] Probably without realizing it, Anderson had hit upon a theme which has persistently affected penal reform in Louisiana from that day until the present—a grudging and sometimes successful rear-guard action by the forces of local tradition against the encroaching professional systems and theories of outsiders.

Initial progress was predictably slow. One year after Cozart's arrival, morale among the convicts had improved, although physically Angola remained largely the same.[97] "Leather bats" and "hickory sticks," long utilized in beating the prisoners, were gone, as were many of the old employees, who had been weeded out by a combination of retirements, resignations, and outright dismissals. Many convict-guards remained on the scene, however, and the "model prison goal" was "still a long way off."[98] Construction of a modern complex of segregated dormitories and cell blocks (designed to replace the scattered and crowded camps) was nonetheless under way. The near completion of this critical facility late in 1955 greatly assisted implementation of other reforms.

But before this milestone in Louisiana penal history was reached, Reed Cozart returned in July, 1955, to the federal prison service in time for retirement.[99] On the eve of his departure, after about three years in Louisiana, Cozart submitted a special report in which he summarized changes made at Angola since 1952. Progress in construction of the new housing facilities was reviewed. Improved convict morale was cited, as was the initiation of "other types of penalties" instead of flogging as a means of punishment. Cozart spoke at length of the professional staff he had recruited, many of whom were "University-trained in special fields." With these people in mind, Cozart pleaded that politics "stay away from the peni-

[96] Quoted in New Orleans *Times-Picayune*, July 20, 1952.
[97] Baton Rouge *State-Times*, June 30, 1953.
[98] *Ibid.*   [99] *Ibid.*, July 20, 1955.

tentiary."[100] Angola, he cautiously asserted, had as yet only "the makings of a real treatment and rehabilitation program." The "true value of the new penitentiary" would be realized only "in the years to come."[101] The New Orleans *Times-Picayune*, for many years a stanch supporter of penal reform, observed editorially that "Louisiana could not have obtained a better man for the job" than Cozart. But, the paper went on, "a dozen Cozarts [would] not suffice to carry on the program" without the continued support of both the people and future governors of the state.[102]

On November 28, 1955, the new Angola was formally dedicated in ceremonies attended by Governor Kennon, Cozart, other dignitaries, and about a thousand visitors. "We now have the buildings," declared Warden Maurice Sigler, one of Cozart's protégés, "but the buildings are only the beginning."[103] Kennon described the event as "the achievement of one of [his] primary objectives as governor of Louisiana," while Cozart warned that "things can get bad here and fast if the people of Louisiana take too much for granted." Cozart implored both citizens and press to "keep the prison officials on their toes."[104]

The uneasy caveats expressed by Cozart and the press were not without foundation. As the gubernatorial election of 1956 approached, and with it an inevitable change of administrations, prison traditionalists began to speak out boldly and loudly. Two months before the dedication ceremonies, an exceptionally sharp encounter between some of these in-

[100] *Ibid.*

[101] Quoted in *ibid*. The *Morning Advocate*, while lauding Cozart, agreed that "the treatment and rehabilitation programs yet have a good way to go." Baton Rouge *Morning Advocate*, July 23, 1955.

[102] New Orleans *Times-Picayune*, July 26, 1955.

[103] Quoted in Baton Rouge *Morning Advocate*, November 29, 1955.

[104] Quoted in *ibid*. One month earlier Cozart had stated in an interview that "the present philosophy will be so implanted in career personnel that the Louisiana penitentiary will continue its progress regardless of political changes." Back in Louisiana during an election year, Cozart had moderated his optimism by November. See *Saturday Evening Post*, October 8, 1955, p. 122.

dividuals and two officials of the administration had taken place in St. Francisville, seat of the parish in which Angola is located.

An organization calling itself the West Feliciana Parish Citizens Committee had been formed in 1953 "to protest a rash of escapes from Angola." Despite the fact that escapes and attempts to escape had declined from 102 in that year to 14 during the first half of 1955,[105] the committee assembled on September 28, 1955, ostensibly to discuss the problem of security at the penal farm. Both the director of institutions, Dr. Edward Grant, and Governor Kennon's executive counsel, Wilbur Lunn, were invited to attend and did so.

It was apparent at the outset that committee chairman Ed Percy had matters on his mind other than prison security. "You are here," he told Grant and Lunn, "to listen to what we have to say. We are not interested in any more high falutin' talk about policy."[106] Percy next affirmed that the interests of both the state and of Angola would be best served if Governor Kennon were to "fire" Director Grant, Warden Sigler, and several other specified officials at Angola. "Morale" at Angola was low, according to Percy, because "these out-of-state people have been brought in here and placed over Louisiana people."[107] Two state senators, neither of whom represented West Feliciana Parish, were also present at the meeting and voiced criticism of Angola's administration. Politics, patronage, and Angola were still close bedfellows.

One week later West Feliciana's sheriff, T. H. "Teddy" Martin, gave a remarkable interview to a reporter for the New Orleans *Item*. Martin had been a member, for a while, of Governor Long's Citizens' Committee, but resigned when the committee began to investigate Angola thoroughly. As told to the *Item*, Martin regarded Angola as "a damn playhouse" where the "damn convicts [were] running the peni-

---

[105] Baton Rouge *State-Times*, July 20, 1955.
[106] Quoted in Baton Rouge *Morning Advocate*, September 29, 1955.
[107] Quoted in *ibid.*

tentiary."[108] What did Martin think of convict-guards? "I'm not at all opposed to convict guards," he replied. "They're the most loyal people you can get on a chase. . . . That's the best way to rehabilitate a man—make him a guard. If I were running the place, I'd keep them. I like convict guards."[109] Would Martin himself accept the position of warden if it were offered to him? "I wouldn't say I would and I wouldn't say I wouldn't," was his answer.[110]

By the end of 1955 Angola's new buildings were only 90 percent completed (and already overcrowded by an inmate population surging beyond earlier estimates).[111] Treatment and rehabilitation were still only in the blueprint stage. The next administration, if ill-disposed toward penal reform, would be able severely to impede, if not to destroy, gains and objectives made and set since 1952. The three-hundred-odd employees at Angola, from the warden on down, were considered safe, for the moment, inasmuch as Kennon had put them all under state civil service.

As the new year dawned, however, supporters of penal reform were expressing concern about the fate of both the new Angola and of the classified employees there. Governor-designate, as the result of an unprecedented victory in the first Democratic primary, was a man who had demonstrated little affinity for penal reform and even less for civil service, which as chief executive before he had once abolished—Earl Kemp Long.[112]

However, Long proved amenable to reform, which was allowed to continue during the four years of his last gubernatorial term. It was not until after 1960 that the forces of reaction firmly reasserted themselves during the second administration of yet another former governor, Jimmie Davis.

[108] Quoted in New Orleans *Item*, October 7, 1955.

[109] Quoted in *ibid*.

[110] Quoted in *ibid*. Martin's "outbursts," the *Item* revealed, "coincided with reports that [he was] interested in becoming warden of Angola or naming the warden or getting the post of state police superintendent."

[111] New Orleans *Times-Picayune*, February 28, 1956.

[112] See "Cozart Reports Prison Employees Worried about Loss of Their Jobs," Baton Rouge *State-Times*, March 21, 1956.

CHAPTER VII

An Unpredictable Future
1956-1968

O NE OF Earl Long's stoutly professed maxims in his later years was that "you don't fool with Angola or LSU if you've got good sense."[1] It is not known precisely when or under what circumstances Long gained this political wisdom, nor what unfortunate experiences he may have had with the state university.[2] During his previous administration, however, Angola's heel-slashers had caused "Ole Earl" an immense amount of embarrassment. He vividly remembered the censure heaped upon him by press and public and was determined to avoid a recurrence of it.[3] As a consequence, Long refrained from meddling with Angola during his last gubernatorial term from 1956 to 1960. He preferred instead to let "the newspapers run" Louisiana's penal system.[4]

In practical terms Long's changed attitude gave penal reform in Louisiana a renewed lease on life and a significant boost. Contrary to the fears of some and the hopes of others,

---

[1] Quoted in Baton Rouge *Morning Advocate*, January 9, 1966, by a close political associate of Long's six years after his death.

[2] Earlier politicalization of Louisiana State University, from which the University's role in the scandals evolved, may have convinced Long that a hands-off policy toward that institution was "good sense."

[3] "I was almost run out of the state," Long recalled impishly in 1958. Quoted in Baton Rouge *State-Times*, February 26, 1958.

[4] Quoted in *ibid.*

the governor did not attempt to replace either Institutions Director Edward Grant nor Angola Warden Maurice Sigler, both professional carryovers from the Kennon-Cozart era.[5] Although Grant and Sigler subsequently resigned while Long was in office—largely as the result of a policy disagreement with each other—the governor allowed their successors to come from the seemingly inexhaustible pool of professionals brought to Louisiana by Cozart. With Long's support and cooperation, Angola's penologists were able to reach previous objectives and to inaugurate additional reforms by 1960. Especially was this the case with post-custodial rehabilitation, the area in which Louisiana's entire correctional apparatus was most deficient. With Angola functioning adequately under professional supervision during the late fifties, the governor was able to let the penal farm take care of itself while direct- ing his attention to the urgent problems of parolee super- vision and job placement of released convicts.

During his final year in office in 1955, Governor Robert Kennon's penologists had issued a clear statement describing Louisiana's modernized penal policy. In order to comfort those who suspected their regime of convict-coddling, assur- ances were given that Angola's inmates were "not treated with kid gloves" and did not "live off the fat of the land."[6] Angola was not a country club, but a humanely run penal institution where every effort was made—through rehabilita- tion—finally to release convicts as "decent, law-abiding cit- izens." It was stated that "to do less than this would not only be foolish but also more expensive in human life and dollars in the long run."[7]

Earl Long, voted back into the governorship in 1956, had yet to be fully convinced of the soundness of rehabilitative penal measures. Commenting in 1957 that "reform and reha-

[5] "A lot of my good friends were disappointed when I didn't change both of them," Long admitted candidly. Quoted in *ibid.*

[6] State of Louisiana, *Department of Institutions: Annual Report 1955* (Baton Rouge, 1955), 29.

[7] *Ibid.* Kennon's penologists were the first in Louisiana to invoke fiscal conservatism in support of penal reform.

bilitation is [*sic*] a hard thing to come by," he hoped that he would be "disillusioned in [his] belief that it won't work."[8] Memories of the heel-slashings and their unpleasant aftermath, however, succeeded in keeping Long's skepticism passive. Although Angola's penologists continued to experience opposition and harassment, Earl Long was no longer among their tormentors. In fact, by 1960 when he left office (to die later that year) he had become a firm friend of penal reform, if not an avowed reformer himself. The most significant and progressive developments during Long's final administration were: creation of an incentive pay system for Angola's convicts; the opening of a correctional facility for first offenders; and the appointment of a special gubernatorial committee to overhaul the parole system, with the objective of making possible the early release and outside employment of more of Angola's forgotten men.

As has been typical of most prisons, Angola's inmates for many years had received upon release, depending upon duration of time served, only the traditional ten or twenty dollars, which was hardly enough money to provide complete support until some form of employment could be obtained. The result in many cases was an immediate reversion to crime, generally followed by arrest, trial, conviction, and return to Angola. By 1956 both legislators and penologists were in agreement with the Baton Rouge *State-Times* that if convicts could "earn enough money in prison to last them a month or so after discharge," then possibly the chances of their return to society as contributing members would be substantially enhanced. The post-custodial rehabilitative value of incentive pay was not its only attraction; for if fewer discharged convicts committed fewer subsequent offenses, an already overcrowded penal system would have its burden lightened by having to accommodate fewer future inmates.[9]

With no dissenting votes in either house, the legislature

[8] Quoted in New Orleans *Times-Picayune*, November 10, 1957.

[9] Baton Rouge *State-Times*, June 26, 1956. Here again was an aspect of penal reform promoted as an economy measure.

of 1956 enacted a program under which the inmate population would be divided into three groups according to "dili-
gence and skill." Those in the top group would earn five
cents an hour, the middle group three and a half cents an
hour, and everyone else two cents an hour. Convicts in the
lower groups could be promoted on the basis of performance
on their jobs and good behavior. Financed by penitentiary
revenues, the incentive wages were to be divided evenly, half
given to the convict for purchase of incidentals while in
prison and half put aside for him until his release.[10] Warden
Maurice Sigler estimated that within two and one-half years
a discharged inmate would have between $75 and $150 to
take with him into the "free" world.[11] Although neither of
these sums could be considered a fortune, and though a much
more fundamental problem, post-custodial supervision, had
been ignored, the incentive pay program of 1956 was not a
negligible gesture.

Several studies of the inmate population were made by
Angola's classification department and by the research division of the Department of Institutions between 1956 and 1960.
These studies revealed that increasing crime was a corollary
of urbanization in Louisiana, and that the state's convicted
criminals were predominantly young, black, inadequately
educated, and poor.[12] Even though not all of these findings
were novel—Edward Livingston and others in the nineteenth
century, for example, had pointed out that convicts were
disproportionately poor and ignorant compared with the rest
of society—the political climate in mid-twentieth century Louisiana seemed more propitious for corrective action than at
any time before. Especially was it deemed necessary to isolate

[10] State of Louisiana, *Department of Institutions: Annual Report
1956–57* (Baton Rouge, 1957), 12.

[11] Baton Rouge *State-Times*, January 2, 1957.

[12] Baton Rouge *Morning Advocate*, July 15, 1956; Baton Rouge *State-
Times*, January 15, 22, 1958. In a footnote to one of these studies, Institutions Director Edward Grant shrewdly observed that "prisoners" were
a "special group of criminals"—the ones who are apprehended and convicted. "The criminal who is not caught might be very different," Grant
continued "and no one has suggested a way [of testing] him."

the expanding number of young first offenders within a facility of their own where they could be more effectively rehabilitated before discharge.

Upon the recommendation of Governor Kennon's penologists, the legislature of 1954 had authorized construction of a first-offender institution. Located at DeQuincy in western Louisiana, the $2.4 million facility was completed in September of 1957. Because of a lack of operational funds, however, DeQuincy was inhabited only by a small maintenance crew for an entire year, and no Angola convicts were transferred there until September 22, 1958.[13] Fifty-eight years had elapsed between 1900, when the Prison Reform Association of Louisiana, upon termination of the last James lease, petitioned the General Assembly to implement separation of first offenders, and the year in which this basic principle of penal reform was at last effectively carried through in Louisiana. No other feature of Louisiana's penal history more vividly illustrates the uphill struggle against public apathy, official inertia, and fiscal conservatism that reformers faced throughout the twentieth century. Since 1958 DeQuincy, like Angola, has had its problems, principally with budgets and personnel. But it has continued to operate in its double function of relieving Angola's "population explosion" to some extent and of providing special rehabilitative programs for first offenders.

Dating back to 1914, Louisiana's parole system had functioned with limited effectiveness at best. At their worst, actions of past parole boards had been scandalous. Often charged with political favoritism, board members had been accused of granting "quickie paroles" to prisoners with "connections" and of flagrantly selling early releases to those who could pay.[14] While the undeserving were thus released from custody,

[13] Baton Rouge *State-Times*, November 4, 1957; September 22, 1958.

[14] Files of Baton Rouge, New Orleans, and Shreveport newspapers contain accounts of repeated parole scandals since 1930. For a brief but accurate history of parole laws and administration in Louisiana since 1914, see State of Louisiana, *Department of Institutions, Biennial Report 1962–1964* (Baton Rouge, 1964), 69–71. See also John Maurice Hyde, "Developments in Correctional Services for Adult Felony Offenders in Louisiana," (M.A. thesis, Louisiana State University, 1955), 39–40; 43–48; 55–59.

many convicts whose records merited consideration remained neglected and forgotten at Angola. Even when the board, which consisted mostly of elected officials and gubernatorial appointees, strove conscientiously to perform its duties, the number of cases to be reviewed was usually more than could be judiciously considered within the time allotted. As a result, many inmates were paroled who should not have been, while potentially better risks were kept behind bars.

On top of all this were glaring deficiencies in post-custodial rehabilitation. Parole officers were too few in number to supervise their charges satisfactorily and there was hardly any systematic effort to place released inmates in positions of employment. Discharged into a bewildering if not hostile society, the former Angola convict often failed to find a niche for himself. Reverting to crime out of frustration, necessity, or both, he soon found himself back at Angola to become, once again, a burden upon the taxpayers.

By 1958 it was apparent that a more modern penal system, even with incentive pay, could not, by itself, solve the problems of discharged and paroled inmates. Further corrective measures would be needed if Louisiana's former convicts were to readjust to the free world and if the expanding prison population were to be kept within manageable limits. In September, 1958, Governor Long appointed a committee to study the area of post-custodial rehabilitation in its broadest sense. Officially designated as the Parolee Rehabilitation Committee, the body became popularly known as the "Forgotten Man's Committee." With former Governor Sam H. Jones as permanent chairman, this competent and distinguished group also included former Governors James A. Noe, Jimmie Davis, and Robert F. Kennon, judges, legal scholars, penologists, law enforcement officers, and other prominent citizens.

Long welcomed the committee to Baton Rouge on September 22. Conceding (in a ponderous understatement) that it was "hard to keep politics out of anything" in Louisiana, the governor nonetheless urged the members to con-

duct their business in an "absolutely non-partisan" manner.[15]
"Nobody," Long advised them knowingly, "ever made any
votes out of Angola. You're more apt to lost votes from it."[16]

After working at its task for a year and a half, the "Forgotten Man's Committee" submitted its report and recommendations in February, 1960, three months before Long's
term in office expired.[17] Looking back over penal developments in Louisiana since 1952, the committee perceived three
"revolutions," one of which had already taken place—the
rebuilding and professionalization of Angola under Kennon—
and two others on the threshold in 1960. "Revolution 3"
consisted of the "growing number of narcotics violators" in
Louisiana, a problem which the committee did not investigate in detail but considered serious enough to deserve
mention.[18] "Revolution 2," the committee's principal objective, was defined as the need for a "state Department of Corrections *with a pardon and parole system devoid of political
operation* and aimed at genuine rehabilitation where it is
possible."[19]

Specifically, the committee made nine proposals, all of
which are quoted below as phrased in the committee report:

1. A Department or division of Corrections to coordinate
   the rehabilitation of prisoners.
2. A full-time, professionally trained Parole Board, with
   jurisdiction over prisoners after they have served one
   year, except for narcotics violators or those sentenced
   for "life."
3. A parole Staff and Service Unit at Angola and DeQuincy
   to assist and prepare prisoners for their eventual release
   —thus getting at the very root of the "forgotten man"
   problem.

[15] Quoted in Baton Rouge *State-Times*, September 22, 1958.
[16] Quoted in *ibid.*
[17] The committee's proposals thus came before the legislature of
another administration, which rejected most of them.
[18] Shreveport *Times*, February 7, 1960.
[19] *Ibid.* An editorial digest of the report and not a quotation from the
report itself. Italics added.

4. An expanded, non-political, professionally trained parole and probation supervision system.

5. A mandatory pre-sentence investigation report on all non-capital felony cases, so that circumstances of the crime and environment can be known.

6. A permanent Citizen's Advisory Committee to help in job training and placement.

7. A change in the Pardon Board membership, adding the full-time Parole Board members so as to secure the benefits of their training and knowledge of the prisoners.

8. The removal of bars to the state employment of parolees in certain jobs.

9. A special committee to study narcotics laws, so as to deal with the growing problem of narcotic addicts in the state.[20]

Viewed in retrospect, the year 1960 surpasses even 1901 (when leasing of convicts ended) as the high-water mark of penal reform in Louisiana. Although several characteristics of the lease system had for many years survived the lessee, little remained of the "old Angola" as Earl K. Long's last gubernatorial term drew to a close. Twice during the 1950s (and each time, incidentally, under Long's authorization) committees of concerned and able Louisianians had urged radical changes in the state's penal operations. Largely as a result of recommendations by Long's Citizens' Committee of 1951, Angola's physical plant was modernized and its overall objective shifted away from profit to rehabilitation. In 1960 it was expected that the "Forgotten Man's Committee" would be similarly heeded, and that its proposals for improving parole and post-custodial rehabilitation would also be enacted. Had this desirable consequence ensued, Louisiana's penal history might have terminated in 1960 with a "happy ending." As it was, a coalition of skeptics and traditionalists, aided by a fiscal crisis in 1962, succeeded not only in shelving some of the committee's proposals for eight years, but also

[20] Quoted in *ibid.*

brought about a near-return to the "old Angola" before preventive measures were at last taken to stem a retreat into the dismal past.

For while Long's policies were consistently reformist between 1956 and 1960, reactionary attitudes had survived and frequently manifested themselves during the governor's final administration. These episodes foreshadowed a sudden and massive reaction which would occur following Governor Davis' return to office in 1960. Long himself, to the surprise of many, had become more sympathetic to penal reform, but several influential legislators continued to believe that Angola's primary objective was to make money and that requiring a full day's work was the best way to rehabilitate a convict. Additionally, Angola's high command, which by 1956 included more "outsiders" than Louisianians, remained vulnerable to attack by resentful natives and frustrated patronage seekers who wanted to regain control of what they conceived to be "their" penal system. Unresolved while Long was governor, these tensions boiled over after 1960 as penal traditionalists, fiscal conservatives, and political spoilsmen joined forces to regain ground lost since 1952.

Early in 1957 a joint legislative committee, formed the year before to investigate state institutions, inspected Angola. The committee chairman, Representative Lloyd Teekell of partially rural Rapides Parish, was particularly interested in the penal farm's financial operations. While there was no direct admission that committee members felt Angola was not doing enough to support itself, Teekell created this impression when he stated that, "the people don't like to pay so many taxes. Their demands, especially for education, would curl your hair."[21] Nine months later, Teekell's committee again visited Angola, this time to look into four murders committed by inmates on each other. Angola officials

[21] Quoted in Baton Rouge *State-Times*, February 7, 1957. What Teekell seems to have meant was that if heavy taxation had to be endured, then the "people" preferred that the revenues be applied to education (or some other desirable objective) rather than invested in the penal system.

blamed overcrowding for the crimes (DeQuincy had not yet opened), but the prison grapevine indicted "resistance to and retaliation for homosexual advances."[22] Teekell's group, however, was inclined to believe that lax discipline, a casual inmate workload, and "apparent lack of respect" for Warden Maurice Sigler himself had brought about the violence. Especially condemned was an occasion on which "all work ceased in order to watch the world series on television."[23] Despite his sweeping criticism of prison operations, Teekell somewhat inconsistently professed full confidence in Sigler.[24]

Shortly afterward a nasty scandal erupted when the warden's secretary was discovered to be a female inmate named Penny Kent, a one-time strip tease dancer convicted of a narcotics violation. Sigler insisted that, as warden, he possessed the authority to select his own staff, and that Miss Kent was a much more efficient secretary than could be hired at the prevailing salary. A whispering campaign, alleging improper relations between Sigler and his inmate-secretary, helped persuade Institutions Director Edward Grant that the former dancer would have to be replaced. Sigler agreed to relieve Miss Kent of her secretarial duties, but continued to retain her for several months, asserting that no satisfactory replacement had been found.

In February, 1958, Grant went to Angola and virtually demanded that Sigler get rid of Miss Kent. Sigler did so on the spot, informing his secretary that her duties had terminated "as of this moment."[25] The warden himself then insisted on resigning, angered by what he considered to be a trespass upon his authority. Tempers soon cooled, however, and Sigler did not resign—then.

Several days after his confrontation with Sigler, Director

[22] *Ibid.*, November 4, 1957.
[23] New Orleans *Times-Picayune*, November 8, 1957.   [24] *Ibid.*
[25] Quoted in Ed Clinton, "Just Plain Politics," Baton Rouge *State-Times*, February 26, 1958. This article presents as full and balanced an analysis of the Sigler-Kent episode as could, in all probability, be discreetly submitted.

Grant affirmed that hiring policy "within the [penal] organization" should attempt "to make the best use of our qualified people who are Louisianians—you can understand why."[26] Perhaps, then, the real source of official displeasure with Miss Kent was not the rumored impropriety between herself and Sigler, but simply that she was an inmate who, however competent, occupied a position that could otherwise have been given to a salaried employee. And although only a clerical position had been at stake in this particular squabble, Grant's remark might have possessed an even broader meaning—that "qualified Louisianians" should be employed on all levels at Angola. The domination of Angola by "outsiders" had been, after all, a local grievance since 1952, and the employment of convicts within the administration of the penal farm was an even older source of irritation.

In any event, Teekell's committee did not hesitate to use the Penny Kent episode for their own purposes. Teekell himself promised to clear up "the new turbulence at Angola," justifying his belief of a year earlier that "certain policies of Warden Sigler would lead to trouble."[27] A committee report made public on June 30, 1958, asserted that Angola was "still a very rotten institution." The penal farm, despite implementation of reform programs, remained "an excellent place for a youthful and noncriminal type prisoner to get a full education in criminal inclination and crime."[28] Staff morale was found to be low, a condition ascribed by the committee to Sigler's being "far more interested in the welfare and contentment of his prisoners than [in] harmony among his employees."[29] While commending Sigler's "excellent character" and "devotion to duty," the committee disparaged the warden's rehabilitative policies, convinced that they would "never be very productive at the Louisiana State Penitentiary."[30]

[26] Quoted in *ibid.*   [27] Quoted in *ibid.*, February 27, 1958.
[28] Quoted in Shreveport *Times*, June 30, 1958.
[29] Quoted in *ibid.*
[30] Quoted in Baton Rouge *State-Times*, June 30, 1958.

The Teekell committee's antidote for Angola's "new turbulence" was expansion of farming and other agricultural operations so as to make possible a "full day's work for all" inmates.[31] A specific recommendation of the committee (which consisted entirely of rural legislators) was that more acreage be devoted to cultivation of cotton and sugar cane. Critics of the committee quickly pointed out that acreage expansion of either crop would not only require federal approval, but, if implemented, could seriously impede Angola's rehabilitation program, because employment opportunities in staple agriculture were steadily diminishing. The committee's charges of lax discipline and light work schedules were considerably vitiated when critics also observed that increased mechanization and a rising convict population had combined to produce an unavoidable surplus labor problem at Angola.[32] Rehabilitation of inmates would be better accomplished and idleness more effectively reduced by continued diversification of Angola's industrial program than by an anachronistic reemphasis of farming, which Teekell's committee of ruralites had automatically assumed would "always be the backbone of the economics [sic] at Angola."[33]

Shaken initially by the furor over Penny Kent, Warden Sigler had meanwhile resigned, disgusted by the charges and implications of the Teekell report, which he branded in part as "character assassination" and described as "not unbiased."[34] (A number of convicts who were questioned by the press shortly afterward charged that the report contained several statements that were "the exact opposite" of what members of the committee had been told by inmates whom the com-

[31] Shreveport *Times*, June 30, 1958.

[32] Baton Rouge *State-Times*, July 22, 1958.

[33] Quoted in Shreveport *Times*, June 30, 1958. Members of the committee, in addition to Teekell, were Senators W. J. Cleveland (Acadia Parish), B. C. Crothers (Concordia Parish), and W. D. Folkes (West Feliciana Parish), with Representative Shelby Alford (St. Helena Parish).

[34] Quoted in Lake Charles *American Press*, July 20, 1958. Institutions Director Edward Grant had already resigned in March, the breach having widened between himself and Sigler.

mittee had interviewed.) [35] The day after Sigler's announce-
ment, more than two thousand Angola inmates "refused
breakfast and stayed off their jobs" in protest until persuaded
by Sigler himself to return to work. Most of the demonstrators
were convinced that Sigler had been placed in an untenable
position by politicians determined to oust him.[36]

Both "inmates and free personnel alike" at the penal farm
were "disturbed" over Sigler's resignation, which many believed had been engineered to facilitate a restoration of the
"old Angola."[37] But, as in 1956, the continuity of reform
policy was again unexpectedly maintained. Possibly upon
the governor's recommendation, and certainly not without
his approval, the Board of Institutions nominated still another
alumnus of the federal prison service to succeed Warden
Sigler. Their choice was Victor G. Walker, on Angola's staff
since 1954.

The speed and apparent thoroughness with which Louisiana's penal system had been rebuilt according to modern
standards and its objectives realigned with current penal practice, served to relax the zeal of reformers during the late
fifties. Governor Long's surprising change of heart, demonstrated by support rendered in various ways throughout his
second administration, contributed further to a triumphant
notion that the "old Angola" was gone forever.[38] Traditionalists and patronage seekers remained to be dealt with, but were
no longer in the ascendancy, as the smooth transition from
Sigler to Walker had substantiated.

Earl Long, who had surprised those who feared his policies,
was succeeded by a man who surprised those who hoped for
much from his policies. Jimmie H. Davis, Louisiana's gover-
nor-elect in 1960, had been an outspoken critic of flogging

[35] Baton Rouge *State-Times*, July 21, 1958.   [36] *Ibid.*
[37] Baton Rouge *State-Times*, July 22, 1958.
[38] A somewhat millennial view of Angola, prematurely written in 1960,
may be found in Ed Clinton, "Angola: The Story of Louisiana State
Penitentiary," *American Journal of Correction*, XXII (November–December, 1960), 4–8.

during his previous administration. He had also authorized
the Sanford-Jenkinson survey, constructed a modern hospital
at Angola, and was a vice-chairman of the "Forgotten Man's
Committee." His approaching inauguration, therefore, cli-
maxed the euphoria of high hopes for penal reform in Louisiana. Even at Angola, "probably for the first time in its history," an incoming administration was welcomed rather
than feared.[39]

The Davis administration soon revealed that penal reform
was not among its priorities, for it stood by in near apathy
while the legislature of 1960 "bypassed almost in full" the
recommendations of the "Forgotten Man's Committee."[40] The
committee, of which he was himself a vice-chairman, had
"some good ideas," said Governor Davis one year later, "but
some of the things they wanted to set up [would] cost a lot of
money."[41] By 1962 there had been piecemeal enactment of
other committee proposals, "but the major legislation" providing for "training and jobs for prisoners" remained, like
the "forgotten men" themselves, in limbo.[42] The Shreveport
Times, one of the more conservative Louisiana newspapers,
had nevertheless been a supporter of penal reform since the
1951 heel-slashings, for it was convinced that reform could
save both money and human dignity. The paper scolded
"some Legislators" of the 1960 session for continuing to "believe that a prison sentence is intended to place a man—or
a youth—under conditions of cruelty and hardship making
it impossible for him ever to be a trustworthy citizen again."[43]

[39] Baton Rouge *State-Times*, May 16, 1960. While noting an "edgy"
mood at Angola, the reporter nonetheless found a "prevailing attitude"
of "hope that there [would] be no changes" in personnel or programs
by the Davis administration.

[40] Shreveport *Times*, March 30, 1961.

[41] Quoted in Baton Rouge *State-Times*, March 10, 1961. Cost-
consciousness did not prevent Davis from building a new governor's
mansion. During the 1959 campaign Earl Long had said that "Jimmie
Davis loves money like a hog loves slop." Quoted in A. J. Liebling, *The
Earl of Louisiana* (New York, 1961), 113.

[42] Baton Rouge *State-Times*, May 30, 1962.

[43] Shreveport *Times*, March 20, 1961.

Despite these and other criticisms, nothing more was done about the committee's recommendations until 1968. Failure to implement measures which could free more eligible parolees from Angola placed a burden upon the institution itself by complicating the problem of overcrowding.

In 1962 a political disaster again befell the penal system. The Davis legislature, "staggered by a deficit resulting from intemperate spending in other areas," cut Angola's operating budget from $3,444,780 (1961–62) to $2,522,541 for the fiscal year 1962–1963.[44] This action, lamented the Baton Rouge *State-Times*, made it "hard to see anything but retrogression for Angola," which could "find once again a label pinned on it of the worst [prison] in the country."[45]

Damage reports began to pour in. James Wayne Allgood, assistant warden, professional penologist, and the highest ranking native Louisianian on Angola's staff, resigned (effective August 31, 1962) to join the faculty of Louisiana Polytechnic Institute, his undergraduate alma mater.[46] By the date of Allgood's departure, 108 correctional officers, 4 classification officers, and 2 teachers had been discharged.[47] Correctional officers who remained were put on a sixty-hour week, while convicts soon replaced those who had gone. Angola's educational and vocational programs, so painstakingly built up since 1952, were practically abandoned. The Classification Reception Center was "virtually . . . closed down," thus fulfilling Warden Walker's gloomy prediction that departure of the classification officers would "shoot [the program] to hell."[48]

[44] New Orleans *Times-Picayune*, April 9, 1967. See also State of Louisiana, *Acts of the Legislature, Regular Session, 1961* (Baton Rouge, 1961), 23; *Acts of the Legislature* (1962), 161.

[45] Baton Rouge *State-Times*, May 25, 1962.

[46] *Ibid.*, August 3, 1962. Allgood had come to Angola in 1952 as classification director. In 1956 he was awarded the degree of Master of Arts in sociology by Louisiana State University.

[47] *Ibid.*, August 27, 1962. Several other employees, like Allgood, resigned.

[48] Quoted in *ibid.*; Baton Rouge *Morning Advocate*, September 23, 1962.

The number of escapes increased, violence among prisoners broke out more frequently, and convict-guards resumed their traditional vocation of brutalizing and killing fellow inmates.[49] As the last year of the Davis administration got under way, the concerned Shreveport *Times* found Angola "back in the days of [inmate] guards, allegations of virtually barbarous administration in some instances, and poverty in funds provided for its administration. It is not the medieval slave camp of the past, but it is skidding."[50]

The Davis administration was obsessed with futile attempts to prevent any desegregation of Louisiana's public schools and to keep Negroes from voting. It appropriated money for projects ranging from a multimillion-dollar governor's mansion to an immense (and unnecessary) toll bridge across the Mississippi River. And in 1964 it careened discreditably into history, leaving a ravished penal system as one of many headaches to plague the next governor.[51]

Earl K. Long's death in 1960, along with his nephew Russell's continued absence from Louisiana as United States senator, disrupted the succession within the Long movement on the state level. Two aspirants to Earl's mantle entered the gubernatorial primaries of 1963–1964. One, Gillis Long, was a distant cousin of Huey and Earl and congressman from Louisiana's eighth district. The other, John J. McKeithen, a member of the Public Service Commission, had once been a Longite floor leader in the legislature and in 1952 had run for lieutenant governor on the Longite Spaht ticket. Anti-Long contestants were former Governor Robert F. Kennon, State Education Superintendent Shelby M. Jackson, and the

[49] In December of 1962, two black inmates (aged 17 and 19) were shot to death and five others wounded by convict-guards when the group allegedly tried to escape from a work formation. See New Orleans *Times-Picayune*, December 14, 1962; and Baton Rouge *State-Times*, December 19, 1962.

[50] Shreveport *Times*, May 25, 1963.

[51] When a searching account of the second Davis administration is written, "Singing Jimmie" may well emerge as a twentieth-century Samuel Douglas McEnery.

perennial bridesmaid of recent Louisiana gubernatorial races, Mayor deLesseps S. Morrison of New Orleans.[52]

Morrison, an active campaigner with a solid constituency, led the field in the first primary. By astutely cultivating both Long and anti-Long elements, McKeithen ran second (ahead of Gillis Long). Unable to shed the burdens of his Roman Catholicism and his "city slicker" image, Morrison then lost to Protestant McKeithen, who was born in a rural Anglo-Saxon parish (Caldwell) in North Louisiana. That many Negroes had voted for Morrison in the first primary, and that Morrison was a Kennedy sympathizer, also contributed to the triumph of McKeithen, the subsequent victor over a Republican contender in the general election.

Because he was "both a Long and an anti-Long," McKeithen's election further obscured Louisiana's already hazy Democratic bifactionalism.[53] Two years later, in 1966, the state's voters approved a constitutional amendment removing the prohibition (in effect since 1898) against an incumbent governor's running for reelection.[54] Opposed only by nonentities and a maverick freshman congressman, McKeithen coasted to an effortless victory in the 1967 primary. With no Republican opposition, there was no need for a general election, and in 1968 John McKeithen emerged at the very summit of Louisiana politics, as unopposed as anyone since

[52] Morrison ran unsuccessfully for governor in 1955, 1959, and 1963. An effective and charismatic mayor, Roman Catholic "Chep" Morrison had many loyal supporters in New Orleans and throughout French South Louisiana. His urbanity and religion, however, hurt him in rural North Louisiana and among Protestants everywhere. Earl Long liked to ridicule the mayor (as he had Sam Jones in 1940), "always calling Morrison 'deLasoups' and mocking his 'tuppy' (toupee)." Michael L. Kurtz, "Earl Long's Political Relations with the City of New Orleans: 1948–1960," *Louisiana History*, X (Summer, 1969), 250.

[53] Charles W. Tapp, "The Gubernatorial Election of 1964: An Affirmation of Political Trends," *Proceedings of the Louisiana Academy of Sciences*, XXVII (December, 1964), 87.

[54] It was affirmed in some quarters that fear of another potential Jimmie Davis administration induced many voters to endorse the succession amendment.

Huey Long, and the first governor since Murphy J. Foster to
be elected twice consecutively.

McKeithen's broad-based popularity was both a result and
a reflection of his successful subordination of factional legacies
within the state Democratic Party to his own monolithic
leadership. Under radically different circumstances, Governor
Foster had engineered an identical accomplishment between
1892 and 1896.[55] Pursuing other lines of similarity between
these two governors, it can be said that each inherited a
troubled and vexing penal system from his predecessor.
Convict leasing had prevailed in Louisiana when Foster became governor, and he opposed the lessee for several reasons.
After two Foster administrations, however, the state was still
leasing convicts, although arrangements had been made to
end the lease system in 1901. When McKeithen became
governor in 1964 the penal system was in serious disrepair
as a result of budget cuts imposed two years before. Angola's
wardenship changed nine times between 1964 and 1968; and
during that same interval the damage inflicted upon facilities, programs, and personnel by the Davis regime was never
fully repaired. Most significantly, politics, patronage, and
profit were allowed to retain at least some of their traditional influence over Louisiana's penal operations.

Serious deficiencies still afflict Louisiana's correctional system, as disclosed in a recent symposium held at Louisiana
State University.[56] Governor McKeithen's second administration, which will not be dealt with here past the 1968 legisla-

[55] Interestingly enough, one of McKeithen's recent appointments to
the Louisiana State University Board of Supervisors was Murphy J.
Foster, Jr.

[56] See "Employee Needs Told in State Penal Study," in Baton Rouge
Morning Advocate, November 9, 1969. This article summarizes the conclusions of an investigation conducted for the Louisiana Commission on
Law Enforcement and Administration of Justice. Findings of this state
commission almost parallel those of a survey conducted nationally for
the federal Joint Commission on Correctional Manpower and Training,
which released its conclusions to the press one day later. See "Prison
Reform Study Issued by Commission," in Baton Rouge *Morning Advocate,*
November 10, 1969.

tive session, has less than one year left in office at this writing. Recently the governor and his top aides have sought to arouse public interest in and concern for the problems of Angola and related agencies. Thus far, these efforts have met with limited success. Whether sufficient support for hiring needed personnel and constructing all necessary additional facilities can be obtained by 1972 remains to be seen.

No better evidence could be offered of the chaos into which the penal system had fallen by 1964 than the continuous procession of wardens to and from Angola during the next four years. At no time since 1901 had policy implementation been more confused or attrition so high among top administrators. Warden Victor G. Walker, transferred from Angola to DeQuincy in October, 1963 (while Davis was still governor), was called back to Angola in June, 1964, only to resign altogether from Louisiana's penal service a month later. The warden's letter of resignation was accepted on July 15, 1964.[57] In the letter Walker cited as reasons for his departure the unrestored budget cuts of 1962, reemployment of convict-guards, and inability to get along with T. H. Martin, a man totally opposed to penal reform, whom McKeithen had appointed to the Board of Institutions. (Martin condemned Cozart's Angola in 1955 as a "damn playhouse" and was evidently still determined in 1964 to effect a restoration of the old ways at the penal farm.) Also an object of Walker's disapproval was the reemphasis by McKeithen's board upon commercial operations at the expense of rehabilitation. "They [the Board of Institutions] seem to be more worried about the sugar cane crop and the canning factory than about the prisoners," Walker charged several days later.[58]

The last member of the original Cozart team, Walker

[57] Baton Rouge *State-Times*, July 15, 1964.
[58] Quoted in *ibid.*, July 23, 1964. Perusal of the Board of Institutions' *Biennial Reports* for the mid-1960s will confirm Walker's accusation. For further indictment of the board's emphasis on money-making see New Orleans *Times-Picayune*, January 3, 1965 and April 10, 1967; Baton Rouge *Morning Advocate* (editorial), September 3, 1967.

left Louisiana with a pessimistic view of Angola's prospects: "The place is so large, so complex, and has so many prisoners. . . . Angola needs more than one man there. It needs a team of trained men dedicated to their jobs and given the money to do them. I hope that will come about some day."[59] To replace Walker the board appointed as acting warden H. L. Hanchey, a former guard who had progressed up the ladder to become Angola's meat-packing supervisor. Hanchey was also a native of Governor McKeithen's hometown, Columbia.[60] This fact annoyed the Baton Rouge *Morning Advocate*, which criticized the appointment, observing editorially that Hanchey's main claim to the job of warden was "apparently the fact that he is a neighbor of Governor McKeithen's."[61] (The next day McKeithen reacted with "surprise" to Hanchey's nomination.)[62] In any event, the governor's "neighbor" remained in charge at Angola for the next seven months while a qualified, permanent warden was sought.[63]

James Wayne Allgood, Walker's assistant warden, was persuaded to return to Angola as top man in January, 1965. He in turn resigned within a year, complaining that he was given no control over personnel selection or financial operations.[64] The source of Allgood's difficulty seems to have been Institutions Director Wingate White, another McKeithen appointee and former Louisiana police official, who "apparently rode herd on the prison at all times," cutting Allgood

[59] Quoted in Baton Rouge *State-Times*, July 23, 1964.

[60] *Ibid.*, July 16, 1964.

[61] Baton Rouge *Morning Advocate*, July 19, 1964.

[62] Baton Rouge *State-Times*, July 20, 1964.

[63] Serving under Hanchey as "executive assistant" (at a $600-a-month salary) was T. H. Martin, Jr., whose father had recently joined the Board of Institutions. The New Orleans *Times-Picayune* condemned the appointment of the junior Martin as "reprehensible." New Orleans *Times-Picayune*, August 30, 1964.

[64] Baton Rouge *Morning Advocate*, January 9, 1966. Allgood was the only professionally qualified native Louisianian ever to serve as Warden of Angola. And yet his one-year tenure was one of the shortest in history, hardly an encouragement for qualified Louisianians to enter the penal service.

out of the picture entirely.[65] At this point Mrs. Margaret Dixon, a prominent Baton Rouge journalist and former member of Governor Earl Long's 1951 Citizens' Committee, charged that "administration of . . . Angola is one area where the McKeithen regime has failed completely."[66] White continued to direct Angola as de facto warden for two years. (Acting Wardens J. D. Middlebrooks and Hayden J. Dees were successively in nominal command during White's satrapy.)[67]

By the spring of 1967 Governor McKeithen had come to realize that in Angola lay a threat to his political career. The system was not working well financially, unrest among inmates was increasing, none of his appointees seemed to know how to deal with the situation, and criticism was mounting. As he was planning to succeed himself, it would certainly not harm him politically if the mess at Angola could be straightened out. The primaries, after all, were only several months away.

In May, McKeithen appointed as director of institutions recently retired Lieutenant General David Wade, USAF. A native Louisianian, Wade had just concluded a successful military career in which he had demonstrated keen administrative and leadership abilities. He also possessed a military "no-nonsense" attitude, of which many individuals, including Warden White, were destined to run afoul.[68] Early in 1968 another series of scandals broke at Angola. Not as dramatic (nor as novel) as the 1951 heel-slashings, the discovery of a sodomy ring among inmates, narcotics peddling on the premises, moonshine whiskey operations, and apparent mismanagement of $400,000 worth of prison funds nonetheless

[65] *Ibid.*

[66] Mrs. Margaret Dixon, "Administration of Penal System Reflects on State," *ibid.*

[67] For an excellent summary of the confusion prevailing at Angola in 1967, as well as criticism of the "difficulties, intrigue, and pure politics that have beset [Angola]," see New Orleans *Times-Picayune*, April 9. 1967.

[68] After shaking up the Department of Institutions, Wade became adjutant general of Louisiana. He next served as director of public safety (state police), before becoming adjutant general again.

spelled the end for Wingate White, whom General Wade
insisted had to go. Governor McKeithen upheld Wade's
demand and White resigned.[69] Hayden Dees again served as
acting warden until February 29, 1968, when an out-of-state
professional (the first since Walker to head Angola) was
appointed permanent warden. Charles M. Henderson, a former warden at both the Iowa and Tennessee penitentiaries,
has done a commendable job stabilizing Angola, where he
remains at this writing.[70]

The McKeithen administration was saddled by Davis with
a penal system in dreadful shape, which may account in part
for the board's determination to make Angola "pay." Mc-
Keithen was further restricted by the political obligations
every incoming Louisiana governor must necessarily satisfy,
possibly explaining the appointment of T. H. Martin, a
thorough traditionalist, to the Board of Institutions. But it
is still difficult to argue with Margaret Dixon's assessment
of McKeithen's penal policy, in its initial years at least, as
a complete failure. Whatever good intentions or positive goals
the governor may have formulated for Angola were in no
way demonstrably apparent until the appointment of Wade
in 1967, and did not become clearly discernible until after
White's removal (and McKeithen's own reelection) one year
later. Angola's annual operating appropriation, moreover,
was not raised above the pre-slash figure of $3,444,780 (for
fiscal 1961–62) until 1967, McKeithen's third year in office,
when the legislature provided $3,560,088 for fiscal 1967–
1968.[71] Even so, the increase in convict population, rising
costs, and neglected services must have devoured this modest
increase immediately.

Like Earl Long, his mentor, together with all other polit-

[69] McKeithen reportedly promised to find "other state employment"
for White. Baton Rouge *State-Times*, February 8, 1968.

[70] For an editorial commending Henderson's appointment, see *ibid.*,
February 29, 1968. Henderson was recruited by General Wade. Governor
John J. McKeithen, conversation with author, January 5, 1970.

[71] State of Louisiana, *Acts of the Legislature, Regular Session 1967*
(Baton Rouge, 1967), 25.

ical agents of penal reform in Louisiana, Governor Mc-
Keithen seems to have become genuinely concerned about
Angola only after serious deterioration within the system
prompted enough critics to howl.[72]

Penal and parole reform were major planks in McKeithen's
reelection platform in 1967.[73] Since then, and in the face
of a statewide financial crisis triggered by Davis' spending
and made worse by recent legislative inertia, the McKeithen
administration has endeavored to bring Louisiana's custodial
and parole facilities up to acceptable standards of operation.
The legislature of 1968 substantially enacted the remaining
proposals of the "Forgotten Man's Committee," without, however, providing sufficient funds for effective implementation—
a formula employed several times in the past to render other
aspects of penal reform relatively impotent. A gubernatorial
commission on law enforcement and administration of justice
has been established. In the tradition of its numerous predecessors, this body is packed with various experts and has
been charged with both investigatory and promotional functions. Limited educational programs, supported in part by
the federal government, have been reestablished at Angola.[74]

As recently as November, 1969, however, Louisiana's correctional system was 2,000 employees short of an acceptable
employee-inmate ratio. At Angola 239 convict-guards were
still used, while the classification system itself was not handled
by professionals but by 23 inmates. Medical and psychiatric
personnel were in great demand throughout the system, and
construction of a penitentiary in New Orleans, "where 50
per cent of Angola's inmates come from," was urgently

---

[72] Early in his first administration, McKeithen's solution for Angola's
problems was stated as follows: "I believe all that is needed right now
is for the people [at Angola] to use a little energy and a little cleaning
up, a little painting up and a little straightening up." Quoted in Baton
Rouge *State-Times*, July 31, 1964. By 1967 the governor's Angola policy
was less simplistic.

[73] For a full-page McKeithen campaign advertisement, on the eve of
the 1967 primary, see *ibid.*, November 3, 1967.

[74] See "Angola Education Program," Baton Rouge *Morning Advocate*,
January 22, 1967.

needed. Pardon and parole operations, although based upon forward-looking legislation, were failing to work out, as each of the state's parole officers was compelled to handle an average of 162 cases, with 35 considered the "highest likely [number] to permit effective supervision and assistance."[75] The "average Louisiana inmate" is released after only two years in custody, but "for maybe half of these offenders, there is a return to crime."[76] As recently stated by a group of Louisiana specialists: "The true goal of correction is to help the offender break out of this circle of recurring crime and punishment. The cost of keeping an offender in the system is incalculable in terms of both harm to society and dollars and cents."[77]

Throughout the years, progressive penology has been held back in Louisiana by several forms of resistance. Patronage-minded politicians, having nothing to gain and much to lose from thorough professionalization of the penal service, have fought this trend accordingly. The traditional view of incarceration as punishment (especially of Negroes in past years) has often frustrated programs aimed at rehabilitation.[78] But the major barrier to successful reform efforts has been an economic one. Neither the public nor significant numbers of state officials—except in times of obvious crisis—has been willing to furnish the penal system adequate funds for projected requirements. They have, on the contrary, adhered just as tenaciously in penal matters as in racial ones to the philosophy of "deferred commitment," preferring to risk

[75] Report of Louisiana Commission on Law Enforcement and Administration of Justice, quoted in *ibid.*, November 9, 1969.

[76] Quoted in *ibid.* On a nation-wide basis, and according to the FBI, more than 60 percent of prisoners released from custody commit further crimes. *Ibid.*, November 10, 1969.

[77] Quoted in *ibid.*, November 9, 1969.

[78] As recently as 1964, Angola's inmate population was 55 percent Negro, while in 1960 blacks comprised only 32.1 percent of the state's population as a whole. State of Louisiana, *Department of Institutions, Biennial Report 1962–1964* (Baton Rouge, 1964), 25; James R. Bobo and Sandra A. Etheridge, *Statistical Abstract of Louisiana* (3d. ed.; New Orleans, 1969), 6.

long-term cost, which is vague and remote, than to pay short-term costs, which are precise and immediate. Underlying even this basic attitude is a further conviction that prisoners are unworthy of financial assistance on any level. The New Orleans *Times-Picayune* concisely pointed out several years ago that "the main reason why Angola is not a well regarded operation and why related parts of the system such as the parole board fall short, is that recent administrations and legislatures have been indifferent. They have preferred to allot revenues to purposes and activities backed by louder popular demand while cutting back the support for the penal system."[79]

Thus, for the past seventy years Louisiana's penal system has been unable to devote its full energies to its proper function—rehabilitation of inmates. Instead, it has had to be constantly preoccupied with commercial operations, knowing full well that self-support is its only certain source of revenue.[80] With a recalcitrant legislature currently failing to overhaul Louisiana's twenty-year-old tax structure, and with popular demand waiting to urge generous appropriations for roads, schools, welfare, and other priority services once funds do become available, it seems most unlikely that Louisiana's custodial and parole systems will function any more effectively in the future than they have in the past—that is, if state

[79] New Orleans *Times-Picayune*, August 9, 1964.

[80] While "profit" has been a locally recognized fact of life at Angola for decades, it is almost amusing how Louisianians become incensed when "outsiders" point to it. A special report on the Arkansas, Mississippi, and Louisiana penal systems, issued in 1968 by the Southern Regional Council, devoted two and a half pages to a concise, generally accurate, and up-to-date appraisal of Angola. The report stated that "actions of the Board of Institutions suggest the members believe that their chief function is to produce a profit," which at the time was perfectly true, even if it was equally correct that the "profits" in question were used to support the penal system and its various activities. Reaction in Baton Rouge, however, expressed indignant denial. See *The Delta Prisons: Punishment for Profit*, Southern Regional Council Special Report (Atlanta, 1968), 7; "Punishment for Profit Study on Prisons labeled Hearsay," in Baton Rouge *State-Times*, March 22, 1968; and "Our Suspicions are Confirmed" (editorial), in *ibid.*

support alone is considered. Current federal proposals appear to envision assistance to state correctional facilities as well as law enforcement agencies. With ample funding from Washington, Louisiana's penal system could certainly be administered at less direct cost to Louisianians. On the other hand, federal aid to correctional systems in the South and elsewhere could create similar disputes along the objective, operational, and jurisdictional lines that have arisen from federal aid to education, highways, and welfare. Thus the traditional problems of Louisiana's penal establishment, which have been local in origin and are not yet resolved, could soon be compounded rather than alleviated as a result of being drawn into the federal sphere of operations. This risk could be avoided, of course, were the state to increase its support of custodial and rehabilitative services to sufficient levels. But nothing in the history of Louisiana's penal system gives any assurance that such a sustained commitment is forthcoming.

CHAPTER VIII

Conclusion

ONLY WITHIN the last twenty years has Louisiana's penal system begun to evolve into a genuine correctional apparatus, administered by professional penologists, with rehabilitation of convicts its actual, as well as its professed, objective. Prior to 1952 the system was essentially a business enterprise, administered either by politicians or by lessees, with both forms of management seeking to extract as much money as possible from the labor of thousands of semi-skilled "state slaves." And if the study of history seeks, among other goals, to explain the tension between the forces of continuity and the forces of change, the history of Louisiana's penal system must lean overwhelmingly toward continuity, for even by 1968 the transition noted above had not been completely effected.

Underlying and sustaining the deficiencies of Louisiana's system have been three interrelated and historically pervasive factors: (1) public opinion, the ultimate arbiter of policy formation in a democracy, has in Louisiana generally ignored the penal system and has been disinclined to bestow upon it the kind of support readily bestowed upon other state agencies; (2) political control of the penal system has easily occupied the near-vacuum caused by public apathy, with the result that penal policy on all levels in Louisiana has been formulated exclusively by politicians, who have been able until recently to subordinate completely penological objectives to political considerations of cost, race, and patronage; (3) modern penology, with its necessarily higher costs, professional personnel, and popularly exaggerated overtones of convict-coddling, has had a difficult time supplanting the old ways in Louisiana, where public officials have preferred to utilize the penal system as a patronage mill, where public opinion has been satisfied when it could be assured that convicts were being punished, and where both public officials and public opinion have long agreed that the least expensive penal system is the most desirable one.

No more than twice during the past century have changes of any magnitude been imposed upon Louisiana's penal system. The first transition was initiated by abundant evidence of brutality inflicted upon convicts by lessee Samuel L. James. But those who ultimately succeeded in ending the lease system were not motivated so much by humanitarianism as by political considerations, for the major's worst offense in their eyes was that he divided their party, and not that he brutalized or failed to rehabilitate convicts. It was the lessee, in fact, rather than the lease system itself which Louisiana's Democratic oligarchy moved to rid itself of during the 1890s, a distinction made vividly clear by the type of "new" penal system erected by the state following James's death and his company's departure—a system patterned closely after the lease system, but without the lessee. While treatment of convicts was substantially more humane after 1901 than before, brutality was not ended altogether, profit and patronage continued to afflict the system (as profit and politics had continuously afflicted it since 1844), and rehabilitation was given little more than lip service.

Exactly a half-century following resumption of state control came the second major alteration in Louisiana's penal operations, this (like the first) an outgrowth of crisis and undeniable scandal within the system. The heel-slashings of 1951 surpassed even the James regime in shocking Louisiana's usually apathetic public and, as a result, most of the old camps at Angola were torn down and replaced by a modern prison facility. Professional penologists were also, for the first time in Louisiana's history, given direct charge of implementing yet another "new" penal policy. But in 1962 tradition again reasserted itself and much of the progress made by Angola's professional staff was blunted if not eradicated. Thus in each case, in 1901 as in the 1950s, change was superficial and of short duration, a pattern which may well continue to characterize penal reform in Louisiana for the foreseeable future.

For the past is still alive and in fair health at Angola. Emphasis upon agricultural pursuits dates back to the 1870s, when James and other southern lessees abandoned cells and walls for penal farms so as to capitalize to greatest advantage upon the known abilities of a majority of the convicts— former slaves. It was during this same period that enthusiasm for rehabilitation became (in Louisiana as doubtless elsewhere in the South) inversely proportional to the number of black convicts either known or believed to be within the system. And, finally, it was lessee James who dazzled a generation of Louisianians (including many who opposed him for one reason or another) with easy money from convict labor, and, thus, did more than anyone else to legitimate profit-making as the continued and overriding goal of Louisiana's penal system.

Leasing of convicts ended more than two generations ago in Louisiana, and penal farms are much less viable today, either as rehabilitative vehicles or as economic hubs of well-run prisons, than they were in years past. Rehabilitation has, at last, acquired official status as a priority objective while profit for its own sake has been correspondingly deemphasized. But the farm is still there. A majority of the convicts are still black. And in fact, if not in theory, self-support still seems to have precedence over rehabilitation at Angola, where the legacy of Major James, who resided there for a generation, remains persistently in evidence.

Some discussion is due of the problem of comparisons, which for two reasons have not been abundantly cited within this study. Because this is the first full-length, up-to-date penal history of Louisiana ever to be undertaken by anyone in any of the social sciences, it was necessary to explore the local sources as inclusively as possible and to utilize them as extensively as possible. Thus, neither the scope of the investigation nor the priorities involved would permit extensive incorporation of comparative penal history.

But then there is no comparative penal historiography worthy of the designation. Advised by a colleague some months ago that literature in this area was largely "nonexistent," I have since discovered on my own that her assessment was correct.[1] To my best knowledge, there is no comprehensive history of the federal prison system, fantastic as this is. Nor have most of the state systems received thorough investigation.[2] Just as convicts are generally ignored by society as being unworthy of assistance, so penal systems have been largely dismissed by scholars as being unworthy of histories. With the secondary literature thus scattered, out-of-date, and mostly unwritten, I would have had to delve through endless volumes of outside source material in order to obtain substantial historical comparisons between Louisiana's penal system and systems elsewhere, and this was simply not feasible.[3]

[1] Professor V. K. Andreason of the Department of Sociology, Louisiana State University in Baton Rouge.

[2] Two unpublished studies of Border State penal systems are Robert G. Crawford, "A History of the Kentucky Penitentiary System, 1865–1937" (Ph.D. dissertation, University of Kentucky, 1955) ; and Herman L. Crow, "A Political History of the Texas Penal System, 1829–1951" (Ph.D. dissertation, University of Texas, 1964).

[3] A tribute is due Hilda Jane Zimmerman, "Penal Systems and Penal Reforms in the South Since the Civil War" (Ph.D. dissertation, University of North Carolina, 1947). Utilizing a broad range of source material and drawing upon the limited monographic literature available, Zimmerman's pioneer study is still the best comprehensive history of Southern penal systems. Its chief virtues are its mass of factual data and an inclusive bibliography covering the period from 1840 to 1940. On the other hand, Zimmerman frequently equated a law passed with a reform substantially achieved, and like Elizabeth Wisner, *Public Welfare Adminis-*

There is, of course, an extensive literature dealing with penology—numerous textbooks, monographs, articles in many professional journals, and reams of statistical data (most of which emanates regularly from Washington)—but this literature is diffuse, conflicting, frequently jargonized, and almost totally devoid of useful historical perspective. Having little historical focus, penological literature therefore possesses little historical value, except as source material for histories of penology, which would possess considerable merit indeed.

Despite the lack of enough reliable penal histories, some tentative comparisons between Louisiana's experience and those of the South and the rest of the nation are offered, together with some final remarks on the possible uniqueness of Louisiana.

Both the facilities and the philosophy of prisons in the South, especially in the Deep South, were tailor made for black convicts as viewed by their white former masters in the post-Civil War period. Today, despite gradual alterations and nominal progress, these institutions remain much as they were at the turn of the century, and are thus penologically, racially, and economically two generations out of date. Systems which have managed most successfully to diversify their operations away from farming, thereby serving more effectively the needs of modern rehabilitation, are located where there are fewer blacks and, hence, fewer black convicts—the border states and Texas. Those systems within the states having large Negro populations, where adherence to racial segregation widely persists, are the least diversified economically and the least able to carry out modern programs of rehabilitation. Among these states of the Deep South, the penal systems of three were pointedly criticized in a recent report issued by a responsible agency. The three states were Arkansas, Mississippi, and Louisiana—the same three states in which (according to George Washington Cable in 1885) the worst

<hr>

tration in Louisiana (Chicago, 1930), she overestimated the influence of the Prison Reform Association of Louisiana, whose account of their own significance both Wisner and Zimmerman accepted at face value.

features of the convict lease system had existed.[4] Whether these three systems at present are necessarily the "nation's worst," or which is the worst of the three, cannot be determined as there are simply too many variables, known and unknown, that are involved. But as all three continue to stress farming in an age of computer technology and to employ convicts of both races at "black" jobs increasingly closed to either race, it would appear that the Arkansas, Mississippi, and Louisiana penal systems—measured by national penological standards—have the most modernizing to do in the least amount of time.

Comparisons between Louisiana's penal system and those in the North or West are more difficult to make. No state outside the South (except Nebraska) ever leased its convicts or penal facilities to private contractors or corporations. As a result, the same kind of profit motive that was so firmly established as an objective of penal policy in the South was probably less firmly established, if at all, in Ohio, for example. Penal farms, black majorities among convicts, and relatively poor state economies have also been uncharacteristic of nonsouthern penal systems. As for public support of penal systems, the rest of the nation does not seem to be any more enthusiastic or reliable than Louisiana. Correctional programs are nationally unpopular, according to a contemporary authority, because "support means more expenditures" and because offenders are feared and distrusted by the public.[5] And if, as recently asserted by a well-known psychiatrist, "we need criminals to identify ourselves with, to envy secretly, and to

[4] *The Delta Prisons: Punishment for Profit,* Southern Regional Council Special Report (Atlanta, 1968) ; George Washington Cable, *The Silent South: Together with the Freedman's Case in Equity and the Convict Lease System* (New York, 1885) , 168–69. For what it is worth, one index of deep-rooted conservatism, though by no means the only one, is how a state votes in successive presidential elections. Only three states supported Thurmond in 1948, *and* Goldwater in 1964, *and* Wallace in 1968. All, needless to say, were in the South. Louisiana and Mississippi were two of them. (Alabama was the third.)

[5] Peter G. Garabedian, "Challenges for Contemporary Corrections," *Federal Probation,* XXXIII (March, 1969) , 5.

punish stoutly," then Louisianians are no different from other Americans in perversely retaining "the crime and punishment ritual as part of our lives."[6]

If Louisiana's penal history is unique in any respect, the uniqueness may be found in the total politicalization of the system since it was initially leased in 1844. Whether administered by lessees, state appointees, or even by professional penologists, Louisiana's penal system has been a hostage of politics and a haven for politicians for more than a century. Education, highways, and hospitals, of course, are also supervised (and their budgets determined) by politicians. But Louisiana's public schools have never been compelled to support themselves, much less produce a revenue for the state; former governors have not been hired to construct freeway interchanges; and major surgery has not been performed by untrained political appointees. Along with class politics and race politics, Louisiana has also sustained a durable "politics of punishment."

[6] Karl Menninger, "The Crime of Punishment," *Saturday Review* (September 7, 1968), 22.

Essay on Authorities

Only the principal sources for this study are discussed below. For a complete bibliography the reader should consult the footnotes that accompany the chapters.

Because Louisiana's penal system has never been an object of general or prolonged speculation, scarcely any manuscript collections were found to contain references to it. Two political leaders who mentioned the system, albeit briefly, were Albert A. Batchelor, a legislator from Pointe Coupee Parish during the 1890s, and his contemporary, Joseph E. Ransdell, planter-lawyer and United States senator from East Carroll Parish. Both the Batchelor and Ransdell papers are in the Department of Archives and Manuscripts, Louisiana State University, Baton Rouge.

Official publications of the state of Louisiana, several of which may not have been utilized before, comprise the nucleus of documentation for this study. Journals of the legislature contain a gold mine of information relative to all aspects of official policy in Louisiana, especially those published during the nineteenth century when these documents frequently included verbatim transcripts of debates, explanations of legislators' votes on controversial measures, reports of state agencies, gubernatorial addresses, petitions, speeches, and similarly revealing material. Following the inauguration of the reactionary Governor Murphy J. Foster, the journals became progressively more sterile and today contain little more than titles of bills in the various stages of consideration plus the vote of legislators on final passage. However, the journals are better indexed now than previously, and they remain valuable sources of information for those who know how to use them

and what to look for. Because most changes in penal policy
originated in the upper house, the more valuable of the two
journals for this undertaking was the *Official Journal of the
Proceedings of the Senate of the General Assembly/Legisla-
ture of the State of Louisiana* (Baton Rouge, 1850–52; New
Orleans, 1869–78; Baton Rouge, 1884–1930). But also illu-
minating, particularly for the years 1875–1894, was the
*Official Journal of the Proceedings of the House of Represen-
tatives of the General Assembly/Legislature of the State of
Louisiana* (New Orleans, 1870–78; Baton Rouge, 1884–1932).

Reports by the penal system itself have been irregularly
issued and are extremely uneven in quality. Often these
reports disclose more by what they omit, and always they
sustain a feeling that state officials have had something to
hide. The *Annual Report of the Board of Control* (New
Orleans, 1868–72, 1875, 1878) and the *Biennial Report of the
Board of Control* (Baton Rouge, 1890–1900) were issued, in
the main, by conscientious but powerless officials under the
domination of lessee Samuel L. James. These reports contain
no financial details of penal operations after 1870, but should
be consulted for the comprehensive vital statistics occasionally provided. After the state resumed control of the system
in 1901, the financial side of penal operations was again
included in the *Biennial Report of the Board of Control*
(Baton Rouge, 1904–14). But as in all respects these reports
were heavily slanted in favor of the system, considerably less
than the whole story emerges from their pages. The *Report
made by Hy. L. Fuqua, General Manager of the State Penitentiary to the Governor and General Assembly for the Regular Session of 1918 Covering the Biennial Period of 1916 and
1917* (Baton Rouge, 1918) was the last official document to
emerge from the penal system until 1932. It contains a pro-
fusion of financial data, but its convict vital statistics are erratic and self-contradictory. Not until Huey P. Long came to
power did the penal system again officially disclose the details
of its operations: the *Louisiana State Penitentiary Report to
His Excellency, The Honorable O. K. Allen, Governor of
Louisiana, and to The Honorable Senators and Representatives of the General Assembly of the State of Louisiana* (Baton
Rouge, 1932) and the *Biennial Report of the Louisiana State

Penitentiary (Baton Rouge, 1934–40) span the decade during which Longites ran the penal system. Well-written, orderly, and informative, these reports were saturated with promotionalism by General Manager R. L. Himes between 1932 and 1936. The scattered *Annual/Biennial Reports of the Department of Institutions* (Baton Rouge, 1942–68), submitted during years of scandal, reform, and transition within the penal system, reflect the official line of successive administrations. Reports submitted by appointees of Governor Jones and Governor Davis (1940–48) are rather bland and superficial, while those prepared by professional penologists under Governor Kennon and Governor Earl Long are relatively candid and cautiously optimistic. Reports since 1960 have neglected the problem of rehabilitation almost entirely, concentrating instead upon finances and promotionalism. Two issues of the *Biennial Report of the State Board of Charities and Corrections* (Baton Rouge, 1908; New Orleans, 1938) were valuable. (This visitorial agency led a disjointed and subdued existence.) The first extensive and professional indictment of Angola's many shortcomings can be found in *Recommendations for Reorganization of the Penitentiary System: A Survey Report by the United States Department of Justice, Bureau of Prisons, and Federal Prison Industries, Inc.* (Baton Rouge, 1946). Largely neglected until the 1950s, this report inspired subsequent reforms and improvements. Providing consistent and revealing insights into financial aspects of penal operations were the *Annual Report of the State Treasurer* (New Orleans, 1874–79) and the *Biennial Report of the State Treasurer* (Baton Rouge, 1882–1940). While the number of state agencies in Louisiana has proliferated greatly since World War II, systematic and comprehensible accounting of their activities has declined. For financial data relative to penal operations since 1940, one must consult collectively the legislative journals, infrequently issued executive budgets, reports of the Department of Institutions and of the Division of Administration, and major Louisiana newspapers. All laws affecting the penal system may be found in the *Acts of the General Assembly—Legislature of the State of Louisiana* (New Orleans, 1844, 1869–75; Baton Rouge, 1886–1968).

NEWSPAPERS

For illumination of nineteenth-century events, the Louisiana newspapers most useful in this investigation were the New Orleans *Daily Picayune*, the New Orleans *Times-Democrat* and the Baton Rouge *Daily Advocate*. A comprehensive and responsible organ, the *Daily Picayune* stood far above other state papers in its day. While its accounts of legislative proceedings were sometimes more detailed than the *Picayune's*, the *Times-Democrat* was otherwise second best of the two papers, which merged in 1914 to form the *Times-Picayune*. A small-town paper devoted to advertisements and local gossip, the Baton Rouge *Daily Advocate* was Louisiana's official journal from the mid-eighties into the early twentieth century. As such, it was the organ of Louisiana's Bourbon elite and was consulted accordingly. Louisiana's newspapers in the present century have abundantly fulfilled their obligation to keep the public informed, if occasionally to no avail. When state officials are evasive, reticent, or silent—and this occurs frequently in Louisiana—the New Orleans *Times-Picayune*, the Baton Rouge *State-Times* and *Morning Advocate*, and the Shreveport *Times* can be relied upon to fill the vacuum with detailed and generally judicious commentary. Angola's history since 1940 had to be drawn largely from the files of these papers and no student of anything controversial in Louisiana should fail to consult them.

OTHER PRIMARY SOURCES

Indispensable for identifying and locating official sources for the nineteenth and early twentieth century was Lucy Foote, *Bibliography of the Official Publications of Louisiana, 1803–1934* (Baton Rouge, 1942). Two informed and responsible critics of state penal policy during the post-lease era were Robert H. Marr, "The Institutions of Louisiana," *Proceedings of the Annual Congress of 1902 of the National Prison Association of the United States* (Pittsburgh, 1903), and F. S. Shields, *Prison Reform: Its Principles and Purposes—What It Has Accomplished—Work yet to be Done* (New Orleans, 1906). Frederick H. Wines, a penologist of national repute during the Progressive Era, visited Louisiana's facilities and recorded his valuable observations in a *Detailed Report upon the Penal and Other State Institutions and upon Thirty-Nine Parish Jails for the Prison Reform Association of Louisiana* (New Orleans, 1906), and in "The Prisons of Louisiana," *Proceedings of the Annual Congress of 1906 of the National Prison Association of the United States* (Indianapolis, 1906). Much concerning the attitudes and objectives of the Prison Reform Association of Louisiana, an enthusiastic and repeatedly frustrated organization, is revealed in its *Memorial to the Senate and House of Representatives on Prison Reform and on the Necessity of a State Reformatory with the Opinions of Judges, District Attorneys, and Sheriffs* (New Orleans, 1900). The most celebrated and formidable exposé of the southern convict lease system is in George W. Cable, *The Silent South: Together with the Freedman's Case in Equity and the Convict Lease System* (New York, 1885). A candid portrait of Louisiana Bourbon Democrats drawn by Louisiana Bourbon Democrats is *The Convention of '98: A Complete Work on the Greatest Political Event in Louisiana's History, and a Sketch of the Men who Composed It* (New Orleans, 1898). Equally revealing for leaders of a somewhat later period is Alcée Fortier, *Louisiana: Comprising Sketches of Parishes, Towns, Events, Institutions, and Persons, arranged in Cyclopedic Form* (n.p., Century Historical Association, 1914).

SECONDARY MATERIALS

It would be pointless and presumptuous to enumerate a vast body of southern historiography, most of which shed no light on the subject of this investigation. Among the relevant articles the following were especially useful. A persuasive view of why the progressive penal theories of Edward Livingston were unacceptable in antebellum Louisiana is contained in Mitchell Franklin, "Concerning the Historic Importance of Edward Livingston," *Tulane Law Review*, XI (1937). (For a broader perspective on Livingston, see one of his better biographies, William B. Hatcher, *Edward Livingston: Jeffersonian Republican and Jacksonian Democrat* (Baton Rouge, 1940).) An early but still valuable study of the southern convict lease system is Blake McKelvey, "Penal Slavery and Southern Reconstruction," *Journal of Negro History*, XX (1935). For a more recent and comprehensive treatment, see Fletcher M. Green, "Some Aspects of the Convict Lease System in the Southern States," in Fletcher M. Green, (ed.), *Essays in Southern History Presented to Joseph Grégoire de Roulhac Hamilton* . . . (Chapel Hill, 1949). More than forty years ago, blacks who had held public office in Louisiana after Reconstruction were rediscovered and their names compiled in an invaluable article which has remained forgotten and unused until the present. See A. E. Perkins, "Some Negro Officers and Legislators in Louisiana," *Journal of Negro History*, XIV (1929). Although several studies now exist of the Louisiana State Lottery Company, the best, in the opinion of this writer, is Berthold C. Alwes, "The History of the Louisiana State Lottery Company," *Louisiana Historical Quarterly*, XXVII (1944). A competent evaluation of treatment accorded the lottery by the state press is R. H. Wiggins, "The Louisiana Press and the Lottery," *Louisiana Historical Quarterly*, XXXI (1948). Mortal enemy of the lottery (and of the Louisiana convict lease) was Governor Murphy J. Foster, who is treated sympathetically and superficially in Sidney J. Romero, Jr., "The Political Career of Murphy J. Foster," *Louisiana Historical Quarterly*, XXVIII (1945). Highly critical of Angola at a time when the prison deserved such criticism are John Lear and E. W. Stagg, "America's Worst Prison," *Collier's*, CXXX (November 22, 1952). The professional views of Reed Cozart, who initiated the reformation of Angola, are spelled out in Reed Cozart and E. W. Stagg, "Our Prisons Need Not Fail," *Saturday Evening Post*, CCXXVIII, No. 16 (October 8, 1955). A judicious summary of reforms made at Angola by Cozart and his staff is Ed Clinton, "Angola: The Story of Louisiana State Penitentiary," *American Journal of Correction*, XXII (November-December, 1960). Unfortunately, only two years later these reforms were vitiated by an indifferent administration. The election in 1963–1964 of Governor John J. McKeithen is perceptively analyzed in Charles W. Tapp, "The Gubernatorial Election of 1964: An Affirmation of Political Trends," *Proceedings of the Louisiana Academy of Sciences*, XXVIII (December, 1964).

Several theses and a dissertation provided valuable information and useful leads. The only comprehensive investigation of southern penal history is Hilda Jane Zimmerman, "Penal Systems and Penal Reforms in the South since the Civil War," (Ph.D. dissertation, University of North Carolina, 1947). Although spread thinly in places, this was a monumental pioneer effort in its time. Zimmerman amassed an extensive bibliography, and her study remains the necessary point of departure in secondary literature for any history of southern penology. A definitive treatment of the southern convict lease system has yet to be written. In the meantime, a readable study of some merit is Dan T. Carter, "Prisons, Politics and Business: The Convict Lease System in the Post-Civil War South" (M.A. thesis, University of Wisconsin, 1964). An uneven survey of Louisiana's early penal system is Leon Stout, "Origins and Early History of the Louisiana Penitentiary" (M.A. thesis, Louisiana State University, 1934). Perceptive sociological studies of Angola, by three professional penologists who served there in recent years, are James Wayne Allgood, "A Sociological Analysis of the Transition of the Louisiana Penal System" (M.A. thesis, Louisiana State University, 1956) ; Joseph Clarence Mouledous, "Sociological Perspectives on a Prison Social System" (M.A. thesis, Louisiana State University, 1962); and Raymond P. LeBlanc, "Selected Limitations on the Organization of Treatment in a 'Modern' Prison" (M.A. thesis, Louisiana State University, 1964). Of the three, Allgood and Mouledous are the more historically useful. The Louisiana parole system receives fair treatment in John M. Hyde, "Developments in Correctional Services for Adult Felony Offenders in Louisiana" (M.A. thesis, Louisiana State University, 1955).

There exists an extensive literature dealing with criminology and penology, none of which embodies much comprehensive historical focus. The two works consulted for this study were Harry Elmer Barnes and Negley K. Teeters, *New Horizons in Criminology* (Englewood Cliffs, 1959) ; and Robert G. Caldwell, *Criminology* (New York, 1965). One of the best general works on the antebellum South is Clement Eaton, *The Growth of Southern Civilization: 1790–1860* (New York, 1963). Indispensable authorities for the post-Reconstruction period are

C. Vann Woodward, *Origins of the New South: 1877–1913* (Baton Rouge, 1951); and George B. Tindall, *Emergence of the New South: 1913–1945* (Baton Rouge, 1967). In 1956 Allan P. Sindler fairly observed that "with but few exceptions, neither the general nor special histories of Louisiana are very satisfactory." Fifteen years later Sindler's verdict remains substantially valid. None of the general histories is sufficiently free of omissions or distortions, and only a handful of special studies could be added to Sindler's list of exceptions. Among the latter, those which were useful in this investigation include Sindler's own *Huey Long's Louisiana: State Politics 1920–1952* (Baltimore, 1956). More concerned with Longism than with Long himself, Sindler's analysis of Long is nonetheless persuasive and his statistics on voter behavior are revealing. Following a similar path of analysis is Perry H. Howard, *Political Tendencies in Louisiana, 1812–1952* (Baton Rouge, 1957). Sindler and Howard together provide the only scholarly analyses of Louisiana's political history for any of the period since Long's death in 1935. For Long himself see the possibly definitive T. Harry Williams, *Huey Long: A Biography* (New York, 1969). An unscholarly and yet thoroughly enjoyable and revealing portrait of Huey's younger brother, Earl K. Long, is A. J. Liebling, *The Earl of Louisiana* (New York, 1961). For Louisiana's antebellum history, nothing has surpassed the durable classic, Roger W. Shugg, *Origins of Class Struggle in Louisiana: A Social History of White Farmers and Laborers During Slavery and After* (Baton Rouge, 1939). The victim for years of local fantasy and scholarly neglect, post-Reconstruction Louisiana has recently found its able historian in William I. Hair, *Bourbonism and Agrarian Protest: Louisiana Politics 1877–1900* (Baton Rouge, 1969). The first published work to deal with Louisiana's penal history was Elizabeth Wisner, *Public Welfare Administration in Louisiana* (Chicago, 1930). Fairly sound for the antebellum period and for the 1920s, Wisner is most skimpy in treating the years between.

Index

Act 55 of 1869, p. 17. *See also* Huger-Jones lease
Act 56 of 1870, pp. 17–18. *See also* James, Samuel Lawrence; James, S. L., and Company
Act 22 of 1875: motives and passage of, 24: significance of, 25; repeal of in 1878, p. 36; attempted revival of, 50, 50n, 53; mentioned, 68. *See also* Convicts: competition with free labor; Negro legislators; Plantation work
Act 72 of 1886, p. 54, 54n. *See also* Commutation of sentence
Act 112 of 1890, p. 54. *See also* Commutation of sentence
Act 114 of 1890, p. 60–70 *passim*. *See also* James, S. L., and Company
Act 70 of 1900: provides for state control of penal system, 80–81; Board of Control established by, 90–91; reformatory authorized by, 95–96; classification of convicts in, 99–100
Act 290 of 1926, p. 118
Act 350 of 1950, p. 147. *See also* State use system
Agricultural operations. *See* Angola; James, S. L., and Company; Louisiana state penal system; Negro convicts; Plantation work
Allain, T. T., 63. *See also* Negro legislators
Allgood, James Wayne, 181, 181n, 186, 186n
Anderson, Sam, 161, 162–63
Angola: purchased by S. L. James, 20; purchased by state, 92; convict population at, 119–20, 190n; flood damage to, 93, 96, 98, 116, 120; patronage appointees at, 105–106, 107, 125–26, 154–55, 155n, 158–59, 188; brutality at, 131, 131n, 137, 152–54, 155, 182, 182n; scandals at, 136, 150, 176, 176n, 187–88; investigations of, 140–42, 151–56 *passim*, 175–76, 175n, 177–78; reform of, 142–43, 146, 147, 159–61, 168–69, 178, 189, 189n; opposition to reform of, 144–45, 148–49, 158–59, 162–63, 164–65, 177–78, 181–82, 191, 191n, 194–95; rehabilitation at, 148–49, 153–54, 161–62, 168–69, 178, 184, 184n, 191; convicts on staff of, 149, 177, 189; homosexuality at, 153, 155, 176; retrogression at during 1960s, 174–75, 185–88, 189–90; influence of S. L. James upon, 194–95. *See also* Louisiana state penal system; Louisiana State Penitentiary; Penal reform
Anti-lease amendment of 1894; passage of, 74–75; defeat of, 78. *See also* Anti-lease bills; Convict lease system
Anti-lease bills: opposition to by Negro legislators, 66, 66n, 67. *See also* Parlange anti-lease bill (1884) ; Downing anti-lease bill (1886) ; Bossier anti-lease bill (1888) ; Provosty anti-lease bills (1888, 1890) ; Anti-lease amendment of 1894; Constitutional Convention of 1898; Convict lease system
Arnaud, Aurel, 44, 44n. *See also* Negro convicts

Baker, Joshua, 16
Batchelor, A. A., 64, 64n
Baton Rouge *Daily Advocate*, 52, 56, 82